Horizons of Difference

ENGAGING WITH OTHERS

FRED DALLMAYR

UNIVERSITY OF NOTRE DAME PRESS

NOTRE DAME, INDIANA

University of Notre Dame Press
Notre Dame, Indiana 46556
undpress.nd.edu

Copyright © 2020 by the University of Notre Dame

Published in the United States of America

Library of Congress Control Number: 2020940632

ISBN: 978-0-268-10849-6 (Hardback)
ISBN: 978-0-268-10850-2 (Paperback)
ISBN: 978-0-268-10852-6 (WebPDF)
ISBN: 978-0-268-10851-9 (Epub)

To the memory of Jacques Maritain (1882–1973),

visionary of a just and humane democracy,

and of Hans-Georg Gadamer (1900–2002),

practitioner of hermeneutics and of an "other" humanism

The essential is the difference (*Unter-schied*) as such;
neither (worldly) beings nor Being suffice to capture this difference.

—Martin Heidegger, *Vier Hefte*

The rift between Being and beings is the reticence
of an original belonging together.

—Martin Heidegger, *Beitraege zur Philosophie (Vom Ereignis)*

CONTENTS

PREFACE

It is a melancholy experience when, at an advanced age, one finds the world hell-bent on proving one wrong. I am now in the ninth decade of my life, and everywhere things seem to be falling apart. Wherever one turns, one finds hateful or vitriolic language, a likely prelude to hateful and destructive deeds. Here are some recent words of the secretary-general of the United Nations António Guterres: "States are seeking security, not in the proven collective way of diplomacy and dialogue, but in developing and accumulating new weapons. And the situation is particularly dangerous as regards nuclear weapons. . . . We simply cannot afford to return to the unrestrained nuclear competition of the darkest days of the Cold War." Yet, notwithstanding these sober words, the "return" is already well underway.

For me, the situation recalls the earliest days of my life. Living in Germany, my childhood was spent under the dark clouds of the Hitler regime and the disasters of World War II. In my mind's eye, I still see burning or devastated cites, the result of firebombing or direct military action. I still see dead or mutilated bodies and long lines of starving people. Later in my life, I also visited the aftermath of utter destruction in cities such as Hiroshima and Nagasaki. But I also recall, after the end of the war, the massive upsurge in my generation of the fervent counterplea: "Never again!" Never again this descent into bloodlust, into xenophobia and chauvinism, into inhuman hatred and destruction. What gripped my generation then, not only in Germany but in many parts of Europe and the world, took deep roots in own my heart and mind. Indeed, the fervent plea of "Never again!" became the dominant leitmotif for the rest of my life. Both my actions and the long list of my publications testify to this commitment.

In this book I have assembled a fair number of my writings linked together by the "Never again!" plea. Some of these writings are new, some are older and have been published before. I have assembled these texts in order to demonstrate that dialogue and multiple peaceful engagements are, for me, not a sudden or occasional inspiration but have served as *basso continuo* throughout the many decades in my life. I should add that dialogue, for me, is not a restricted or ephemeral enterprise, but it extends broadly to the most important domains of experience: philosophical, cultural, religious, ethical, and political. One dimension that is too often neglected in modern times is the dialogue between religious and secular commitments, between faith and reason. This aspect, it seems to me, is particularly important in our time since both faith and reason can give rise to dangerous and destructive types of extremism, fanaticism, or idolatry. The same interactive engagement also operates within religious traditions: there is insufficient dialogue between and among Catholics, Protestants, and Orthodox Christians, as there is between Sunni and Shia Muslims. Some purely secular ideologies also tend to operate like religious zealotry, especially capitalism and socialism. In all these areas, "Never again" has been my persistent motto.

So, after having spent my life dedicated to this plea, it is sad to note that the storm signs of our time seem to point back to my beginnings. What kind of delusion possesses people when they long back to a time of hatred, carnage, and destruction? Contrary to the promise of "security" held out by political and military leaders, why would they want to plunge headlong into mayhem and disaster? Would it not be high time to abandon the reckless machismo of these so-called leaders, not in order to jettison politics altogether, but to listen again to the "good news" of genuine religion and also the genuine political teachings of Plato and Aristotle (and Gandhi and Confucius)? Clearly, these legacies are meant to serve not just as ornaments decorating schoolrooms or sanctuaries, but, rather, their real significance emerges only when they are confronted with the agonies and ordeals of real-life human sufferings.

When invoked in these lived situations, the legacies surface as brightly shining guideposts illuminating our human existence. Another bright beacon or guidepost is the realm of art, especially music and painting.

I have chosen as cover for this book *An Undying Love: Around Her* by Marc Chagall. As the painting shows, in a genuine loving engagement, everything around the beloved is transfigured into beauty, harmony, and peace.

Fred Dallmayr
University of Notre Dame
October 2019

Postscript: Since the above lines were written, the world has been gripped by a vast health pandemic. In a broad sense, this pandemic has produced two main consequences: first, a further tightening of national boundaries; and second and unexpectedly (despite the policy of social distancing) sporadic upsurges of interhuman solidarity.

ACKNOWLEDGMENTS

Some material in this book has been previously published in different forms. I have drawn from the following sources:

"After Babel: Journeying toward Cosmopolis," in *Being in the World: Dialogue and Cosmopolis* (Lexington: University Press of Kentucky, 2013), 47–58.

"Apophatic Community: Yannaras on Relational Being," *Comparative Philosophy* 10 (January 2019): 3–17.

"Befriending the Stranger: Beyond the Global Politics of Fear," *Journal of International Political Theory* 7 (2011): 1–19.

"Confucianism and Public Life: Five Relations Plus One," *Dao: A Journal of Comparative Philosophy* 2 (June 2003): 193–212.

"Gandhi and Islam: A Heart and Mind Unity," in *Peace Talks: Who Will Listen?* (Notre Dame, IN: University of Notre Dame Press, 2004), 132–54.

"Hermeneutics and International Dialogue: Linking Theory and Practice," *Ethics and Global Politics* 2 (2009): 23–39.

"Self and Other: Gadamer and the Hermeneutics of Difference," *Yale Journal of Law and the Humanities* 5 (1993): 1–13.

Introduction

A Paradigm Shift?

Charles Péguy once distinguished between two types of historical time: "periods" and "epochs." Interpreting broadly the intent of his distinction, one can say that "periods" are basically times of normalcy, times when things are running or conducted along established routines. "Epochs," on the other hand, are times of trouble, when routines are changed or disrupted and when novel vistas (suddenly or haltingly) open up or make their appearance.[1] Given their disruptive and innovative character, one can also call epochs the times of paradigm shifts when there is change not only in details but in constitutive frameworks or frames of meaning. Judged in terms of this distinction, our time in the twentieth and early twenty-first century is definitely an epoch, a time of paradigm shift. In this respect, our present situation resembles the opening phase of Western "modernity" (four hundred years ago) when European societies broke loose from the medieval structure of the "Holy Empire," a broadly homogeneous, religiously inspired and guided Christian commonwealth.

The paradigm shift inaugurated by this breakup was accompanied by much unrest and turbulence, by successive religious wars, and even by a Thirty Years' War. Once the dust settled, a new framework emerged. In a nutshell, the dawn of the modern age brought into existence a novel constellation basically anchored in two pillars: the autonomy of the ego (individual subject) and the autonomy (sovereignty) of the nation-state, with

I

the two pillars lodged in tension if not radical antinomy. The first pillar was established by modern philosophy, especially by René Descartes and his principle of the "thinking subject" (*ego cogitans*); the second pillar was sanctioned by the Peace of Westphalia (1648), which inaugurated the modern state system. The first pillar gave rise to the ambivalent legacy of a more or less self-centered individualism; the second launched the still more ambivalent agendas of nationalism and chauvinism. In addition to these foundational anchors, the modern age also spawned a deep religious or spiritual rift: not only the antagonism between Catholics and Protestants but (more importantly) the rift between the "two worlds," between the transcendent realm of faith and the "secular" world. The Peace of Westphalia terminated the preceding religious wars, but did so at the price of the politicization and/or privatization of faith. With its principle of "the one who rules the land, rules the faith" (*cuius regio, eius religio*), the Peace tied faith firmly to political rule. However, this linkage at the same time stirred up a profound countermovement: the exodus of church members either into private faith or else (and with time more and more massively) into "secularism" or unbelief.

As it seems to me, we today are entering, or have already entered, a new historical period, that is, a time of basic paradigm change. What is happening is the rise of radically new perspectives, new horizons, and new experiences. These perspectives are putting pressure on the old paradigmatic pillars, robbing them of their self-evident and foundational status, a pressure that is fiercely resisted. Hence, the unstable and even contradictory quality of our period. Just because of their increasingly fragile character, the pillars of the modern age reassert themselves with a vengeance and with unprecedented ferocity. This is true both of egocentrism and of nationalism (centered in a "state" or not). As Charles Taylor and many others have shown, the character of modern selfhood or individualism during recent centuries has increasingly become "buffered," that is, self-enclosed and divorced from others and the world.[2] Thus, we witness everywhere the unchecked pursuit of self-interest and selfish will to power—to the point that social life in the West resembles or replicates the Hobbesian "state of nature" (war of all against all). Moreover, buffered selfishness is not limited to individual lives, but today radiates out into the conduct of organized groups, including political parties and racial, ethnic, and even religious factions or communities. A similar hardening of self-enclosure can also be found in the second pillar of the modern age, epitomized by the nation-state. Despite the dismal experiences with nationalism and nation-state policies in the twentieth century, our time faces the renewed upsurge of nationalistic or chauvinistic rhetoric in many parts of the world. Not-withstanding the increased potential of nuclear destructiveness, political leaders seem again willing to sacrifice their people on the altar of "national greatness."

Seen in the light of broader trajectories, however, the forceful resur-gence of the modern pillars is futile and artificial. Basically, it is out of sync with deeper historical currents of our period, with the result that the resurgence has increasingly the character of contrived "theater" or a nos-talgic déjà vu. Differently put: the theater no longer corresponds to the genuine cultural and existential experiences of people, what one can call the lived world or "life-world" of peoples. This noncoincidence of lived experience and contrivance can be detected in both pillars of the modern age.[3] In the course of modern history, the linchpin of individualism—the Cartesian *ego cogito*—shriveled steadily into buffered self-possession or egocentrism. In elevated philosophical language, the linchpin for a long time was termed "subjectivity," seen as the validating anchor of human thought. The role of this anchor persisted in the nineteenth century, in the midst of a growing scientism or materialism, and even to the onset of "phenomenology," a perspective that traced all experience back to the con-stitutive function of "consciousness" (or subjective awareness). In one of his early writings, the founder of phenomenology, Edmund Husserl, still paid tribute to Descartes as the discoverer of a purified (or transcendental) consciousness lodged in the "subject." In his later life, however, Husserl made another startling discovery, namely, that the thought and experience of the subject is always embedded in a presupposed matrix or framework of multiplicity transgressing individual constitution, a matrix he called the "life-world." This insight was continued and further deepened by his stu-dent Martin Heidegger, who defined human existence not as subjectivity or egocentric will but as "being-in-the-world" in a caring way.[4]

The discovery of "life-world" or "world" as the underpinning of human life dislodged the *ego cogito* from its place as the warrant of human iden-tity, just as it called into question the nation-state or the state based on unified exclusionary ethnicity. No doubt, the changes occurring with regard to identity and nationality are unsettling, but they are (or can be) also hopeful, productive, and transformative. Thus, state structures that have become outdated and oppressive can give way to new cross-cultural and cross-national combinations more in tune with emerging exigencies and needs. The same is true of identity conceptions, which no longer fit the emerging diversity of life-world experiences. The most important feature characterizing our epoch, in my view, is the upsurge of pluralism and multiplicity in the place of older unitary entities and/or polarized dichotomies or dualisms. This is what one means by "difference" in the contemporary "postmodern" sense. The point is not that everything differs from other beings in a purely binary or else negative sense (A is not B). Rather, difference in the new sense is a mode of relationship or "transversality" where commonality remains a lived background and hence a constant task and searched for possibility. For this reason, solidarity and stability today cannot simply be imposed or presupposed but have to be explored through mutual dialogue and interaction. As one should recall here, dialogue is a "logos" not of the ego but of the interface (*dia*) between people. Philosophically, the upsurge of relationality or difference has been initiated or heralded by a number of thinkers and a series of foundational texts. At least some of these texts should be mentioned here.

Basically, the philosophical breakthrough to the new paradigm was accomplished by Heidegger with his move from subjectivity to the lived world or life-world. As he pointed out in *Being and Time*, the move shatters the dualism of inside and outside, between immanence and transcendence, replacing it with a "differential" relationship. The effect of this change on human identity was spelled out in his *Identity and Difference*; at the same time, the transition from a centered humanism to an "other," differential humanism was delineated in his *Letter on Humanism*. Partly under Heidegger's influence, some phenomenologists, hermeneuticists, and "postmodernists" have fleshed out the implications of the paradigm shift. Thus, Maurice Merleau-Ponty pursued this line of thought in *Sense and Non-Sense* and (magisterially) in *The Visible and the Invisible*. Jacques Derrida is well known for his *Writing and Difference* and *The Other Heading*. Other writers have drawn their inspiration from Platonic sources, especially from his ideas of "chiasm" and "metaxy." Thus, the French writer

Simone Weil has invoked the Platonic "chiasm" as signaling the "interlinking" of different realms or entities; in a similar vein she employed "metaxy" as a term denoting a distance or separation that simultaneously connects.[5] In Indian philosophy, the notion of "nondualism" (*Advaita*), which also signifies "nonmonism," has a long and important tradition (exemplified in this book by Gandhi and Raimon Panikkar). In Chinese philosophy, the emphasis on relationships points in a similar direction.

To repeat an earlier point: This described paradigm shift—the shift from stable identity and state structures toward difference—is far from painless and trouble-free. The problem is the fierce tenacity of the structures of the older and vanishing "epoch" and its defenders. In many ways, the paradigmatic shift affects or calls into question the concrete life-interests of leading champions of the old order. Thus, once transformed into a buffered "egotism," the individualism center-staged in the past period reveals itself as the backbone of a rigid social class structure at variance with the demands of contemporary democracy. In its most prominent form, this class structure involves the basic defense of private wealth and property, a defense that sometimes shades over into the quasi-religious celebration of neoliberalism and laissez-faire capitalism. This tightening or buffering is also evident in the second pillar of the modern paradigm, where an earlier cultural nationalism is replaced by the stress on uniform ethnic nationality as the backbone of the modern nation-state. The dismal effects of this celebration of ethnic nationality are still in vivid memory from the experiences of the last century, especially the horrors of two world wars. Recently, partly in response to the paradigm shift of our time, some of the horrors affiliated with ethnic nationalism are making a vicious comeback. Suffice it to mention the warmongering endemic to nationalist policies, the phobias promulgated by nationalist leaders (from anti-Semitism to Islamophobia and xenophobia), and the demonization of immigrants or strangers.

The evils resulting from the backlash to the ongoing shift have been analyzed by numerous authors. In my view, nobody has captured this scenario better than Jacques Maritain. For Maritain, the basic defect of the modern age was its binary character, the assumption of fixed entities facing each other in rigid dualisms or dichotomies: self versus self, ego versus community, nation versus nation, race versus race, and secular science versus faith. As he wrote in 1939, shortly before the eruption of Europe into chauvinistic frenzy, racial nationalism fascist-style is nothing but a "demonic para-theism" (that is, idolatry); although it strives for total national unity, it "seeks this community in human animality (or pure ethnicity)—which, separated from the spirit, is no more than a biological inferno." Together with this inferno, he also deplored the headlong plunge into economic acquisitiveness and materialism at the heart of contemporary social decay. Above all, however, he denounced the spiritual divisiveness of the modern age, its insistence on the binary antinomy between secularism and faith. "One of the worst vices of the modern world," he stated, "is the dualism [manifest in] the dissociation between the things of God and the things of the world." Under the aegis of this bifurcation, the things of the world have been "abandoned to their carnal law," while the teachings of religion have been turned into abstract "formulas or slogans" that have little or no genuine effect and have effectively been "vassalized" by temporal powers.[6]

To the divisive logic governing the modern paradigm, Maritain opposed an entirely different perspective: the perspective of correlation and tensional interaction he called a "philosophy of culture." What renders his designation apt is the fact that it is in "culture" (broadly conceived) that the different aspects or tendencies of life interact, collide, or else coalesce. It is in the milieu of culture that we find the correlation of noble ideas and aspirations with the "concrete logic" of historical events, that is, a meeting ground of lofty possibilities and real-life constraints. What is important is that cultural life always transcends or overarches the division between separate spheres, especially between the "two worlds" of the sacred and the secular, which remain "different" in this correlation. From the angle of his perspective, "there is not occasion to choose, so as to sacrifice one or the other, between the vertical movement toward the eternal life . . . and the horizontal movement whereby the substance and creative forces of 'man' are progressively revealed in history."[7] In this way, the paradigm shift envisaged by Maritain clearly links together the warring modern factions of secularity and faith, of scientific knowledge and religion, and it does so not by conflating or submerging the two but by preserving the "difference" of their correlation.

A crucial ingredient of Maritain's perspective is his novel vision of "humanism," which he also called "integral humanism" because of its porously diversified and comprehensive character. "A new humanism ought to be viewed in a singularly profound sense: it ought to evolve within the movement of history and create something novel in relation to those four centuries that are behind us [i.e., the modern age]. If it has not such power to renew, it is nothing." Here we find Maritain's clear assertion of a paradigm shift, that is, of a change in the prevailing frame of reference. The shift would be like a "Copernican revolution," a change "in the relative importance of the [constitutive] elements in the universe of action."[8] In greater detail, the vision was further spelled out in his *Integral Humanism* (1936) where, metaphorically speaking, the shift was said "to cause the 'old man' to die and to give place to the 'new man' who is formed slowly, in the history of the human race as in each of us, and in whom are accomplished the deepest desires of our being." In less metaphorical language, the shift was described by Maritain as the move from binary oppositions to a new correlation or relationality: "Let us remark, first of all, that it seems that the dualism [or binary character] of the preceding age is at an end. For the Christian [or Western man], separatism and dualism have had their day, whether they be of the Machiavellian [power politics] or the Cartesian type. An important process of integration is taking place in our time, by a return to a wisdom at once theological [or spiritual] and philosophical, a return to a vital synthesis."[9]

A key feature of the dawning age for Maritain is "pluralism," not a pluralism of dispersal and mutual negation, but a pluralism of compatible differences. In another context, I have described this kind of compatibility as "integral pluralism" (borrowing the term in part from the French thinker). In a modern democratic context—firmly endorsed by Maritain—this integral pluralism can also be called a *sensus communis*, that is, a sense that cannot be appropriated or instantiated by any faction or group, but that always hovers in the background as the ultimate source of legitimacy. *Integral Humanism* contains some beautiful and appropriate lines about "the very ambiguous word 'democracy.'" For Maritain the meaning of this word is "affective and moral," having reference to the "dignity" of common people, and it consequently excludes "the heterogeneous domination of one social category over the mass of people." The togetherness of the emerging "pluralist city" he has in mind is as distant from the "liberal [or egocentric] conception" favored in the nineteenth and early twentieth centuries as it is from a placid consensualism or communitarianism.[10]

The distinctive features of the emerging historical "epoch" have been analyzed by many other writers from various angles, but I find Maritain's formulation most succinct and persuasive. Basically, what is involved is the move from the self-centered and state-centered focus of the modern period to an upsurge of diversity, multiplicity, and transversality, but not of utter heterogeneity (of self-enclosed units). In a different idiom, one can describe the change also as the move from monologue to a diversified dialogue or plurilogue. The change is evident in the steadily increasing diversity of self-identities, coupled with the growing need to coordinate and integrate competing models of selfhood. The change is also manifest on the level of nationality where the growing interaction and interpenetration of national communities engenders the need for the integration and coordination of citizenships or civic engagements.[11] The change is palpable even on the plane of religious or spiritual commitments, a level governed by deep human loyalties. As theologians and church leaders attest, multiplicity has penetrated even into the domain of church membership and religious affiliation, yet one surely has to distinguish here between a shallow trendiness or hybridity and the serious effort of interreligious learning that requires competence in more than one religious "language game."[12]

Horizons of Difference: Engaging with Others is divided into two, closely related parts. Titled "Relationality and Difference," the first part explores the emergence of diverse loyalties and attachments in different social and cultural contexts. The assumption here is not that different commitments are necessarily synchronized or "naturally" compatible, but rather that they are held together precisely by their difference and potential antagonism. Part I opens with the discussion of one of the most difficult aspects of social and political multiplicity: the search for a viable global order of peace. As chapter 1 makes clear, the search does not start from a preordained global commonality or cosmopolis, but from the dispersed variety of cultures and languages resulting from the collapse of the Tower of Babel. At the same time, the goal cannot be some abstract universalism or uniform structure of power neglectful of differences; instead, differences have to be taken seriously in intensive efforts of cross-cultural engagement. The result is likely going to be a rich tapestry of crisscrossing loyalties and commitments, perhaps (and I hope) with an upward orientation toward global peace. In sketching the path toward such order, chapter 1 invokes some teachings of Plato and Aristotle, especially the former's construction of the city in speech and the latter's distinction between survival (*esse*) and the "good life" (*bene esse*). What was not (and could not have been) fully thematized by classical writers is our present diversity of cultures and religious beliefs and also the emergence of the modern market economy and financial capitalism with their corrosive effects on social cohesion and public life. By way of conclusion, chapter 1 discusses efforts to correct these effects, especially efforts in line with the renewal of public ethics and civic virtues.

The following chapters deal with multiple, possibly agonal commitments found in the works of a number of religious and/or political thinkers, exploring how diversity can or might be mediated or sustained. Chapter 2 returns to the sprawling life-work of Maritain, who is well known for a variety of intensely held intellectual engagements, which, on the face of it, seem to be at odds or in collision. On the one hand, he is famous for his quasi-medievalism, that is, his renewal of the Thomistic legacy attesting to the Scholastic symbiosis of faith and reason. On the other hand, in the face of the "antimodernist" tendencies of the Catholic Church, his name is also associated with his valiant defense of features of modernity, especially the rise of modern democracy. To complicate matters further, the latter defense was divided between his critique of old-style egocentric liberalism and his endorsement of an emerging spiritual-social solidarity. The chapter's title, "Continuity and Historical Change," captures his tensional commitments. A similar tension can be found in the writings of the Catalan-Indian theologian Raimon Panikkar, the topic of chapter 3. One of the key phrases of his work is "sacred secularity," which seems to bestow the blessings of divinity on the secular world. At the same time, Panikkar was keenly aware of the "fallenness" and growing corruption of modern secular life, an insight that fueled his intense striving for social justice. The chapter's title, "Sacred Secularity and Prophetism," seeks to capture the gist of this antagonism. The review of the two Catholic thinkers is rounded out in chapter 4 by a discussion of the Greek Orthodox writer Christos Yannaras, well known for his key emphasis on the general "relationality" of engagements. The question I raise in this chapter is whether his notion of

an "apophatic community" is limited to the traditionally existing Orthodox Church, or whether it can also make room for an emerging democratic society as envisaged by Maritain.

The final two chapters in part I open my horizons toward India and
the Far East. Chapter 5 focuses on the multiple engagements of Mahatma
Gandhi. A faithful Hindu believer, he found a major source of religious
inspiration in the *Bhagavad Gita* (*Song of the Blessed One*), a text inserted
into a great epic tale of a battle of clans. Notwithstanding his awareness of
the pervasiveness of social conflict, Gandhi put the emphasis of his struggle for Indian independence or "home rule" (*swaraj*) on the possibility of
peaceful, ethical interaction (*satyagraha*). This commitment was put to the
test by the simmering rivalry between Hindus and Muslims in India, a
rivalry to which he opposed his fervent commitment to a "heart unity"
of peoples, which ultimately cost him his life. Basically, home rule for
Gandhi did not equal Hindu rule or Muslim rule but rather the coexistence (nondualism) of different faiths in a public community that is neither dominated by nor hostile to faith.[13] This balanced kind of Gandhian
commitment also guides my reflections in chapter 6 on the role of Confucianism in China. As spelled out in traditional texts, Confucianism is
basically a philosophy of relationships, with a focus on five different relations. Keeping in mind the need for ethical interaction among all commitments, my argument in this chapter centers around the need for an
additional linkage, namely, a public relation between all citizens to preserve the integrity of specific engagements.

Titled "Engagement through Dialogue and Interaction," part II deals
with the pursuit and practical performance of self–other engagements.
The focus is on engagement with "others," where others include racial or
ethnical others, economic or class-based others, national others (determined by the structure of nation-states), religious or denominational others, and sexual or gender-based others. In all these cases, difference has to
be negotiated in some fashion. Several chapters explore the road to understanding opened up by exegesis, hermeneutics, and interpretation. Other
chapters examine the possible contributions of cultural or diplomatic dialogue to the cause of social justice and/or the pursuit of global cooperation and peace. Still others focus on the intrinsic meaning and possible
plural purposes or connotations of dialogical interaction. At this point,

a problem is likely going to arise. Readers of these chapters are bound to notice the distance separating the arguments from their own contemporary life-world. As it seems to me and many observers, a cold, even freezing climate has entered our world, a climate not hospitable to engaged dialogical interaction. By comparison with the relative calm prevailing in many classical and humanistic texts, our world today witnesses the upsurge of bare-knuckles politics where harsh words are followed and/or accompanied by still harsher, often violent actions or deeds. Scholars and intellectuals do not have the ability or the power to change this situation. What they can and must do is to present alternative, more peaceful or humane, possibilities—and do so relentlessly and insistently.

PART ONE

Relationality and Difference

CHAPTER ONE

After Babel

Journeying toward the Global City of Peace

Jerusalem aedificata ut civitas

—Psalm 122:3

We have no choice but to be cosmopolitans *and* patriots,
which means to fight for the kind of patriotism that is open
to universal solidarities against other, more closed kinds.

— Charles Taylor, "Why Democracy Needs Patriotism"

In the earliest times, after the great flood, the Bible tells us (Gen. 11:1–9), "the whole earth had one language and few words." The people took hold of a stretch of land in order to settle there and gain means of subsistence. They soon developed skills as artisans and craftsmen and even ventured into the fields of construction and engineering. After they had acquired sufficient competence and self-confidence, they said to each other: "Come, let us build ourselves a city and a tower with its top in the heavens, so that we make a name for ourselves and not be scattered upon the face of the earth." As the construction of the tower was beginning to take shape, the Bible story continues, God was not pleased with the endeavor and said to himself: "Look, they are one people ... and this is only the beginning of what they will do and nothing [in their view] will seem impossible for them." Hence, God came down and "confused the language" of the people and "scattered them from there over the face of all the earth." Therefore, the story concludes, the place was called "Babel" because there "the Lord confused the language of all the earth."

The story is memorable at all times, but especially in our age of globalization when there are initial glimmers of "cosmopolis" or an emerging global city or community. The biblical account holds several lessons worth pondering, but especially these two. First, the present global convergence happens "after Babel," that is, after the scattering of languages and peoples. This means that we cannot proceed from a presumed unity or univocity of humankind, but have to take seriously the diversity or multiplicity of languages, customs, and cultural traditions. Hence, any move or journey in the direction of cosmopolis today can only occur in the mode of sustained dialogue, the mode of cross-cultural and interreligious interaction. Second, the biblical account should caution us against placing our trust exclusively or even predominantly in our engineering capacity, that is, our capacity for instrumental fabrication or construction. The journey toward cosmopolis, one might say, cannot rely solely or even predominantly on our quality as *homo faber* or designing architect. Going beyond the narrow confines of anthropocentrism, the journey has to make ample room for dialogue and listening, for the humanizing demands of education, ethics, and spiritual insight. Differently put: *homo faber* has to yield pride of place to *homo loquens, homo quaerens,* and *homo symbolicus.*[1]

BUILDING A (GLOBAL) CITY

Thus, in embarking on a global endeavor today, we cannot take as our model the work of the early peoples after the great flood. A better model to follow would be the teaching of Plato, but even here we have to make several corrections or modifications. Plato in the *Republic* sets out to discuss the meaning of "city," or political community (*polis*), and especially to specify what is required for a city, particularly a good or well-ordered city, to exist. For Plato, or rather for Socrates as the protagonist of the dialogue, the origin of the city resides in human need: "A city, I take it, comes into being because each of us is not self-sufficient but needs many things." Since different people need many different things, the point is to "gather many persons into one place as partners and helpers, and to this common settlement we give the name of 'city' [*polis*]." The most basic and commonly shared need is for survival or subsistence, and to satisfy this need provision must be made for foodstuffs "so that we may live and be." Closely connected with this requirement is the need for clothing, for shelter or housing, and for different utensils. So room must be made in the city for farmers, weavers, builders, shoemakers, and the like; soon other occupations will be added. In this way, Socrates says, "carpenters and smiths and many other such craftsmen become partners in our city and make it big." Traders and merchants will also be added as the city becomes more affluent or opulent. At this point, however, a query or objection is raised whether we are in the presence of a properly human city or whether we have built only a "city of pigs" (or fit only for pigs), since the sole concern seems to be survival or physical well-being. Responding to this query, Socrates introduces the higher concern for ethical well-being and justice. To meet these demands, the city needs to be well-ordered and well-governed, a task placed into the hands of a caste of "guardians" and ultimately a philosopher-king.[2]

Plato's imaginary *polis* constructed "in speech" remains memorable and instructive. Its great value resides in its insistence on a "higher" purpose, or *telos*, namely, the goal of justice and ethical well-being as the loadstar of civic life. Despite its inspiring quality, however, we need to modify Plato's city in a number of respects, especially if we shift our focus from the city to cosmopolis. First of all, the contemporary striving for cosmopolis happens "after Babel," that is, after the dispersal of humanity into a multitude of languages, customs, and cultural traditions. Thus, we cannot accept or take as a model the relatively uniform or homogeneous character of the Greek city. Although Plato recognizes different individual aptitudes and functions, his model does not start from the premise of different languages and cultures. The second aspect in need of modification is the vertical caste structure of the Platonic city, a structure predicated on the sharp distinction between physical survival needs and "higher" ethical aspirations, between material and spiritual dimensions of human life. This aspect was already criticized by Aristotle, who objected to the presumed superiority of an ethical elite, saying, for instance, that the quality of a food depends not solely on the opinion of the cooks but also, and importantly, on that of the eaters. For Aristotle, and for us following his lead, the concern for survival (*esse*) and for ethical well-being (*bene esse*) are more closely linked or interdependent. What we *do* want to retain from Plato's model is chiefly the accent on justice and shared well-being, what Aristotle called the "good life."[3]

To some extent, we also follow Plato's dialogue in trying to build the global city from the ground up: by proceeding from material survival needs to normative concerns, or from nature to culture. Like any city, cosmopolis cannot exist or flourish without adequate natural and material resources, that is, without sufficient provision for livelihood and material well-being. Here, we in our time introduce a consideration that was not yet prominent in Greek antiquity: the awareness that civilization or city life cannot be purchased at the price of ecological spoliation or the devastation of natural resources. When nature is eroded or wasted, the preconditions of civil life are jeopardized. Awareness of this correlation was not entirely lacking in ancient times. One of the many lessons of the Babylonian epic *Gilgamesh* is that proper human life depends on the symbiosis of nature and culture, poetically expressed in the friendship between the city ruler Gilgamesh and Enkidu, the man of the wilderness. In modern times, however, this insight has been largely forgotten or shunted aside. Progressively, science and technology have been celebrated as cure-alls for social and material ills, but today it is clear that the "cure-all" cannot cure itself or is itself a source of disease. The process of global warming and a host of natural catastrophes demonstrate the fragility of our natural habitat and the fact that nature's resources are not infinitely renewable.

MATERIAL INEQUALITY

In addition to ecological resources, the material conditions of human life are dependent on modes of economic production and exchange. Here, another huge problem arises for cosmopolis, equal to global warming, namely, the haphazard, lopsided, and largely inequitable distribution of wealth and economic resources. Under the influence of modern liberal individualism and market economics, economic activities are undertaken less and less with a view to the common good (in Aristotle's sense) and more and more for the sake of private gain. As this development proceeds, social solidarity increasingly gives way to inequality, and particularly to class division or stratification. In recent times, this process has reached its culmination in the system of corporate and financial capitalism, a culmination that revealed its grim side in the financial crisis of 2008–2009. As detailed in a report of the Economic Policy Institute in Washington, the income of Americans from wages or salaries declined significantly between 1959 and 2007, while the shares derived from dividends and from interest more than doubled; moreover, income from capital gains rose from 1.6 percent to 8.2 percent in the same period. In the words of Harold Meyerson analyzing the report: "The big money, in other words, was in big investment, and it went overwhelmingly to the rich. In 1962, the wealthiest 1% of American households had 125 times the wealth of a median household. By 2009, that gap had increased to 225 times the median."[4]

Such a steep disparity of wealth clearly is incompatible with any idea of social well-being or the common good. It is also at odds with a measure of social stability, which requires the reining in of extreme wealth and poverty in favor of a common middle ground. In the sage words of Aristotle, as "the best way of life is one which resides in the mean [or middle]" so "the best form of political society is one where power is vested in the middle class. . . . [Hence] it is the greatest of blessings for a state that its members should possess a moderate and adequate property."[5] Obviously, what goes for a single *polis* also goes for the emerging cosmopolis. Unfortunately, under the effects of globalization and neoliberalism, the system of economic stratification evident in the United States is projected or transferred to the global arena. The trend, sad to say, has been going on for some time. According to the Human Development Report issued by the United Nations in 1999, global inequalities in income and living standards had by that time reached "grotesque proportions." For example, the combined wealth of the world's three richest families (about $135 billion) was greater than the annual income of 600 million people in the economically least developed countries. Whereas in 1970 the gap between the richest one-fifth of the world's population and the rest of the world stood at 30 to 1, by 1990 it had widened to 60 to 1 and at the end of the century to 74 to 1. The same UN report also disclosed that, between 1995 and 1999, the world's richest people doubled their wealth to over $1 trillion, while the number of people living on less than $1 per day remained steady at 1.3 billion. A similar picture was painted by the World Bank in its World Development Report of 2000/01: at the dawn of the new millennium the average income in the richest twenty countries was thirty-seven times the average in the poorest twenty countries, a gap that had doubled in the least forty years.[6]

Things have not changed much during the first decade of the new millennium. In its Human Development Report of 2010, titled *The Real Wealth of Nations*,[7] the UN noted problems and growing disparities especially in the area of social and economic equality. Despite some advances in terms of people's health and education in some regions, the report stated, the past years "have also seen increasing inequality—both within and across countries—as well as production and consumption patterns that have increasingly been revealed as unsustainable." The disparities are especially evident in the field of global income distribution. "Despite aggregate progress," we read, "there is no convergence in income because, on average, rich countries have grown faster than poor ones over the past 40 years. The divide between developed and developing countries persists: a small subset of countries has remained at the top of the world income distribution, and only a handful of countries that started out poor [like India and China] have joined that high-income group. . . . Hence, the gaps in human development across the world, while narrowing, remain huge." Despite some improvements on the level of average measurements, the report adds, income inequality during the past few decades "has risen in many more countries than it has fallen." Thus, in most countries of the former Soviet Union and many countries in East Asia and the Pacific Rim, income inequality today is higher than it was a few decades ago. The report also points to the connection between economic disparities and the financial crisis in 2008, a crisis that "caused 34 million people to lose their jobs and 64 million more people to fall below the $1.25 a day income poverty threshold."[8]

Anyone seriously yearning for cosmopolis cannot possibly be complacent about this maldistribution of economic means. Close attention to inequality is dictated, first of all, by the looming danger of civil strife, possibly a global civil war. In the crisp language of Aristotle's *Politics*: "The masses become revolutionary when the distribution of property is unequal." But the deeper reason is that stark maldistribution thwarts the striving for human and social well-being in a community. In the felicitous words of the UN report: "The central contention of the human development approach is that well-being [Aristotle's *eudaimonia*] is about much more than money: it is about the possibilities that people have to fulfill the life plan they have reason to choose and pursue. Thus, our call for a new economics . . . in which the objective is to further human well-being."[9] To remedy the plight of maldistribution and to advance the prospect of equity on a global level, some thoughtful people have proposed a number of remedies. Thus, already in the 1970s, the Nobel laureate economist James Tobin proposed a tax on all currency transactions, which then would go into a global distribution fund. Subsequently, the "Tobin tax" idea was reformulated in several ways, especially to include all global financial transactions, but always with a similar purpose. Giving to the idea a religious or theological underpinning, Rabbi Jonathan Sacks in 2002 invoked the biblical notion of "*tzedakah*," meaning a just distribution of resources in light of a substantive conception of the common good. As he stated pointedly, *tzedakah* aims to remedy a social condition where "a few prosper but the many starve," where "not all have access to good education, health care, and other essential amenities."[10]

CULTIVATING THE COMMON GOOD

Removing gross material disparities is an important requisite in the building of cosmopolis. But by itself, it is insufficient and ineffective unless it is coupled with the cultivation of a social ethos, a sense of duty, social responsibility, and shared well-being. Here again, Jonathan Sacks is right on target: "It is difficult to talk about the common good when we lose the ability to speak about duty, obligation and restraint, and find ourselves only with desires clamoring for satisfaction." The blame, in his view, must be attributed to "the dominance of the market" focused exclusively on private gain and, more broadly, to the modern (Western) infatuation with individual self-centeredness that has "eroded our moral vocabulary" and "social landscape." Sacks, in this context, refers appropriately to Alasdair MacIntyre's *After Virtue* and its complaint about the growing incomprehensibility of the older moral vocabulary. As a result of this semantic slide, "virtues once thought admirable, like modesty, humility, discretion, restraint," have become "dusty exhibits in a museum of cultural curiosities." In eloquent language, Sacks seeks to recover the socializing and humanizing quality of virtues, their ability to sustain networks of relationships as an antidote to divisiveness: "The rewards of the moral [or ethical] order are great. It creates an island of interpersonal meaning in a sea of impersonal forces." Differently put: ethics is "an attempt to *fight despair in the name of hope,* and recover human dignity" (emphasis original); it is "civilization's greatest attempt to humanize fate."[11]

What is needed to recover social ethics from oblivion is the good example of elders and public leaders, and the transmission of ethical and religious teachings through education. Here we touch on a crucial fiber in any possible future cosmopolis, but a fiber that is still undervalued and underdeveloped. Sacks refers to an important resolution of the UN General Assembly (2002), which says that, through the intermediary of the World Bank, funds should be provided to ensure universal education throughout the world by 2015. But he also points to the steep hurdle, namely, that education is still "far too unevenly distributed" and that "of the world's children, 113 million do not go to school." Still, the immensity of the task does not dampen his spirit and his conviction that education holds out the best chance of "moving us forward in the long, hard journey to universal human dignity." In this spirited conviction, Sacks is ably seconded by Martha Nussbaum, especially in her *Cultivating Humanity* (1997) and *Not for Profit* (2010). She says in the later study that education plays a crucial role in transmitting and sustaining ethical modes of conduct and invigorating the practice of civic virtues. In performing this role, education relies on schools, but also on many other factors: "Much of the work of overcoming narcissism [or selfishness] and developing concern [for others] has to be done in families; and relationships in the peer culture also play a powerful role. Schools, however, can either reinforce or undermine the achievements of the family; they can also shape the peer culture" for good or ill. For Nussbaum, education is "a huge agenda" that must be implemented with constant awareness of local situations and possibilities.

Above all, "it must be addressed not only through educational content but through exemplary pedagogy," what she calls "Socratic pedagogy."[12]

When properly pursued, the task of ethical education is supported and underscored by religious teachings and good religious practices, but that synergy can be subverted by either secular or religious extremism. It is in this domain that Sacks's text issues its most stirring plea: not to impose a uniform doctrine on people everywhere, but to recognize or discern in the variety of religious faiths glimmers of a dimension that is "not for profit" and that we call "divine." Our global era, Sacks states, summons the world's faiths to a supreme challenge: "Can we find, in the human other, a trace of the Divine Other? Can we recognize God's image in one who is not in my image?" More concretely put: "Can I, a Jew, hear the echoes of God's voice in that of a Hindu or Sikh or Christian or Muslim or in the words of an Eskimo from Greenland speaking about a melting glacier?" (Quite appropriately, the cover of his book carries a painting by Pieter Brueghel the Elder titled *The Tower of Babel*.) For Sacks, religions at their best are not accomplices of worldly powers, but rather expressions of "deep dismay" at some of the features of our world, "its inequities, its consumerism and exploitation, its failure to address widespread poverty and disease." Different religions express this dismay in different languages and with attention to different local or regional conditions. At this point, Sacks introduces one of his most startling thoughts, that the proposition at the heart of monotheism is "not what it has traditionally been taken to be: *one God, therefore one faith, one truth, one way.*" Rather, the contrary needs to be affirmed (in our time "after Babel"): that "*unity creates diversity*," that "the glory of the created world is its astonishing multiplicity." This, he adds, is "what I mean by *the dignity of difference.*"[13]

GLOBAL CITIZENSHIP

Recognition of difference, to be sure, does not entirely cancel mutual bonds or a sense of interconnection. This is particularly true when (following Plato's *Republic*) we move from the level of material needs and social arrangements to the normative level, and first of all that of citizenship. As in any city, members of cosmopolis must be able to claim the status of citizen irrespective of their economic, ethnic, or religious background; differently put, they must enjoy a qualitative (or normative) equality, especially in and before the law. Aristotle is emphatic on this point: citizenship is not a matter of kinship, lineage, or any personal association, because it is established in public law: "A citizen is best defined by one criterion: an individual who shares in the public administration of justice and in [the possibility of] holding public office."[14] This does not mean that relevant distinctions are entirely discarded. There are in all republics certain age qualifications for the exercise of political rights and the holding of public office; usually, a distinction is also made between natural-born and naturalized citizens. Above and beyond these factors, recognition of the "multicultural" character of most present-day countries or states may entail acceptance of certain differences inside the citizenship category itself. This point has been particularly advanced by political theorist Iris Marion Young in her critique of "the ideal of universal citizenship." Although it is morally appealing, this ideal—in Young's view—has often forced marginalized or minority groups to assimilate to a dominant cultural and civic model neglectful of their situated needs. To correct this bent to conformism, she argued, "we need a group differentiated citizenship and a heterogeneous public where relevant differences are publicly recognized as irreducible," but without abandoning concern for the "common good" and the need "to decide together the society's policies."[15]

Pursuing this line of thought further, we need to remember our condition "after Babel," that is, the dispersal of humankind into different cultures and languages. In this situation, cosmopolis cannot possibly be a uniform legal and political structure hegemonically controlling the world; it can only mean a shared aspiration nurtured and negotiated among local or national differences. In the prudent words of Charles Taylor: "We have no choice but to be cosmopolitans *and* patriots, which means to fight for the kind of patriotism that is open to universal solidarities against other, more closed [or chauvinistic] kinds."[16] What this comment brings into view is the need for a layered or "multiple" citizenship where people might be citizens both in a particular city (or cities) and the cosmopolis. This idea is favored especially by proponents of "cosmopolitan democracy," that is, a cosmopolis making room for national or local forms of democratic self-government. According to Richard Falk, one of the defenders of this view, the idea of a multiple (including cosmopolitan) citizenship is designed to impose ethical restraints both on national chauvinism and on the ambitions of hegemonic global elites; what is needed for its functioning is not properly a global state but "a global community providing protection against the overwhelming power of the nation-state to its citizens and the power of multinational corporations over people's lives." In particularly eloquent language, the constraining and enabling role of layered citizenship is emphasized by Falk, who describes cosmopolitans as "citizen pilgrims," that is, as citizens journeying toward a just and peaceful cosmopolis. "I have used the metaphor of 'citizen pilgrim' to describe the spirit of a sojourner, committed to transformation that is spiritual as well as material, that is promised on the wholeness and equality of the human family."[17]

INSTITUTIONAL ARRANGEMENTS

Although largely ethical and aspirational, cosmopolitanism cannot entirely ignore the need for institutional arrangements. In this area, supporters of cosmopolitan democracy have advanced numerous proposals aimed at reforming and strengthening existing global institutions. Thus, Falk has made a strong plea for a restructuring of the UN: including a reform of the Security Council (to provide for a more equitable representation of the world's major regions), the establishment of a new People's Assembly, and the granting of broader jurisdiction to the World Court. In addition, he has also argued in favor of the extension of "geo-governance" into the domains of environmental protection and global market regulation.[18] Proposals of a similar kind have been sponsored by many international political theorists, such as David Held, Daniele Archibugi, and others. Held, in particular, has introduced a long list of "cosmopolitan objectives" for both the short and the long term, a list whose implementation is designed to lend to cosmopolitanism a measure of institutional concreteness and stability. What one might wish to add to his list is the provision for a global "Truth and Justice" or "Truth and Reconciliation" Commission where peoples and societies would be able to air grievances regarding inflicted wrongs and injustices in the hope of accomplishing a more equitable settlement. What none of the global democrats advocate, however, is the erection of a global state or superstate—a modern "tower of Babel"—endowed with the power of centralized management and control. In Held's words, global democracy "is the only grand or 'meta-narrative' which can legitimately frame and delimit the competing 'narratives' of the good. It is particularly important because it suggests a way of relating 'values' to one another and of leaving the resolution of conflicts open to participants in a political dialogue."[19]

Held's comments are clearly pertinent to our situation "after Babel," throwing into relief the question animating or, rather, troubling my presentation here: Can we or should we reconstruct the ancient tower, now in the form of a global superstate? Not surprisingly, the sidelining of this option (by defenders of global democracy) is unsatisfactory and a provocation for international "realists" wedded to the primacy of "sovereign" power and the imperative of a central command structure. Although it is frequently advanced as a firm dogma, this primacy has been called into question by a long line of political or ethical-political thinkers, from Plato and Aristotle to Hegel and beyond. With specific regard to cosmopolitanism, the danger of an imperial despotism (implicit in a global state) has been clearly outlined by Immanuel Kant in his famous treatise *Perpetual Peace*, in which he opted for a lose federation, or lateral *Bund*.[20] As is evident already in its title, Kant's treatise expressed an ethical vision, or what Sacks calls a "covenant of hope": a hope predicated on the progressive maturation and transformation of humanity.[21]

At this point, we come back to the notion of *homo symbolicus* and also to Falk's metaphor of "citizen pilgrims" journeying toward a state of "wholeness" or cosmos in the world. Seen from this angle, cosmopolis itself is ultimately a metaphor or parable: a parable for a condition of humanity that exists not only *propter peccatum* (for the correction of evil through force) but as a projection and anticipation of the good life. Another traditional metaphor for this condition or cosmos is "Jerusalem" (or else Mecca or Banares). As the Psalmist says, "Jerusalem is built like a city, bound firmly together" (Ps. 122). And he adds: "Pray for the peace of that city; may they prosper who love you. Peace be within your walls, and abundance within your towers!" This agrees with an inspiring line placed over the entrance to the basilica at Montserrat, Spain: *Urbs Jerusalem beata dicta pacis visio* (Jerusalem is called the beautiful vision of peace).

CHAPTER TWO

Continuity and Historical Change

Remembering Jacques Maritain

> You only transform the social regime of the world by effecting,
> at the same time, and first of all within ourselves, a renewal
> of spiritual life and of moral life, by digging down into
> the spiritual and moral foundations of human life.
>
> —Jacques Maritain, *Integral Humanism*

On the occasion of the eightieth anniversary of *The Review of Politics* (*TRP*), I was asked to offer some reflections on an article by Jacques Maritain in the first issue in January 1939. This was certainly a pleasant and stimulating request. Maritain counts as one of the brightest Catholic thinkers of the past century, one who renewed the doctrinal structure of the Church while opening its doors to modern democracy and modern ways of life. The title was "Integral Humanism and the Crisis of Modern Times," a phrase that, in my view, can be read as a passkey to his entire work. Throughout his life, he was a "humanist" (not of the narrow anthropocentric type) and a religious believer open to or reacting to the crises of modernity, especially political crises. With this accent, he established a standard for *TRP*, a standard suitable for emulation during the following eighty years and beyond.

But the yardstick is not limited to the pages of *TRP*; it extends also to the university where it is located. Although founded and sustained by a religious order, the University of Notre Dame does not exist for itself but is (or is meant to be) open or responsive to the challenges of the world, sometimes critically responsive. I recall Pope Francis's famous saying that the Church does not live for itself but for the sake of the world, which is badly in need of the good news, a saying quite in accord with the biblical passage that religious faith should be "the salt of the earth" (Matt. 5:13). In terms of this passage, faith cannot be separated or divorced from the world nor be collapsed into it.[1] In this context, I also recall Father Hesburgh's (Notre Dame president from 1952 to 1987) repeated insistence that faith is supposed to be a "leaven" or transformative agent in society and the world at large. As it seems to me, Maritain had taken sayings of this kind to heart in his life and writings, offering a valuable beacon to his readers and friends—including me.

RELIGIOUS TRADITIONALISM

Here a caveat is in order, however. Although respectful of his entire work, I am not a follower of the doctrinal or strictly theological teachings of Maritain. Apart from being a humanist and a supporter of democracy, Maritain is also known (and perhaps chiefly known) as the founder of neo-Thomism, that is, of the revival of Scholastic metaphysics. Here my attachment to modern philosophy, and especially to phenomenology, existentialism, and hermeneutics, intervenes. With this attachment came for me an accent on perspective, lived experience, and interpretation. When I joined the University of Notre Dame in 1979, I was told that the Philosophy Department (and to some extent Theology too) had until a few years earlier been firmly neo-Thomist. This predominance, however, had vanished and been replaced by the "analytical" perspective, that is, a basic emphasis on pure logic and epistemology, which also affected the status of Maritain. For me, this change was by no means a good bargain. As I saw it (and still do), both neo-Thomism and analytical philosophy are anchored in cognition, or in rational-epistemic knowledge (of objective data). Veering away from this cognitive stance, I have preferred to see philosophy as a quest or inquiry, that is, as a loving striving for truth and goodness (without a possessive claim). To this extent, I was drawn early on to St. Bonaventure's and Nicholas of Cusa's notion of thinking as an "itinerary" (*itinerarium mentis in Deum*), and to Schelling's emphasis on striving, or "yearning" (*Sehnsucht*), over cognitive possession.[2] Still later, I was attracted to the Eastern Orthodox notion of *apophasis* (experiential intimation) over doctrinal *cataphasis*.[3] But most recently I was drawn to phenomenology and hermeneutics.

At this point, I probably should add a few comments in light of my long-standing involvement with Martin Heidegger's philosophy. In many of my writings I have traced Heidegger's efforts to extricate himself from dubious ideologies of the 1930s, efforts that, in my judgment, were basically successful.[4] However, the narrower issue here is the status of Thomism or neo-Thomism, which he critiqued as an incident of abstract "metaphysics." As it appears, a curious interplay was at work among the thinkers. In his early years, Maritain had been strongly attracted to the work of Henri Bergson with his accent on the dynamic flux of time; however, what was missing for Heidegger in this flux was a stabilizing transtemporal anchor, which he detected in Aristotle's notion of "being" (*ousia*), a notion taken over by Thomas Aquinas under the label of *essentia*. As it happens, Heidegger too in his early years had been influenced by Bergson (and by some Scholastic thinkers, such as Duns Scotus); however, he refused to switch from temporality simply to essence viewed as nontemporality (or as "endless" time). His first magnum opus was titled *Being and Time*—where "Being," although adopted from Aristotle, is by no means equated with essence or an abstract "concept" (*Begriff*) but seen as a constitutive mode of "being-in-the-world." In his later writings, this revised notion is elaborated in many novel ways—for instance, in the texts on *Ereignis*, which signals human participatory praxis without subjective will power or epistemic cognition.[5]

The controversy between Aquinas (or some versions of Thomism) and Heidegger has been a staple of philosophical discussion in recent debates, debates that need not be rehearsed in the present context. Opposed to a relapse into Scholastic essentialism, Heideggerian sympathizers and hermeneuticists have defended Heidegger's treatment of "Being" and "truth," a treatment that sometimes acquires the flavor of "apophaticism," or a nonconceptual vision.[6] The same can be said about Heidegger's approach to faith, religion, and theology broadly conceived.[7] Leaving aside this difficult issue, I want to return to Maritain's 1939 article. Maritain showed there he was not the strict essentialist that he sometimes claimed (or was charged) to be: "My point of view is that of the philosophy of culture, and not that of metaphysics." Explicating the meaning of this kind of philosophy, he adds that it involves a correlation of ideas or aspirations with the "concrete logic" of historical events, a correlation that may be called "dialectical," though not in a strictly Hegelian or Marxist sense. What stands opposed to such dialectical correlation is the modern infatuation with antithesis, with the rigid bifurcation of time and essence, of immanence and transcendence, of concern with "this" world and concern with the divine. In Maritain's words, from the angle of a dialectical philosophy, "there is no occasion to choose, so as to sacrifice one or the other, between the vertical movement toward eternal life . . . and the horizontal movement whereby the substance and creative forces of 'man' are progressively revealed in history." "One of the worst vices of the modern world," he adds a bit later, "is the dualism, the dissociation between the things of God and the things of the world." Under the aegis of this dualism, the things of this world have been "abandoned to their own carnal law," while the teachings of religion (especially of Christianity) have been turned into abstract "formulas and slogans," which in turn have been effectively "vassalized" or instrumentalized by temporal powers for their own purposes.[8]

DIALECTICS AND HISTORICAL CHANGE

Here we are moving in a quite novel terrain. In fact, are we here not close to the "dialectical theology" formulated by Karl Barth and Paul Tillich during the same time? And with his opposition to "dualism," is Maritain not really in the proximity of Heidegger's "being-in-the-world," where human being is seen as radically open to concrete "others" and to the otherness of transcendence? Raimon Panikkar, a Catholic priest of Catalan and Indian background, has taken up the accent on nondualism and linked it with the great Indian philosophical tradition of *Advaita*, which was also a loadstar for Mahatma Gandhi. Exploring further the notion of nondualism, which simultaneously means also nonmonism, Panikkar is led into a completely new framework that was not perceived by traditional Western logic and that, in fact, constitutes the hidden tremor running through Western philosophy in recent centuries. What the tremor opens up is the possibility of new horizons: those of a "difference" that is neither the same nor totality "other," neither synthesis nor antithesis. An important feature of this difference is the correlation of "being" and "nonbeing" (or nothingness) as mutually constitutive, which in recent times has led to the fruitful exploration of Buddhism and Asian thought by Western theologians.[9]

Awareness of this tremor is present though not fully examined in Maritain's piece. His "philosophy of culture" is critically directed at dominant features in the world of 1939: fascism, racism, National Socialism, communism, and materialism. No doubt, the relevance of the targeted topics has changed in the course of the past eighty years. Thus, National Socialism Hitler-style was defeated in World War II. In the same way, Soviet communism (in the rigid Stalinist mode) has vanished in the wake of Russian perestroika and other changes. However, other targets have not disappeared; on the contrary, they have been revived and even strengthened in recent times. This is true of fascism taken in the sense of aggressive chauvinism; of a racism coupled with elitism and social oppression; and, of course, it is true of materialism in the sense of the worship of material goods and their egocentric appropriation. On all these topics, Maritain's comments are powerful and right on target, but they might sometimes be sharpened in the light of current experiences. Regarding fascism, he treats the term largely as equivalent to the state-centered ideology found in his time in Italy and Spain, but today we may want to redefine it as brute (chauvinistic) power politics wedded to the rule of the strongest. Regarding racism, his comments are sometimes a bit simplistic, as when we read that racism is "above all an irrational reaction," a "protest of the man in the street against the scholar," even "a pathological protest of nature with all its forces of vitality and ferocity rising out of the depths of mother-earth." Statements like these may indeed capture the primitive countercultural animus found in some racists, but they bypass a deliberate or calculated racist strategy, a strategy allied often (and increasingly today) with advanced technological methods of domination and oppression.[10]

Without question, his strongest and most persuasive arguments are directed against materialism evident in the egocentric (capitalist) pursuit of material goods. In this respect, he strikes one of the central nerves of the contemporary malaise in the West (and in the world at large). Today, a convenient and widely used term for the malaise is "neoliberalism," which perverts the legitimate striving for freedom into the cult of self-centered acquisitiveness and control. It is at this point that Maritain's key idea of "integral humanism" enters the picture as a remedy for our public ills. The idea stands as a corrective to a faulty kind of humanism prevalent in past centuries, sometimes called "classical humanism," which was basically egocentric and anthropocentric, a conception viewing "man" and nature as "self-enclosed or self-sufficient," as "shut up in themselves and exclusive of everything not themselves." In opposition to this legacy, Maritain does not marshal a "counterhumanism" proclaiming the "end of man" but an "integral" or relational conception able to overcome every type of antithesis (or dualism). Such a new conception is able to rehabilitate and "dignify" the human creature "not in isolation, in a closed-inness of the creature in itself, but in its openness to the world [of others and] of the divine and super-rational." This implies in practice "a work of sanctification of the profane" where "man would direct social work toward an heroic ideal of brotherly love."[11]

As it seems to me, the cited passages contain the truly crucial and forward-looking message of Maritain's thought. To be sure, his argument fits into a broader discourse about humanism, which was beginning to unfold at that time. Heidegger at the end of the war penned his famous "Letter on Humanism" where he distanced himself from the anthropocentric "existentialism" of Jean-Paul Sartre and portrayed *Dasein* (human being) as an "ecstatic" creature standing out into the solicitation of the world and the transcendent call of "Being."[12] A few decades later, Charles Taylor penned his magisterial *Sources of the Self: The Making of Modern Identity*, where he traced the vicissitudes of modern selfhood and bemoaned the progressive narrowing or stiffening of its horizons. In this and subsequent works, Taylor pinpointed as a central feature of the "malaise of modernity" a basic shift in human self-conception: a shift leading from a "porous" social relationship to an increasingly "buffered" egocentrism wedded either to economic acquisition or private emotional enjoyment.[13] Drawing my inspiration partly from Heidegger and partly from Taylor, several of my own writings in recent years have focused on the meaning and status of "humanism," always with an edge against economic or emotive self-enclosure and in favor of human "integration" (distantly reminiscent of Maritain's thought). As I have tried to show, "human being" should be taken not as a fixed empirical object but, rather, as an open-ended possibility, as a wayfarer steadily in need of further humanization, which points to the transhuman, but not to the counterhuman or inhuman.[14]

What this conception of humanism and steady humanization implies is a shift—a paradigm shift—also in terms of social and political philosophy. Whereas Western modernity was anchored in a number of "dualisms"—self and community, freedom and solidarity, secular immanence and sacred transcendence—the shift I am talking about does not mean an option in favor of one of the binary terms. Thus, what emerges into view is a relationality without synthesis or antithesis, that is, a gathering difference. This is precisely what one means by "paradigm shift": a change where all the elements of a previous view are placed into a new "constellation" that gives new meaning to each element. As it seems to me, such a shift is adumbrated in a series of currently fashionable terms. Thus, a term such as "postmodernism" implies a critique of the malaise of modernity, but not necessarily a return to the "premodern" or else leap into the "antimodern," which would be a binary negation. Likewise, the term "postsecularism" does not signal a rejection of the entire secular world or a leap into religious dogmatism (as the negation of secularism).[15] Finally, "postliberalism," the politically most pertinent and pregnant term, must not be taken in the sense of a denial of freedom or an endorsement of autocratic totalitarianism. Though clearly denoting a critique of egocentric connotations of liberty (evident especially in neoliberalism and psychic narcissism), the term "postliberalism" also has a positive or constructive significance by bringing into view and promoting a politically responsible kind of "public" freedom necessary for a viable democracy.[16]

INTEGRAL HUMANISM, INTEGRAL DEMOCRACY

Here my presentation can rejoin Maritain again. For in advancing his notion of "integral humanism," he seems to be quite aware that he is advocating a paradigm shift, in fact, a shift urgently needed in our time. When introducing his novel view, he insists on the breadth and depth of this conception. "A new humanism," he writes, "ought to be new in a singularly profound sense: it ought to evolve within the movement of history and create something new in relation to those four centuries that are behind us. If it has not such power to renew, it is nothing." He adds that the change envisaged would not only affect a cultural or clerical elite, but also it would permeate society as a whole. It would "care for the masses, for their right to work and to a spiritual life, and for the movement which historically brings them to an historically full age." In this manner, it would "radically transform the temporal order," thus unleashing a "Copernican revolution," that is, "a great [paradigmatic] change in the relative importance of the elements in the universe of action." However, sheltered behind the temporal-historical process, something else is unfolding or making its way. For, the very movement seeking to "better man's condition here on earth" at the same time and in a recessed way "prepares in history the Kingdom of God which, for each individual person and for the whole of humanity, is something meta-historical."[17]

Here we have in plain view the broad latitude of Maritain's commitments, a latitude that holds in balance—a tensional balance—dimensions that elsewhere tend to drift apart. The term he used to capture this tensional balance is "integral," a word pointing to the difficulty of integrating or correlating differential perspectives. To round out my presentation, I want to go beyond his 1939 piece and look at some of his other (better-known) writings. His *Integral Humanism: Temporal and Spiritual Problems of a New Christendom* (1936) indicates already in its subtitle the broad range of its concerns because it aims to deal with both the "temporal" (worldly) and the "spiritual" problems of his time in the twentieth century. The crux of the matter is that Maritain endeavors to uphold and celebrate "humanism," but not its increasingly defective, self-enclosed, or "anthropocentric" kind. The latter kind "believes that man himself is the center of man and therefore of all things." If this conception is shown to be false, one understands "that anthropocentric humanism merits the name of *inhuman* humanism, and that its dialectic must be regarded as the *tragedy of humanism*." In opposition to this tragedy and perversion, in *Integral Humanism* Maritain aims to uphold an entirely "new" conception, which implies the "liquidation" of the anthropocentric (or "bourgeois") type. "In the eyes of the new humanism of which I am speaking, it is necessary" to change the paradigm. In biblical language, we aim "to cause the 'old man' to die and to give place to the 'new man' who is formed slowly—in the history of the human race as in each of us—even to the plenitude of age in which are accomplished the deepest desires of our essence."[18]

As one should note, the envisaged change is not purely spiritual or religious, but also involves the "temporal" realm and the "transformation of the social regime." "Let us remark," Maritain observes, that at least from a Christian perspective, "the dualism of the preceding [modern] age is at an end." From this angle, "separatism and dualism have had their day, whether they be of the Machiavellian [power-political] or the Cartesian [philosophical] type." Looking at it closely, "an important process of 'integration' is taking place in our time, by a return to a wisdom at once theological and philosophical, a return to a vital synthesis." Importantly, within this broader synthesis or symbiosis, the things of "the political and economic realm" must also be integrated, despite obvious difficulties; for, quite apart from pure spirituality, there is also what can be called "the proper mission of Christian secular activity with regard to the world and culture." Maritain at this point cites the words of Charles Péguy: "The revolution will be ethical [spiritual] or it will not be at all." And he interprets these words as follows: "The meaning is: you only transform the social regime of the world by effecting, at the same time, and first of all within ourselves, a renewal of spiritual life and of moral life, by digging down to the spiritual and moral foundations of human life, by renewing the moral ideas which govern the life of society as such." This digging down and renewal will be "a work of sanctity" that is "turned toward the temporal, the secular, the profane." Thus, what is called for is a new style of sanctity, which one can characterize above all as "the sanctity and sanctification of secular life."[19]

Although stressing the need for integration or correlation, Maritain is far from equating or simply identifying the secular and spiritual realms. To be sure, the secular can no longer be "opposed to the sacred as the impure is to the pure." What "secular" designates is just "a certain order of human activities whose specifying end is temporal" as compared with another such order "consecrated to the preaching of the word of God and the distribution of the sacraments." Thus, without being opposites, the two orders are different in their correlation, the difference deriving, as Maritain says, from the fact that the secular order is inherently ambivalent or "deficient" by belonging at once to God, human beings, and the "Prince of this world."[20] Despite this acknowledged deficiency, Maritain proceeds to sketch in bold strokes the essential features of the "temporal city" (borrowing both from Aristotle and Aquinas). In his own language, such a city is marked basically by two features: "communal" (though not communitarian) and "personalist" (though not individualistic). The first feature means that "the proper and specifying end of the city and of civilization is a *common good* which is different from the simple sum of the individual goods and superior to the interests of the individual insofar as the latter is part of the social whole." In this sense, the feature demarcates essentially "the right earthly life" of the social multitude. But this goal is not the ultimate end, for it is itself oriented toward something better—"the transtemporal good of the *person*, that is, the conquest of perfection and spiritual freedom." Thus, a crucial task of the common good is "to respect and serve the supratemporal ends of the human person."[21]

In addition to the communal and personalist features, the "temporal city" for Maritain is marked by an additional trait, which he could not have borrowed from either Aristotle or Aquinas, its "pluralist" or "pluralistic" character. As he points out, this trait is different from the homogeneous unity (or communalism) of the Middle Ages, and also from the purely contractual relations of individuals in the modern state. Rather, the pluralism that is emerging today is an *integral* or *organic heterogeneity* that respects the integral "freedom" of all participating persons or citizens. Thus, the conception that is *in statu nascendi* is that of a "pluralist body politic" bringing together in organic unity a diversity of persons and social groupings, "each of them embodying positive liberties." Compared with more traditional types of societies, the emerging city provides only a "*minimal unity,*" but it is held together by more than abstract laws, that is, by mutual respect and "civil tolerance," which imposes on the state "respect for consciences." Basically, what for Maritain binds the "positive liberties" together is neither sheer force nor a uniform doctrine but rather civic affection and care, making the temporal city that "which it is essentially and by nature: a simple unity of friendship."[22] The entire argument leads Maritain finally to offer a beautiful paean to the meaning of "democracy" properly understood:

> I have in mind a meaning of this word that is affective and moral, having reference to the dignity of the person, a dignity of which the people themselves have become conscious, not of course as possessing or truly meriting that dignity but at least as being called to it. This popular civic awareness consequently excludes the heterogeneous domination of one social category over the mass of the people considered as minor.[23]

The praise of genuine humanism and of a humanistic democracy was continued by Maritain a few years later in *Christianity and Democracy*, penned in the midst of World War II. Given the immense destruction and misery caused by the war, the tenor of the book exuded great sobriety but also incredible determination. "The war will not be truly won," we read there, "the peace will not be won, unless during the war itself a *new world* takes shape which will emerge in victory—and in which the classes, races and nations today oppressed will be liberated." For Maritain, the end of the war was to lead to spiritual renewal, in fact to the "liquidation" of the modern bourgeois age, an age "led by Machiavelli's pessimism to regard unjust force as the essence of politics." To this descent into bloodlust, the book counterposed a renewed "spiritualization of secular existence" and above all a democratic political perspective that, "in the great adventure of our life and our history," is putting its stakes on justice and humanism and is therefore "betting on heroism and spiritual energies." In the remainder of the book, Maritain spelled out the "keynotes of a sane political society," that is, a genuine humanist democracy. Among these keynotes is the "common good" flowing back over all participants, an ethical commitment infusing political life, a "personalist, communal, and pluralist inspiration" of society, and an "organic link between civil society and religion (without religious compulsion or clericalism)." All these elements lead to this conclusion: "A common task inspired by the ideal of liberty and fraternity, tending as its ultimate goal toward the establishment of a brotherly city (Philadelphia) wherein the human being will be free from servitude and misery."[24]

CHAPTER THREE

Sacred Secularity and Prophetism

Notes on Raimon Panikkar

> Neither monism nor dualism—neither pantheism nor atheism nor theism—
> corresponds to the profound experience that persons of our time
> seek to express. The World, humankind and God are . . . intertwined.
>
> —Raimon Panikkar, *The Silence of God*

The Catalan-Indian thinker Raimon Panikkar uses the expression "sacred secularity" as a central category in many of his writings, insisting that the phrase denotes neither a compact synthesis nor a contradiction in terms.[1] Given the centrality of the expression, Panikkar can rightly be described as a "holistic," or irenic, thinker. The propriety of the label is further underscored by another phrase that serves as a recurrent leitmotif in his texts: "cosmotheandric," or "theandrocosmic," vision links together the dimensions of the divine, the human, and the natural/material, or the categories of God, humanity, and nature.[2] Clearly, care must be taken not to misconstrue Panikkar's "holism" in the sense of an empirical, objectifiable framework, or totality. There is in his thought also an "excess" that cannot be contained or domesticated and that points in an "ekstatic" and "apophatic" direction. This means that Panikkar's holism should not be seen as a finished system or life at rest, but as a dynamic (temporal and transtemporal) movement, or what he elsewhere has called the "rhythm of Being."[3] Here I want to explore this predicament of rest and unrest by reflecting on a crucial tension prevailing in his (and any) dynamic holism: the tension between affirmation and radical critique, or between sacred secularity and prophetism.

MODERN CULTURE AND ITS DILEMMAS

The issue is important because of Panikkar's assessment of modern secular culture, which is grim and uncompromising. In their combination, its constitutive features render that culture "unsustainable," a prime example of Nietzsche's "growing desert." Its intrinsic militarism has produced a "civilization of armed reason," where reason is employed to create more and more deadly weapons. Thus, long-distance weapons are invented whose lethal effects are divorced from human reach or sensibility; Hiroshimas are unleashed with the mere push of buttons. Technocracy increasingly destroys the "human scale," leading to the replacement of the "human measure" by "the measure proper to machines." As a result, the human being is transformed from *homo loquens* into "technocratic man" and even into *homo telematicus* (remote-controlling man). Small wonder that, for Panikkar, this battery of calamities calls for radical remedies, for a resolute turning-about. These remedies, he says, cannot be found in such fictive panaceas as "atomic deterrents," "Star Wars," or "new world order," all of which are based on hegemonic ideologies. Rather, the path to recovery presents a steep human challenge: "It is a revolutionary, disconcerting path, a path requiring the suppression of injustice, selfishness, greed." The difficulty is "immense."[4]

Although persuasive in its sheer urgency, Panikkar's presentation here raises important philosophical and theological issues. For, one may ask, is there any evidence of a human capacity or willingness for radical change? More importantly, the grim character of modern culture puts pressure on Panikkar's key notion of "sacred secularity." For, what is at all "sacred" about this secular culture? Are we not really facing here an oxymoron? At some points, Panikkar is willing to speak of "profane" secularity, but given its destructiveness, its propensity to catastrophe, is this term sufficient?

Maybe one should invoke here Paul Tillich's stronger term "demonic" and acknowledge that, in some respects, modern worldliness is abysmally countersacred. What opens up at this point is a gulf inside "sacred secularity" that it seems hard to bridge. Or can one still say that, despite demonic derailments and injustices, the world (the secular world) is still somehow hale or in God's hands? One is reminded here of a phrase of the poet Hölderlin repeatedly invoked by Heidegger: "But where there is danger, there the saving grace [das Rettende] grows." Does this mean that in the midst of Nietzsche's "growing desert" (or perhaps as its consequence) an entirely different growth takes place? Panikkar at one point invokes the puzzling stanza placed by Dante over the gates of hell: "Divine majesty, highest wisdom, basic love."[5]

In addition to raising questions of theodicy, Panikkar's portrayal of modernity—as a looming catastrophe—also puts pressure on his "holism," the irenic outlook pervading his work. Many of his comments clearly convey a sense of intense drama or tragic tension not usually associated with the notion of harmony. Hence, holism here needs to be carefully assessed. As used by Panikkar, holism evidently is not something that can be conceptually grasped or encompassed. This means that holism is always in some way "ekstatic," pointing beyond itself; maybe it can be called "apophatic." At another point, Panikkar enlists for his purposes Heraclitus's statement: "Invisible harmony is stronger than the visible" (Fragments 54). What this phrase suggests is that harmony/holism is always dynamic, self-transgressing, or on the move, a point resonating with Heidegger's teaching that "potentiality" is greater than "actuality." In a different register, the point also resonates with Tillich's emphasis on the necessarily "prophetic" quality of religious faith. One of the crucial bedrocks of Panikkar's holism is what he calls "cosmic trust" or "confidence," that is, trust in the ultimate wholeness or fullness (pleroma) of life. This concept of plenitude is "in complete harmony with the central Christian doctrine of the incarnation," which expresses the telos of humanity and of all creation. But it now seems that this fullness also includes an absence: the cross and the experience of the "desert," including the desert of late modernity. Thus, cosmic trust cannot be trust in a finished "cosmos," but is pervaded all along by a prophetic promise or longing, which, to be sure, is not an empty daydream but anchored (apophatically) in the foundations of the world or reality.[6]

SACRED TRUST AND LIBERATION

What all of Panikkar's writings convey is that neither trust nor holism can be humanly engineered or produced. Although both involve human action or practice, the latter has to be "ontonomous" in character, that is, nurtured and sustained by spiritual engagement. An instructive example of this point is the "preferential option for the poor" favored by liberation theologians. Panikkar fully endorses this motto, but he gives it a special quasi-prophetic twist. The option for the poor, he says, for the "suffering portion of humanity," implies a challenge to the "evolutionary cosmology" underlying developmentalism (perhaps even cosmic trust). In a friendly critical exchange, theologian Paul Knitter at one point chided Panikkar's holistic pluralism as being perhaps too gentle and irenic, thus courting the danger of ideological obfuscation. What needed to be acknowledged more fully, for Knitter, is the reigning wasteland of our age: on the social level, "the specter of poverty, starvation, malnutrition caused not by 'natural forces' but by human choices ensconced in political-economic systems"; on the global level, "the horror of wars that can devastate and have devastated vast portions of civilian populations and that, if launched with the ever-expanding nuclear arsenal, can destroy the world as we know it"; on the ecological level, "a world *already* destroyed and sacrificed on the altar of commerce and consumerism." To face up to these dismal realities, more is needed than holistic rhetoric, namely, "liberative praxis," a practical engagement for the suffering, and the "preferential option" as an exemplary mode of such praxis. Religious people involved in such praxis, Knitter adds, would form not only "base Christian communities" but "base *human* communities" constituted by "co-pilgrims" from different backgrounds committed to the task of "*soteria*": the "struggle for justice and life."[7]

In his response, Panikkar is ready to basically second Knitter's *pathos* or ethical commitment: "I fully share his concern. How could I not? . . . I find the justification of my life in my total dedication to justice." The only thing that troubles him is the notion of "option," which suggests a voluntary decision or autonomy; for "any option reposes in the will, a will supposed to be free—even rational." But a life devoted to justice, service, or love relies on something stronger than options or decisions; it is a matter of "being," not choosing. In his words: "I feel I have no option but to strive for justice . . . no option but to stand at the side of the oppressed . . . no option but to speak the truth." Traditional religious language here speaks of a vocation, of God calling, humans listening (*Shemah*). The call may come from God, but it resonates through the heart, the "innermost core of our being." These comments clearly have relevance for the notion of "cosmic trust" or "confidence." Panikkar states, with definite prophetic and apophatic overtones, "Cosmic confidence is not trust *in* the world, confidence *in* the cosmos. [Rather] it is the confidence *of* the cosmos itself, of which we form a part inasmuch as we simply *are.*" Grammatically this is called a "subjective genitive," meaning that "the confidence itself is a cosmic fact of which we are more or less aware, and which we presuppose all the time." Ultimately, we have to trust what we experience and what we call "reality." Hence, cosmic confidence is not just "our interpretation" of the world: it is "that awareness which makes any interpretation possible in the first place." Differently put: "We cannot disclaim a cosmic order without assuming it already."[8]

As one can see, confidence for Panikkar is a "fact" but it is also a response to a calling that resonates in human life, in a heart purified to perceive the calling. Thus, to return to an earlier point: secularity may be "sacred" all along, but it only discloses itself as such to a heart that is seasoned, having traveled through the desert of our secular world and been liberated from its compulsive dross. In traditional language, purification of this kind means *metanoia*, a "turning-about" or "cleansing," which, at least tendentially, is akin to monastic conduct. Somewhere in the middle of his life, Panikkar wrote a book reflecting on that issue, *Blessed Simplicity: The Monk as Universal Archetype.* In his presentation, "monkhood' is not a special occupation or profession reserved for particularly reclusive types, rather, it denotes a disposition *constitutive* of humanity as such: the disposition to care about existence and the meaning of being as such: "By monk, I understand that person who aspires to reach the ultimate goal of life with all his being by renouncing all that is not necessary to it." In a sense, everybody is meant to strive for this ultimate meaning, so that this quest is a universal human potential; the "monk" (so called) is distinguished only by the radicality of his quest. He adds: "One does not become a monk in order to do something particular or to acquire anything, but in order to *be*" properly human. The basic hypothesis articulated in the text is that "monkhood, that is, the archetype of which the 'monk' is an expression, corresponds to a dimension of the *humanum*, so that every human being has the potentiality or possibility of realizing this dimension. . . . Not everybody can or should enter a monastery, but everybody has a monastic dimension that ought to be cultivated."[9]

METANOIA AS HUMAN CALLING

Given the basic character of the quest for meaning, honoring the "monastic dimension" clearly means also cultivating contemplation, mindfulness, and reflection. It means coming to one's senses, to overcome the "oblivion of being" and thereby also the "abandonment of and by being," as Heidegger called it. But contemplation, for Panikkar, is by no means a mode of solipsism, a retreat into privacy from the world as such—it means a holistic recovery as a prelude to prayerful or "ontonomic" practice. As he states, properly pursued, contemplation "leads to action." Reflection makes us aware of the suffering going on around us in the world, of people dying of hunger, being oppressed and exploited in many ways. Observing this state of affairs, Panikkar says, "I cannot leave it at that; I will have to do something. . . . The real criterion of true contemplation is that it leads to praxis, even if that praxis consists only in transforming one's own life and immediate environment." In this respect, the "monk" or the person cultivating his or her monastic capability has "the strongest moral obligation—to denounce, to cry out, to speak and to act." Contemplation here means consciousness-raising and civic enlightenment, which is "a dangerous activity," as the examples of Socrates, Martin Luther King Jr., and many others demonstrate. Today, Panikkar adds, the "monk" is plunged into the cauldron of the wilderness of the world, with all the dangers this implies. If we do nothing, we become accomplices of all the miseries and injustices of the world; as accomplices "we bless and condone the status quo—which is already a political decision" and also an abdication of our responsibility and our human calling.[10]

Therefore, cultivating our monastic vocation, in Panikkar's presentation, is not like nurturing a fixed human capacity, such as universal reason. Rather, as a reflection on the ultimate meaning of life, monkhood is also responsive to the cultural and linguistic contexts of the quest. Given the embeddedness of any genuine search in language (as an attribute of *homo loquens*, not *telematicus*), the monastic disposition necessarily also reflects the difference of cultural and religious traditions, without making the latter a prison or fetish. "Monasticism is not specifically a Christian, Jaina, Buddhist, or other sectarian phenomenon; it is basically a human and primordially a religious one." Nevertheless, one can practice the vocation in a Christian, Hindu, Buddhist, and even a secular and atheist mode. The main reason is that "we do not speak 'language,'" rather, "when we speak, we use only one language." If this is so, Panikkar adds, "then monkhood is not the monopoly of a few [monastic orders] but rather a human wellspring which may be channeled in different degrees of purity and awareness by different people in many parts of the world." As a summons to holistic awareness, responsibility, and maturity, the monastic vocation calls on all people everywhere to develop seriously, in exemplary fashion and according to their cultural contexts, the "deepest core of our humanness." When this happens, people everywhere emerge as "co-pilgrims" on the path toward a sacred secularity and *soteria*, thereby safeguarding both the natural ecological habitat and the primordial ethical-religious fiber of humanity.[11]

The preceding reflections indicate that there is indeed a tension in Panikkar's writings, but it is not a problem for, but a constitutive feature of, his work. What emerges here is the possibility of a "holism" that is not totalizing or totalitarian; of a *summa* that does not sum up everything. As we know from Heidegger and Adorno, every cognitive totality is exclusionary—by exiling the nontotal or "un-whole"; every cognitive grasp of "being" is exclusionary of nonbeing and the embryonic yearning for being. Hence, Panikkar's formula of "sacred secularity" may not be oxymoronic after all. Once the nexus between the two terms is grasped as a radical potentiality, the irenic and seemingly placid formula becomes inhabited by a prophetic drama. Maybe this is also how one should think of "God." Maybe God is the sum total of everything that is—and everything that is left out. Maybe God is the "one"—and the not-one; the omnipotent ruler of the world—and the world's infinite suffering victim. To the extent that it suggests something like this, Panikkar's work remains a source of endless reflection.

CHAPTER FOUR

Apophatic Community

Yannaras on Relational Being

> The catholicity of knowing through relationship preserves
> the chief elements—otherness and freedom—with which
> we mark out the personal existence of humankind.
>
> —Christos Yannaras, *On the Absence and Unknowability of God*

Martin Heidegger's affection or predilection for Greek thought is well known. The dominant theme of his work—the "question of Being"— was ultimately derived from Aristotle, but with an important twist: his transformation of the Greek concept into an existential issue and challenge. To a large extent, it was the conceptual rationalism of classical Greek philosophy that subsequently led Heidegger steadily in the direction of pre-Socratic thinkers, especially Parmenides, Anaximander, and Heraclitus. In his view, the legacy of the pre-Socratics was sidelined or forgotten in the history of Western philosophy, which, partly under the influence of Plato and Aristotle, developed steadily into the kind of rational-epistemic "metaphysics" he considered a derailment of thought. Yet, irrespective of the beneficial or detrimental influence of the Greek tradition, Heidegger throughout his life remained fond of *Griechenland* seen as a homeland of sustained reflection and imagination. He wrote in a letter of 1957: "Greece remains still the dream which sustains every new initiative of thinking." In 1962, after considerable hesitation and trepidation, Heidegger finally visited the dreamland. He asked in his logbook of the trip: "Can Greece still speak to us in its own language and address us as its hearers—us, people of an age penetrated everywhere by the power and artificiality of technology?"[1]

As Heidegger was surely aware, Greece—if at all able to address us— is bound to speak in different idioms and voices. He did not seem to be aware of a very contemporary voice that, curiously, manages to reconnect present-day reflection with the world of Heraclitus and the pre-Socratics: the voice of Greek "orthodox" theology and philosophy. Here I want to lift up for attention the work of one of the most prominent contemporary Greek thinkers: Christos Yannaras, professor emeritus in philosophy at the Panteion University in Athens. Born in 1935, Yannaras studied for some time in Germany, where he encountered the thought of Heidegger, before he turned to additional philosophical and theological studies in Paris and Greece. What attracted Yannaras to Heidegger was chiefly the critique of Western "metaphysics" with its central focuses on rational epistemology and its disdain for experiential knowledge. In a recessed manner, Heidegger's influence is also present in the rejection of Descartes's *ego cogito* and the embrace of a radical "relationism" on the level of both personal encounters and general ontology. What Yannaras opposes to Western metaphysics is "apophaticism," or an "apophatic faith," which he himself defined as "a *stance* against knowledge and epistemology," a "denial of 'conceptual idols' and of the psychological props of egocentric self-assurance."[2] Given the great number of his publications, I shall focus in the following on a limited number of studies: first, a work dealing explicitly with Heidegger and apophaticism; next, studies devoted to (anti-individualistic) "personalism" and human freedom; finally, I shall offer some comments or afterthoughts on "apophatic community."

HEIDEGGER AND THE AREOPAGITE

Yannaras, as a young man, studied a few years in Germany where he acquainted himself with Heidegger's writings. The details and scope of his acquaintance are not known (to me). But it is clear that his familiarity extended beyond *Being and Time* and included some of Heidegger's work after the "*Kehre*," especially his writings on Nietzsche and "European nihilism." The latter familiarity is evident in one of his earliest texts, published in 1967, titled (in translation) *On the Absence and Unknowability of God: Heidegger and the Areopagite.* The book opens right away with a reference to Nietzsche's proclamation of the "death of God" in *The Gay Science*, put in the mouth of a "madman." For Yannaras, Nietzsche's phrase does not mean the affirmation or celebration of a straightforward atheism, as it appeared to the madman's hearers in the marketplace. Rather, it denotes the absence or vanishing of a certain "metaphysical" conception of God, where the divine is the object of epistemic knowledge. In this sense, he basically endorses Heidegger's interpretation of the proclamation as expounded in his Nietzsche texts in the early 1940s. Yannaras writes: "'God is dead' means that the Christian God, the God of Western metaphysics, is but a dead fashioning of the mind, hardly more than a rational idea, an abstract concept. At best, 'God' stands for an idolized, conventional 'value.'" Since the tenability of this epistemic concept has been shown to be illusory, the place of God in Western thought is now "empty," a marker for divine "absence." Above all, the metaphysical concept is unrelated to human experience and the shaping of Western or European culture. This is what is meant (and what Heidegger meant) by "European nihilism."[3]

The vanishing of God or the divine from Western thought was not a sudden cataclysmic event; rather, it was the result of a long trajectory moving through several centuries. In Yannaras's portrayal, the denial or absenteeism of God "took shape gradually in the West from the fourteenth century onwards, culminating finally in Nietzsche's prophetic proclamation." An important stepping stone was the late medieval, early modern misconstrual of the Greek (both Heraclitean and Aristotelian) notion of *logos* (reason), a term that originally still implied a "reference and relation," the means of establishing knowledge "through experienced relationship or the common potentiality of relationship." The departure from this notion of a relational gathering was dramatic. "The Scholastics and Descartes," Yannaras comments, "introduced into human history the interpretation of [Greek] *logos* as [Roman] *ratio*, and *ratio* as a self-reliant, subjective capacity, the capacity of individual calculation and reckoning which is competent to define the truth exhaustively." It was from this capacity of calculation that Descartes deduced the concept of a perfect or divine being, a being that ultimately "has the same kind of certainty as a geometrical truth." In line with this deductive process, Yannaras notes, God was either identified with "the concept of an impersonal and abstract 'first cause' (*causa prima*)" or else as "the absolute authority in ethics (*principium auctoritatis*)." In both cases, God is the figment of the *cogito*, but unrelated to existential human experience. Yet, seen as a figment or fiction, the concept ultimately was bound to collapse. Thus, "precisely because it offered an absolutized rational affirmation of God, European metaphysics prepared the ground of its own rational refutation."[4]

Regarding Western efforts to obtain epistemic "knowledge" of the divine, Yannaras reviews the sequence of attempted "proofs" of God, ranging from the Scholastic conception of God as "first cause," to Anselm's "ontological argument," to the teleological principle of a necessary "end," finding all of them flawed as exercises of purely mental acrobatics. The weakness of these exercises was already exposed by the Protestant Reformation when Martin Luther presented God as "inaccessible to reason" and basically "hidden" (*Deus absconditus*). Although to some extent accepting Luther's verdict, the Enlightenment and critical rationalism preserved the gist of Scholastic efforts by turning God from a substance or essence into a rational postulate or critical ideal. This transformation was accomplished especially by Kant's critical philosophy. Yannaras states, "Kant counters the dogmatic conceptual rationalism of Scholastic metaphysics with the critical power of pure reason," a power that constitutes God as "the ethical demand of the will of the human subject." In this manner, Kant makes the case for "the moral origin of religion, that is, for the understanding of moral principles as divine commands on the basis of a philosophical anthropology." In modified form, this approach was continued by German idealism, which brought to fulfillment the formation of a "moralistic anthropological a-theism." This anthropological turn was particularly evident in the work of Fichte, who saw the human subject as "the central starting point or axis of any philosophy." Although they sometimes quarreled with Fichte, other idealists (including Hegel) agreed on the necessary anchoring of knowledge in the consciousness of subjectivity or the "monism of the subject."[5]

Pondering the shipwreck of the epistemic knowledge of the divine, Yannaras turns to the alternative: the "unknowability of God" announced in the book's title, that is, to the apophatic path or approach. He emphasizes that this approach does not merely involve a denial of knowledge or the simple acceptance of limits of reason in the sense of a "negative theology" (*theologia negativa*). Such an acceptance was familiar to Scholasticism as a humble supplement to reason, but denial here was unproductive of new or different insights. Although it diverged from traditional theology, Yannaras says, apophaticism appeared first in the West "to demarcate the limits, that is to say, the relativity of cataphatic [positive] affirmation"; however, by merely stressing the limits of reason, this kind inevitably facilitated "the rise of relativism, skepticism, and even agnosticism." Thus, the *via negativa* of the Scholastics ignored or failed to grasp an alternative approach to knowledge and understanding: one that "characterized the entire Greek tradition, both Christian and pre-Christian," namely knowledge or insight as "the experienced immediacy of *relatedness*, of the identity of *truthfulness* and *participation*." Yannaras at this point introduces the distinction between an "*apophaticism of essence*" exemplified by Western Scholasticism and an "*apophaticism of the person*" characteristic of Christian thought in the Greek East. The former merely rallied against an epistemic concept, but the latter involves a personal experience and discovery: "I start from the discovery that my existence and the knowledge that I have are facts of accomplished relationships—and relationship is not exhausted by conceptual analysis. . . . Thus, if God exists he is primarily known as a 'person' (*hypostasis*) in the immediacy of a relationship and not primarily as an 'essence' with its conceptual definition."[6]

This second type of apophaticism, in Yannaras's view, was a distinctive mark of Greek thought from the beginning, reaching back to Heraclitus and the pre-Socratics; it was even present in classical Greek philosophy (which was "distorted" by the Scholastics), but it reached its fullest expression in "orthodox" Christian thought as represented by Gregory Palamas and Dionysius the Areopagite (and his school). In the latter case, the notion of the "unknowability" and "absence" of God implies that God is a nonbeing or "nothingness," not in the sense of a simple vacuum but as an inexhaustible source and potentiality. In the words of the Areopagite: "Indeed, the inscrutable One is out of reach of every rational process. . . .

Mind beyond mind, word beyond speech, it is gathered up by no discourse, by no intuition, by no name. It is and it is as no other being is. Source of all beings, it alone could give an authoritative account of what really is." This teaching was later summarized by Maximus the Confessor: "God is said to be both being and non-being, since he is none of the things that are, but transcends unknowably everything that is; for there is 'nothing' that is known in light of the fact that God is 'nothing.'" Yannaras elaborates: "According to the Areopagitical writings, no existential category, not even the 'most spiritual' among the properties of human nature or being can be ascribed to God as determining his essence." Seen in this light, Greek theological apophaticism constitutes "a transcendence of any epistemic methodology—both of the analogical way of affirmation and negation and of the way of causality."[7] Yannaras at this point returns to Heidegger: "The 'nihilism' of Heidegger—as a refusal to subject God and Being to conceptual constructs—seems provisionally to fit in with what we have called, relying on the Areopagitical writings, apophatic *abandonment*." He also cites one of Heidegger's statements: "Atheistic thought that denies the God of philosophy, the God as *causa sui*, is perhaps closer to the divine God (*ist dem göttlichen Gott vielleicht näher*)."[8]

To be sure, Yannaras does not wish to overstate the affinity between Heidegger and the Areopagitical corpus. Apart from the distance of time and culture, there are two features that seem to him to be missing in Heidegger's perspective: the notion of an ontological relation of "persons," and the linkage of apophaticism to human "freedom" and "otherness." In the Greek perspective, "there is preserved not only the many-sidedness of the subject's faculty of apprehension, but also the *otherness* of each subjective approach to knowledge as well as the freedom of approach, the exclusion of any predetermination. In other words, the catholicity of knowing through *relationship* preserves the chief elements—*otherness* and *freedom*—with which we mark out the *personal* existence of humankind."[9] I do not wish to make too much of this distinction, which seems to be based at least in part on misunderstanding. Thus, the notion of "difference," as used in *Identity and Difference*, signifies for Heidegger both a radical distance or "otherness" and simultaneously a mutual belonging or gathering. In turn the concept of "personhood" (borrowed in large part from Max Scheler) is largely preserved in the idea of existential finitude and "singularity" and in the "eksta-

tic" openness of *Dasein* to Being. The same openness to Being in its ontological "transcendence" also establishes human "freedom" seen as the rupture of empirical determinism. Regarding finally "relationship," no theme is
more pervasive in Heidegger's work, provided the term does not designate
the artificial joining together of isolated elements.

In the concluding chapters of *On the Absence and Unknowability of
God*, Yannaras elaborates more fully on the linkage of apophaticism with
personhood and personal participation, on the one hand, and with loving
"communion," on the other. Distinguishing again between epistemic "essence" and experiential "existence," he writes, "The mode of existence that
we know only 'by participation' we call *personal*. God acts in a *personal*
manner, that is, as a person or rather a community, a trinity of persons."
The notion of "person" or "personal" here is closely connected with experiential participation, of the caring inherence of one in the other. This aspect applies also to the experience of the divine: "Hence, we characterize
God's mode of existence as *personal*, primarily because it corresponds to
the experience we have of human personal existence: an existence with
self-consciousness, with thoughtful relatedness, with 'ekstatic' otherness
and the freedom from any predetermination." One should add that the
aspect of participation and experimental relatedness is always marked
also by a dimension of "absence and unknowability" that exceeds positive
articulation. Hence, experiential participation may be symbolically con-
veyed, but can "never be exhausted" in positive (*cataphatic*) formulation.

The same kind of absence or hiddenness is also found in loving or
"erotic" relationship where the target of love can never be fully known or
possessed, thus always involving an element of "passion" or suffering. The
Greek Areopagitical tradition speaks of "eros" as a "yearning" for and "suffering the divine things." In Yannaras's words, apophatic is in this sense
"an 'erotic' naming of God, the attribution to God of names, symbols and
designations as these emerge from the human erotic relationship with
him." Stressing the transepistemic quality of apophasis, the same tradition
also speaks of the "experience of God as the 'mad lover' of the whole creation and of each human person." What this depiction refers to, Yannaras
concludes, is "to the precisely *ecstatic* existence of God, to the erotic will of
the Godhead, unapproachable and imparticipable in his essence, to be
offered as an active call to personal relationship."[10]

PERSON, LOVE, AND FREEDOM

Yannaras is a prolific scholar, the author of numerous books and other works. Despite the expanse of his writings, however, there is a remarkable continuity and coherence in his outlook; notwithstanding ongoing revisions or modifications, there are a number of key themes in his work. How central these themes are to Yannaras's thinking became obvious a few years later, in 1970, when two major works were almost simultaneously published, titled (in translation) *Person and Eros* and *The Freedom of Morality*. According to an observer, the publication of these books caused quite a stir, even "an explosion" in intellectual life and established the author as a leading philosopher-cum-theologian in Greece. The first book turned the limelight instantly on the meaning of "person" or "personhood" defining it not as a self-centered identity but as an open or "ekstatic" relationship. Turning to the Greek term for person, *prosopon*, Yannaras says, "The preposition *pros* (toward) together with the noun *ops* (which means 'eye,' 'face,' 'countenance') forms the composite word *prosópon*. I have my face turned toward someone or something, thus indicating a reference or relation." Andrew Louth (professor of patristics) elaborates: "A crucial step in the exposition is the analysis of the nature of the 'personal' and the distinction between the 'person' and the 'individual' . . . For whereas an individual is defined in terms of his self-identity and distinction from other individuals, as a kind of irreducible unit or monad, person is defined in terms of relationships: an openness to and acknowledgement of the 'other.'"[11]

Yannaras is quite aware of the difficult status of "person" or "personhood" in Western philosophy, especially of its frequent comingling with "consciousness" and "subjectivity." He agrees with Edmund Husserl and much of early phenomenology that consciousness "appears first of all as a necessary and sufficient condition of the phenomenality of phenomena," the fact that phenomena presuppose "the fact of their disclosure" (to consciousness). As Husserl had argued, consciousness is always a "consciousness of something," meaning that consciousness is "intentionally" directed toward a content. For Yannaras, however, this conception still showed a primacy of the subject and awareness as an individual faculty, thus stopping short of grasping "relationality" itself. He writes (in a Heideggerian vein), "The capacity for consciousness alone is not sufficient to explain the principle of the relation of beings to the person; the former belongs to the referential character of the person, but does not explain it." Thus, there is a primacy of "relation" over subjective consciousness, and this primacy is anchored in the "ekstatic" or self-transgressing character of "personhood." For Yannaras, the person is distinguished from an abstract "*ego cogito*" not only by virtue of its relationality, but also by virtue of its distinctive "personal" quality (what is sometimes called "singularity"). Thus, although it is a general or universal human feature, personhood is also marked by diversity or difference. Yannaras emphasizes (again partly following Heidegger): "The starting point of the ontological question (the question about Being and beings, their relation and their difference) is not the human power of cognitive reason but the much more basic reality of the person itself."[12]

The notion of person or personhood, as articulated by Yannaras, is sharply differentiated from the classical conception of the "rational animal," a being defined by epistemic reason (*zoon logon echon*). This conception, he acknowledges, was "strongly challenged by Heidegger," who demonstrated that it was "far removed from the core of the ontological problem" and ultimately transferred it to the realm of "value judgments," thus making it the starting point of an "axiological metaphysics." In Yannaras's account, this metaphysics was developed first of all by the Scholastics and later by modern Western rationalism, but it was partially overthrown by Kant, who anchored metaphysics in the critical power of human rationality, which, in turn, was anchored in individual "subjectivity." This Kantian approach was modified and refined by German idealist thought, but not basically contested. Thus, it happened that modern Western thought, for Yannaras, was increasingly characterized "by humanity's imprisonment in subjectivity" and, at the same time, "by the effort to obtain absolute 'objectivity' (through science)," centered in both cases in the individual *cogito*. At this point, the text invokes again (what it calls) a "great moment" in modern philosophy, namely, the "new ontology of Martin Heidegger," his attempt to formulate "a non-metaphysical ontology," to transcend, via phenomenology, "the absolute and 'ontic' definition of Being, as well as the subjectivity and rationalism of modern metaphysics." Basically, what Heidegger did was to recast the ontological question as "the *difference* between beings and Being," where the former are disclosed *as* phenomena, while Being itself "loves to hide," thus hovering between absence and presence. It is the aspect of disclosure and the interplay of absence and presence that render epistemic certainty in the traditional sense impossible.[13]

An important aspect of Yannaras's notion of personhood is its distinction from a self-enclosed or atomistic individuality, and this via its open-ended relationality: "The person, as absolute otherness, is differentiated from anything conceived by the intellect as definable (ontic) being." This is why every person's mode of existence is objectively "indeterminable, unique, dissimilar and unrepeatable." In different words, that which makes a person distinctive—"*to idiazon,* his or her otherness"—cannot be epistemically defined but can only be concretely experienced, that is, "as a unique, dissimilar and unrepeatable *relation.*" We should note that relation here is not understood as the mere joining of preexisting (ontic) individualities, because relation, as a concrete engagement, precedes the possibility of separate existences. The person, Yannaras emphasizes, is "that mode of existence which is *actualized* as relation, not merely disclosed as relation. It *is* only as dynamic reference, only as 'opposite-something,' only as unique, dissimilar and unrepeatable relation." Underscoring and further sharpening this point, Yannaras states, "It is evident . . . that here we are very far from any kind of objectified subjectivism, any kind of axiologically determined priority of the subject as the capacity for consciousness and intellectuality." Proceeding to give to this conception a quasi-ontologically grounding, Yannaras adds: "Whatever *is* becomes apparent only with reference to a person, is disclosed only within the terms of the *relation* which reveals the otherness of the person. In other words, person and beings *are* the term of a relation, and this relation poses [or encapsulates] the ontological question."[14]

As one can see, the traditional ontological question—"What is Being?" (and the Being of beings)—is translated here into a question of relationality, and more specifically, a relationality of "persons." What is bypassed (or at least pushed somewhat into the background) is the question of the relation of being and non-being and of presence and absence; as a corollary, the "ontic-ontological difference" resurfaces basically as a difference of modes of personhood. It is on the basis of this shift of accent that

Yannaras returns to Heidegger's thought, in an effort to reconnect that thought with the Greek religious tradition. A key term in this reconnection is the notion of *ekstasis*, or ecstatic openness. In a Heideggerian vein, Yannaras describes his approach as a "transition from the ontic-individual perception of human existence to its ecstatic determination." He elaborates, however, that *ekstasis* here is not defined as "humanity's ability to 'stand outside' its natural identity, to wonder at its *being*" (as it was defined by Heidegger). Rather, *ekstasis* now means the "actualization of the person's otherness, that is, the existential presupposition itself of the person." Differently put, *ekstasis* signifies the transference from the naturally given capacity for thinking to "the otherness of personal actualization." At this point, Yannaras builds a bridge from the self-transcendence of personal existence to the deeper aspirations of Greek Orthodox faith: "The dynamic and always unachieved consummation of personal relation is the *eros* of the Greek Church Fathers, the loving impetus and movement of exodus from individualized existence for the sake of the actualization of *relation* in the highest sense." *Eros* here means "the dynamics of *ekstasy* which finds consummation in personal reference to supreme Otherness" (or God). Yannaras here cites the words of Dionysius the Areopagite: "Divine *eros* is also *ekstatic*, so that the lovers belong not to themselves but to the beloved as target of love."[15]

We can see that the issue of "ekstatic" openness is transcribed into a theistic register, albeit a radically apophatic register. Yannaras returns here to his distinction between the "apophaticism of essence" and the "apophaticism of person," assigning the former basically to the Western tradition and the latter to Eastern or Orthodox thought. Given his emphasis on the centrality of Being—albeit a Being beyond epistemic definition—Heidegger seems to have placed himself somewhere at the boundary of the two modes of apophaticism (a location also revealed by his concern for nonbeing or nothingness). Without fully exploring this issue (or leaving it at the margin),[16] Yannaras in the latter part of his book discovers the fullness of sublime relationality in the Christian Trinity. In his words: "For the Fathers of the Greek East, the fullness of dimensionless erotic unity is the loving interpenetration of the Persons of the Holy Trinity: God is 'the all of *eros*.'" The persons of the Trinity are not divided by essence, nor are they separated by power, or place (*topos*) or energy, since (according to John Damascene) "their abiding in each other and their interpenetration are inseparable." These words are particularly important for the topical placement of the persons (where scripture says that the Son "sits on the right hand"). For Yannaras, one has to banish here all spatial delimitation: the place (*topos*) of God is the "dimensionless personal loving relation, the *eros* of triadic communion." Differently put, love is the "place" of divine existence. As he adds, this loving relationality percolates from the divine throughout creation and the entire world. In the view of Maximus the Confessor, the whole of creation has to be seen as "a unified dimensionless erotic fact, an erotic relation dynamically arranged in a hierarchy and universal erotic movement which constitutes creation," always "with reference back to God." In this universal and hierarchical relationality, humanity plays a special role as mediator and actualizing agent: "Humanity's role as 'mediator' between God and the world is fulfilled in the dynamic recapitulation of the erotic interdependence of creation. Humanity is the unique potentiality of *personal* realization of cosmic *eros.*"[17]

As a mediator and actualizer of universal relationality, humanity also enjoys the privilege of not being fully tied down to the nexus of cause and effect: the capacity for freedom elevates human beings (potentially) out of the maelstrom of natural necessity. This is the central theme of the companion volume published first in 1970 under the title (in translation) *The Freedom of Morality*. The book is a paean to human personal freedom achieved (and only achievable) through participation in the cosmic and divinely inspired relationality. In essence, the book is a critique of and attack on dominant Western theories of morality (from Kant to Jean-Paul Sartre): theories where morality is anchored in individual human autonomy and self-determination or else on abstract moral principles or rules (likewise grounded in autonomy). For Yannaras, all these conceptions are vitiated by their egocentrism and their neglect of the "ekstatic" quality of personhood. Modern Western conceptions tend to leave out of account "the ontological question of the truth and reality of human existence, the question of what 'man' really *is* as distinct from what he *ought* to be." What is ignored is that morality is "first and foremost an existential event: the dynamic realization of the fullness of human life and existence." For Yannaras, being human is principally a mode of "relationship and communion." This means that the human being is "a person and not an *individual,* a segment or subdivision of nature as a whole." A person "represents not the relation of a part to the whole, but the possibility of summing up the whole in a distinctiveness of relationship, in an act of self-transcendence" (*ekstasis*). One needs to note here that self-transcendence is not an individual "project," not an act of willful self-determination; rather, it is induced and supported by participation in a divinely ordained cosmic event: personhood is "the mode of existence shared by God and man; the *ethos* of trinitarian life imprinted upon the human being."[18]

An important point to be taken into account is that personal relationality is not an automatic happening, a simple fact of "nature," but, rather, it involves an ethical transformation or spiritual "*Kehre.*" Differently put: although relationality prevails as an ever-present potentiality or possibility, its actualization requires cultivation, steady care, and "ekstatic" openness. Yannaras writes: "From the moment when the human person rejects the [spiritual] call and communion in which he himself is grounded, from the moment when he seeks merely natural and existential autonomy, he becomes alienated from himself." The reason is that, left to its own devices, human "nature" is fragmented and divided into "individual wills" expressing the individual's effort to survive in "natural self-sufficiency." Viewed from a properly ontological perspective, however, the "natural" need for individual survival runs counter to "the personal freedom and distinctiveness which can be realized only through love and communion." Thus, human divisiveness and fragmentation are actually a "falling away" from or an "alteration" of the personalist call for relationship. To overcome this alteration requires an effort—guided from above—to loosen the shackles of self-contained individuality and thus to gain genuine freedom: human beings must refuse to be "wrapped up in the individuality which sets the individual as an ego against the individual existences of other people." This kind of liberation or emancipation is best achieved through spiritual engagement, and especially through attention to the divine "word," which has removed the "gulf between man and God." Yannaras states: "This regeneration of 'man' in Christ requires only the cooperation of man's freedom, his assent to Christ's 'frenzied love' for him as a person." And he adds: "It thus becomes clear that the 'morality' of the Gospel is the absolute antithesis of any kind of individual ethics, since it presupposes the transformation of individuality into an existential reality of communion and relationship."[19]

COMMUNITY PAST AND FUTURE

This stress on "communion" or "community" and the equation of relationship with community prompts me to offer some afterthoughts and
critical reflections. In lieu of roaming over Yannaras's larger opus, I consider it preferable to step back and venture a tentative (and surely corrigible) assessment of some of his central thoughts. As it seems to me, a major
qualm provoked by his work is his resort to binary opposition, that is, the
tendency to slip into the black-and-white rhetoric of radical antithesis. An
example is the contrast between individual freedom and the "existential
reality" of community or communion. What surfaces behind this contrast
is the collision between (Western-style) modernity and antimodernity,
where the former term stands for critical reasoning (*sapere aude*) and the
liberation of people from social bondage (including the bondage of a coercive, purely traditional community). Yannaras's texts are vehement in
their denunciation of this kind of modernity. As he writes in *The Church
in Post-Communist Europe*, modernity has brought about a way of life that
is "antithetical" to and even "diabolically" at odds with the "ecclesial" basis
of orthodox life in the East. The separation of Christian faith from society
has enabled the growth of a civilization that, in his words, is "barbaric."[20]
Similarly, we read in *Postmodern Metaphysics*: "The modern age signifies a
break in all its aspects. Doubtless the matrix of the modern breaks with
what was formerly permanent, self-evident and authoritative. . . . The
break with established religious tradition and authority defines the aims
of the modern age."[21]

This emphasis on a break caused by modernity is not confined to
Yannaras (and some other defenders of Greek orthodoxy). In different
forms, one finds it in most cultures that are victimized (or feel themselves
victimized) by modern Western culture and technology. Examples of such
cultural backlash can be detected in numerous cultural traditions: in
Islam (in the form of Wahhabism and ISIS), in India (in the ideology of
Hindutva), and in many other countries (in the upsurge of exclusionary
nationalism or chauvinism).[22] In some of these cases, opposition is viru-
lent and even veers toward aggressive violence. To be sure, Yannaras's
work is untarnished by aggressive extremism. Nevertheless, in the confrontation with the modern or contemporary age, his texts often sound
harshly dismissive, and certainly do not betray that generous sympathy

that, in his own view, should characterize interhuman and intercultural relations. To this extent, I tend to agree with Daniel Payne when he depicts Yannaras's work as more nostalgic or backward-looking than forward-looking, more attracted to traditional (now mostly defunct) modes for community life than to contemporary or emerging possibilities. As an alternative to the present situation, Payne writes, "Yannaras seeks to retrieve the Byzantine autonomous communities that developed toward the end of the Ottoman Empire. The life of these communities was centered around the life of the church or monastery found in its midst. . . . [Thus] the ecclesial life becomes the basis for human society. . . . [The community] he is looking for is none other than the Orthodox Church."[23]

Partly for reasons of intercultural sympathy, I tend to shy away from radical breaks or antitheses. Whenever possible I prefer to listen to arguments emphasizing the "dialectic" of cultural developments, and thus also the "dialectic of enlightenment" or the "dialectic of modernity."[24] What dialectic suggests is that, in history, wins and losses are closely entwined and that all wins have losses, and vice versa. Regarding the issue of modernity one can readily agree with Yannaras about the immense detriments and devastations unleashed by the modern age, evident in the rise of self-centeredness, technological mastery, and dehumanization. However, there are also features that cannot simply be dismissed as losses. Among these features I would count the processes of steadily advancing democratization and also globalization. What these processes bring into view (at least potentially) are novel kinds of "community" that can be embraced from a Christian and from broadly spiritual and even secular perspectives. Modern democracy is largely inspired by the revolutionary motto "liberty, equality, fraternity," a motto that can be reconciled with Christian aspirations, as Jacques Maritain and others have shown. In the ambiance of the Orthodox tradition, a possible resonance between democracy and Christian faith has also been explored by a number of contemporary thinkers, such as Miroslav Volf, who states that democracy opens up a space where natives and "others" are integrated and where strangers and immigrants can be embraced in the spirit of loving reconciliation and peace.[25] This quality of openness is further underscored by the process of globalization where people of different cultural backgrounds are brought closer together, thus mitigating and contesting the harsh legacies of racism, ethnocentrism, and xenophobia.

It seems to me that these new kinds of relationality or community are not (or should not be) too far removed from Yannaras's perspective, especially his accent on the "apophatic" character of all beings and relationships, that is, their not empirically closed and thus inexhaustible quality. In a judicious and equitable manner, this aspect is fully recognized by Daniel Payne: "Yannaras's understanding of the human 'person' makes possible the articulation of a manner of existence that necessitates a level of pluralism and difference within [and beyond] society. This is so because, in order to love the other, the other must be different from the self. . . . Because of the modern situation whereby persons participate in multiple identities, an independent perichoretic participation in the life of the other is enabled by the pluralistic nature of human society [and the world]. In this manner, the person engages [or can engage] in a dialogical relationship with others." This open relationality extends also to the church, including the Orthodox Church, in the sense that the church "can function in a pluralistic [democratic] society through dialogue and perichoretic relation with other institutions." Thus, Payne adds, "rather than living a sectarian existence withdrawn from modern society, the church can participate in the lives of modern citizens who seek spiritual answers to existential dilemmas."[26] In this manner, the judgment of a backward-looking nostalgia for past ways of life is tempered or corrected in favor of present-day relevance. At various points, Yannaras himself has endorsed this correction or change of outlook. In 1986, in a festschrift for Jürgen Moltmann, Yannaras stated: "Apophaticism means the refusal to exhaust knowledge of the truth in its formulation," which also means "its past or traditional formulation." The title of the festschrift was *God's Future: Future of the World.* Thus, in his contribution, Yannaras clearly recognized the "futurism," that is, the promised advent of the "kingdom to come."[27]

CHAPTER FIVE

A Heart and Mind Unity

Gandhi and Islam

> There will be no lasting peace on earth unless we learn not merely
> to tolerate but even to respect the other faiths as our own.
> A reverent study of the sayings of the different teachers of
> mankind is a step in the direction of such mutual respect.
>
> —Mahatma Gandhi, foreword to *Sayings of Muhammad*

Not long ago, one of the grandsons of the Mahatma commented bitterly
on the upsurge of communal violence between Hindus and Muslims in
India, and especially in his grandfather's native state of Gujarat. The immediate occasion for his comments was the attack on a crowded train
north of Ahmedabad and the ensuing carnage in many parts of the state.
For Rajmohan Gandhi, these events dishonored the basic legacy of the
Mahatma and the legacy of many saints and poets in that part of the country. "The Gujarat of Gandhi," he noted, "of the poet Narsi Mehta who spoke
of the other person's pain, of the modern Jain saint Rajchandra [who deeply
influenced Gandhi], of brothers to the poor like Ravishanker Maharaj and
Jugatram Dave . . . stands deeply shaken." The culprits behind the events,
in his view, were political and religious agitators who had never accepted
the Mahatma's message of nonviolence and interfaith reconciliation:

"The truth is that the subcontinent's religious extremists never forgave Gandhi his beliefs and his triumphs." What they particularly detested was Gandhi's "standing up for minority rights, religious freedom, justice, and forgiveness" and his success in "persuading millions on the subcontinent to embrace these values." Angered and frustrated by this success, extremists on both sides "put their heads together" and came up with two strategies: "inject hate into Gandhi's Gujarat, and turn Gandhi's healing Ram(a), the Almighty who was also the Compassionate, into an anti-Muslim chariot-riding warrior."[1]

As an antidote to the perpetrated carnage, Rajmohan urged a return to his grandfather's vision of intercommunal harmony and peace-building, to what Gandhi himself on repeated occasions had called the goal of a "heart unity" between Hindus and Muslims in India. Here I explore, once again, the story of India's struggle for independence and, in particular, the role played by Hindu–Muslim relations in this struggle, especially as the latter was carried on under Gandhi's leadership. As will become clear, a central issue during this struggle was the question of priority: whether India's independence (*swaraj*) should have primacy over intercommunal harmony or whether such harmony was in fact a precondition of genuine independence. In the first section, I shall recapitulate, in brevity, the main stages of Gandhi's involvement in the "Muslim question" and his evolving attitude toward the interplay of independence and harmony. The second section will highlight some of the major disputes between Gandhi and prominent contemporary Muslim leaders; a crucial issue at this point will be the dispute between Muhammad Ali Jinnah's formal constitutionalism and Gandhi's grassroots multiculturalism or intercommunalism. The concluding section returns to the early twenty-first century in an effort to derive lessons from Gandhi's intercommunal practices both for present-day India and for our steadily shrinking or "globalizing" world.

A STORY OF INTERFAITH ENCOUNTERS

By general agreement, Gandhi played a central—perhaps *the* central—role in India's struggle for independence from British rule. However, the final outcome did not match the initial aspirations. Until the last stages, the country whose freedom Gandhi championed was not the India after partition but the older "Bharata" where Hindus, Muslims, and other faiths had lived together for many centuries. The goal of the freedom struggle, in his view, was to preserve as much of this multifaith legacy as possible in and beyond the achievement of independence. For this reason, he had to act both as a political leader—organizing an effective insurgent movement against British rule—and as a spiritual leader and interfaith mediator among different religious traditions. It is this combination of talents that, in large measure, accounts for the fascination of his "persona" and the intricate complexity of his actions. Students of Gandhi's life often accentuate his political prowess and the sagacity of his strategic moves, while sidelining his spiritual endeavors (or at least relegating them to an ancillary status). Yet, from Gandhi's perspective, it must have been entirely evident that politics and religious faith cannot be neatly segregated, at least not in a place like the Indian subcontinent marked for centuries as a meeting ground of diverse cultures and beliefs.

Gandhi trained himself for public or political service through his legal studies in London and his extensive participation in roundtables and official commissions, and few would deny his efficacy in this arena. However, his religious or spiritual outlook was even more deeply grounded, so deeply as to give a distinctive tuning to his entire life. Part of this tuning came from his family background, another part from his lifelong cultivation of interfaith encounters. On the side of both parents, the dominant family tradition was *Vaishnava* Hinduism, a tradition that emphasized hymn-singing and devotional practices, with only slight attention to orthodox codes and rituals. The center of devotion of *Vaishnava* faith in Gujarat (then and now) is Lord Krishna, whose teachings are enshrined, above all, in the *Bhagavad Gita.* In terms of that sacred text, there are three pathways, *yogas,* leading to salvation: contemplation (*jñana*), action (*karma*), and loving devotion (*bhakti*). Among these three pathways, Gandhi resolutely pursued the last two, without entirely neglecting contemplation or reflection. In his well-known self-description, he was a *karmayogin,* that is, a practitioner of faith, which, in his case, did not mean a mindless activist or busy-body, because his actions were always suffused with spiritual devotion (*bhakti*) involving self-restraint and self-transgression in favor of others' needs. In Margaret Chatterjee's words:

The *Gita* shows the validity of various paths to the attainment of the highest. This suggests that politics too, a human activity which is built into man's living in community, is a valid path. . . . The purification of politics was to be brought about through an infusion of the non-violent spirit into it. There was no [strict] frontier between the things that were Caesar's and the things that were God's.[2]

With its emphasis on devotion and selfless service, *Vaishnava* Hinduism has always been somewhat close to Islamic faith with its stress on selfless surrender. Above all, the Sufi strand in Islamic religion—a strand often deviating from rigidly orthodox canons—was found to be quite congenial to *Vaishnava* spirituality, and especially to *bhakti* poetry and songs. The historian Muhammad Mujeeb notes that at least since the end of the fourteenth century "the devotional character of Hindu songs and the appeal which the language made to Sufis brought Hindus and Muslims closer together than any other influence," opening the way "for a mutual appreciation of values."[3] Small wonder that Gandhi's family home in Porbandar had an open-door policy for open-minded Muslims and members of other communities. "Muslims were received as guests in the Gandhi home," writes Sheila McDonough. "The political traditions of diplomatic courtesy [inherited on his father's side] seem to have been imbibed by the child as a self-evident way for a civilized life to be conducted." Childhood experiences of this kind, she adds, must have "encouraged the young Gandhi to think of Muslims, Jains and Parsis as natural friends and supporters in common causes." We also know that he had a boyhood friend, Sheikh Mehtab, who lived close to the Gandhis in Porbandar and who often defended him against bullies at school. In Gandhi's *Autobiography*, he recollects some of these early experiences and their beneficial effects on him. His father, he recalls, had "Muselman and Parsi friends who would talk to him about their faiths, and he would listen to them always with respect." He was often present at these encounters, and such things "combined to inculcate in me a toleration for all faiths."[4]

Following his legal studies in London, Gandhi went to South Africa in order to work as a lawyer for a Muslim business firm whose owner he had gotten to know in Bombay. During his prolonged stay there—about twenty years—he was in contact with a large Indian community, many of

whose members were Muslims who originally hailed from Gujarat. Drawing on his childhood experiences, he was able to establish close ties with
these Muslims, to the point that he was sometimes treated nearly as a
member of the family. What solidified these ties, in addition to mutual respect and sympathy, was the discrimination and oppression suffered by
Hindus and Muslims alike at the hands of the white government. Gandhi
reported later that Hindus and Muslims were commonly lumped together
by white South Africans in an inferior, subhuman category described vari-
ously as "Asian dirt," "semi-barbarous Asiatics," and "squalid coolies with
truthless tongues."[5] In response to this treatment, a broad resistance movement was forged largely under Gandhi's leadership and based on a close
alliance between Hindus and Muslims.

It was at this point that a kind of "heart unity" came into being, a
brotherhood of defiance that could draw inspiration from the respective
religious traditions. On the Muslim side, the familiar notion of "righteous
struggle" (*jihad*) could serve as a powerful motivating force in the joint
Indian insurgency. Looking for an equivalent in the Sanskritic tradition of
Hinduism, Gandhi coined the term *satyagraha*, meaning "enactment of
truth" or the resolute commitment to truth and justice irrespective of
consequences. Muslim writer Abid Husain reflected on that critical juncture and stated that encouraged by "the unity of sentiments and purpose"
and "the spirit of mutual friendship and trust," Gandhi at the time
"launched his first *satyagraha* campaign which was at the same time his
first experiment in securing the fraternal cooperation of Muslims . . . for a
non-violent struggle that involved the utmost suffering and sacrifice." Different traditions thus could be seen as converging in their practical results. By navigating easily between religious vocabularies, McDonough
comments, Gandhi demonstrated his "extraordinary facility in using language to inspire and direct the religious awareness of his hearers." On the
whole, the South African struggle fully convinced him of "the validity and
importance of mutual understanding and cooperation" among Indians,
and especially between Hindus and Muslims.[6]

It was this conviction that Gandhi carried with himself on his return
to India during World War I. The conviction was soon going to be put to
the test. Almost immediately on his return, he began to organize a resistance struggle, called the "non-cooperation movement," against British

domination, a struggle relying in great part on the lessons learned in South Africa. As before, many of his cohorts in this movement were Muslims committed to Indian independence, foremost among them the brothers Muhammad Ali and Shaukat Ali and Maulana Abul Kalam Azad. As it happened, in addition to independence, Muslims in India (and the Near East) were greatly preoccupied at the time with the collapse of the Ottoman Empire, and especially with the fate of the caliphate seen as the last remaining symbol of the Muslim *umma* (community of believers). In order to salvage the caliphate from the Ottoman collapse, Muhammad Ali, Kalam Azad, and others organized the "*Khilafat* movement," stressing the crucial role of the caliph as protector of the sacred sites in Mecca.

Sensing the urgency of the issue, Gandhi wholeheartedly joined the movement, greeting it as an opportunity to demonstrate the needed "heart unity" with his Muslim friends and associates.[7] The movement came to nothing, mainly because of the decision of the new Turkish leadership to abolish the caliphate. Combined with the upsurge of communal strife in some parts of India (especially Kerala), the demise of the movement had a severely dampening influence on Hindu–Muslim relations throughout the subcontinent. To counteract the deterioration of communal goodwill, Gandhi in mid-1924 devoted a whole issue of his journal *Young India* to the topic "Hindu–Muslim Tension: Its Cause and Its Cure." As far as the cause is concerned, Gandhi placed it in irritability and in unjust or offensive behavior on both sides. As for the cure, he relied on his South African experience: "I see no way of achieving anything in this afflicted country without a lasting heart unity between Hindus and Muselmans in India." To underscore his conviction and to calm communal hatreds, he embarked on a fast in the house of his friend Muhammad Ali. The final breaking of the fast was celebrated by the recital of passages from the Qur'an and the Upanishads and by the singing of both Christian and *Vaishnava* hymns.[8]

Calming emotions for a time, the fast did not have the long-term effect that Gandhi hoped for. Despite its overt failure, the *Khilafat* movement had at least one tangible domestic result: it strengthened the self-confidence of Indian Muslim leaders, many of whom were becoming increasingly suspicious of the National Congress (dominated by a majority of Hindus).[9] The situation was complicated by the rise to prominence of new Muslim voices, like that of Muhammad Iqbal, which, in lieu of interfaith unity, stressed the economic backwardness of Muslims in India and sometimes privileged pan-Islamic aspirations over national independence. One voice that was becoming increasingly influential in the period before World War II was that of Muhammad Ali Jinnah. Although trained like Gandhi at the London Inns of Court, Jinnah nurtured a completely different vision of the future of India and of the Indian Muslim community.

A cool-headed rationalist and legalist, Jinnah thoroughly disliked Gandhi's penchant for grassroots mobilization and also his intense concern with communal-religious harmony (or "heart unity"). Basically, his inclination was to deal with the British through constitutional negotiation, in the hope of possibly transforming India into an autonomous member within the British Empire or Commonwealth (preferably with separate constituencies for Hindus and Muslims). After assuming leadership of the Muslim League in 1937, Jinnah resolutely pursued his vision, and he was supported by many (though not all) Muslim leaders. From this time forward, Hindu and Muslim policies moved progressively in different directions. While Gandhi was desperately seeking to preserve communal harmony through the shared struggle for independence, Jinnah came to despair of national unity, opting instead for separation or partition. In 1944, a sustained conversation took place between Gandhi and Jinnah on the future of the subcontinent, but nothing was accomplished. B. R. Nanda states, "What was Gandhi's hope was Jinnah's fear."[10]

In the end, independence came in a torrent of blood. Even prior to British departure from India, intercommunal violence rocked many parts of the subcontinent. In August 1946, a bloody and destructive riot broke out in Calcutta, to be followed by Muslim attacks on Hindu villages in East Bengal and Hindu attacks on Muslim villages in Bihar. "From this time until his death by assassination in 1948," McDonough observes, "Gandhi lived his final years in the midst of a sort of hell on earth," for there can scarcely be a worse fate than "outbursts of violence among the very persons one has given one's life to serving." In a desperate effort to quench the flames of violence, the Mahatma during this period traveled on foot to remote, riot-torn villages, ignoring the frailty of his body and the dangers to himself. McDonough again: "The old man who tottered over the logs bridging the main streams in the jungles of Noakhali, and later in Bihar, was in no way confused about his goals: he wanted to communicate with the people in their native places and to teach them to live in peace with each other." Although he finally came to accept the partitioning of the subcontinent, the outcome for him was both a personal disappointment and an unmitigated national tragedy. When, shortly before his death and in the wake of the partition, violence struck Delhi, he undertook his last fast there. During this fast he dictated this message to his secretary:

> Anyone who wants to drive out of Delhi all Muslims as such, must be set down as its enemy number one, and therefore enemy number one of India. We are rushing toward that catastrophe; [but] it is the bounden duty of every son and daughter of India to take his or her full share in averting it.[11]

SOME SUSPICIONS AND CONTROVERSIES

Gandhi's commitment to interfaith and intercommunal harmony was in many ways shared by prominent Muslim leaders. Throughout his life, he enjoyed the friendship or at least close association of influential figures in the Muslim community on the subcontinent. During his early years, these figures included Hakim Ajmal Khan, the first chancellor of the Jamia Millia in Aligarh; Mukhtar A. Ansari, the second chancellor and twice president of the All-India Muslim League; and the brothers Muhammad and Shaukat Ali, organizers of the *Khilafat* movement. During his later years, friendly ties linked him with Abul Kalam Azad, repeatedly president of the Indian National Congress and later India's first minister of education; Zakir Husain, India's third president; S. Abid Husain, educator and writer; and the "frontier Gandhi" Abdul Ghaffar Khan, leader of the Pathans (or Pashtuns) on the northwest frontier. There are many testimonials attesting to Muslim affection and respect for Gandhi. Thus, a manifesto issued by Hakim Ajmal Khan and Mukhtar Ansari in 1922 stated that "our Hindu brothers . . . are our brothers in all truth, for the Holy Qur'an teaches that the friends of the faith are our brothers"; hence, "let us remain faithful in thought, word and deed, faithful to our cause, to our country, and to the leader we have chosen—Mahatma Gandhi."[12] After the bloody Calcutta riots of 1940, Abid Husain declared: "In Calcutta and Noakhali the fire of hatred was put out with the miraculous power of love by Mahatma Gandhi." And on the eve of independence, Abdul Ghaffar Khan stated, "Mahatmaji has shown us the true path. Long after we are no more, the coming generations of Hindus will remember him as an Avatar."[13]

Despite such testimonials, which could readily be multiplied, Gandhi's relations with Muslims were also troubled by various suspicions and points of contention. Ranking them in ascending order of importance, the following issues stand out: suspicions about Hindu terminology; disputes concerning specific incidents; disputes regarding broader strategies (especially nonviolence); and conflicts over constitutional design and the need for partition. Although sometimes emotionally charged, complaints about Gandhi's occasional "Hindu" rhetoric seem least difficult to settle. In order to lift up his countrymen to higher levels of duty and ethical conduct, the Mahatma sometimes invoked the classical image of *Ramarajya*, that is, the virtuous regime and rulership of Rama. Already during his South African period, he compared the Indian struggle against apartheid with the struggle waged by Rama and his followers against the demon-king Ravana. After Gandhi's return to India, Rama's virtuous reign was frequently upheld in his speeches as a counterpoise to British oppression and corruption. Combined with other seemingly "Hindu" preferences (like cow-protection and wearing of khadi cloth), Gandhi's rhetoric antagonized and alarmed numerous Muslims, who perceived it as the opening wedge of a more pervasive and domineering Hindu ideology. On the other hand, some right-wing Hindu leaders—probably against their better knowledge—greeted the rhetoric as a welcome concession to their own program of radical "Hindutva," Hindu majority rule.[14] However, more thoughtful people on both sides could hardly be deceived by such construals. Philosophically trained Muslims, for example, could hardly overlook the parallel between *Ramarajya* and al-Farabi's famous portrayal of the "virtuous city." Even without such training, Indians of all shades could readily detect the moral intent behind the rhetoric. An example is Zakir Husain, who, on becoming India's president, stated:

I have endeavored to follow in my life some of Mahatmaji's teaching . . . and I shall do my utmost to take our people towards what Gandhiji strove restlessly to achieve: a pure life, individual and social, . . . an active and sustained sympathy for the weak and downtrodden, and a fervent desire to forge unity among the diverse sections of the Indian people as the first condition for helping to establish peace and human brotherhood in the world based on truth and non-violence. This is what he called *Ram Raj*.[15]

More aggravating for intercommunal harmony, at least in the short run, were specific communal incidents and some Gandhian responses to them. Most prominent among such incidents was the Mappila (or Mo-plah) rebellion of 1921 in Kerala. The Mappilas were a Muslim community who had long suffered under foreign (Portuguese and British) domination and who also were the victims of a repressive landownership system con-trolled largely by the Hindu majority. Given their history of oppression, the Mappilas reacted favorably and even enthusiastically to the *Khilafat* movement and also to Gandhi's noncooperation policy. As things devel-oped, however, reaction went from resistance and noncooperation to out-right militancy. Starting in August 1921, Kerala was shaken by an increas-ingly violent uprising targeting both the British and the landowning Hindu establishment, an uprising marked by killings, arson, and even forced conversions. In the end, the rebellion was forcibly repressed, with massive costs in human lives for the Mappila community.

Apart from widening the gulf between Muslims and the British colo-nial regime, the events placed a severe strain on Hindu–Muslim relations, even affecting in some eyes the integrity of Gandhi's policies. For some Muslim leaders—including the Urdu poet Hasrat Mohani—the events had tested the Gandhian idea of Hindu–Muslim harmony and demon-strated its futility (given the complicity of many landowners with British authorities). Some others blamed Gandhi directly for the outcome of the rebellion. From Gandhi's side, the situation was relatively straightforward. For one thing, the uprising for him was an isolated incident from which no general conclusion could or should be drawn. For another thing (and more importantly), his sympathies were with the real grievances of the Mappilas, but not with the violent methods used by some of their leaders. To this extent, his criticism of some Mappila actions was not targeting that community, but reflected a general philosophical stance.[16]

Gandhi's attitude toward the Kerala events brings to the fore an issue often singled out as a major bone of contention between him and Mus-lims: the issue of nonviolence (*ahimsa*). Commitment to *ahimsa* was a central pillar in Gandhi's overall perspective and a loadstar in his public actions. It derived mainly from Jain and Buddhist sources, but observers have often claimed that *ahimsa* was not really indigenous to traditional Hindu culture, and certainly not an integral part of Muslim beliefs. During the struggle for Indian independence, the issue surfaced repeatedly as a dividing line between Gandhian and Muslim practices. Thus, on the eve of the Mappila rebellion, Gandhi's associate Shaukat Ali expressed disagreement quite openly: "I tell you that to kill and to be killed in the way of God are both *satyagraha*. To lay down our lives in the way of God for righteousness and to destroy the life of the tyrant who stands in the way of righteousness, are both a very great service to God." In a more conciliatory manner, he added, "We have promised to cooperate with Mr. Gandhi who is with us," but "if this fails, the Muselmans will decide what to do."[17]

In even more forceful terms, Hasrat Mohani defended the Mappila insurgency, including their violent actions, while dismissing *ahimsa*. Muslims who supported Gandhi's idea of nonviolence usually did it for tactical or strategic reasons, not on the grounds of moral principle. Mohammad Ali, the friend of his early period, expressed his view of *ahimsa* concisely in 1921 by stating that Gandhi and Muslims both stood for nonviolence, "he for reasons of principle and we for those of policy." Elaborating on this view, he added somewhat later: "I have agreed to work with Mahatma Gandhi, and our compact is that as long as I am associated with him, I should not resort to the use of force even for the purpose of self-defense," unless there was an overwhelming need to rebuff British oppression.[18]

Although clearly significant, the difference between Gandhi and Muslim leaders on this issue should probably not be overstated. On closer inspection, their respective positions show points of contact and even partial convergence. On the one hand, Gandhi's views were not as categorical or apodictic as is sometimes assumed. Although he proclaimed *ahimsa* as a general maxim of action, he was willing to make exceptions in dire emergencies as a last resort to protect lives. Loath to accept violence as a matter of deliberate policy, he made room for spontaneous retaliation under grave provocation and to relieve unbearable conditions caused by direct assault. As he remarked to Louis Fischer in 1944, he was prepared to go even further and to condone minimal violence if needed to promote economic, especially agrarian, justice.[19] On the other hand, Muslim beliefs do not simply favor violence over nonviolence as a general principle; the reverse is closer to the truth. Although it stresses the importance of struggle (*jihad*), Islamic religion in its basic commitments is oriented toward peace (*salam*) and just and peaceful human relations. Islamic teachings differentiate between a "greater" and a "lesser" *jihad*, with the former denoting a personal struggle for moral righteousness and the latter involving violent confrontations under exceptional circumstances and for limited purposes (mainly for the sake of self-defense). It was because of the primary emphasis in these teachings on "greater" or "righteous struggle" that Gandhi in some of his campaigns and speeches could use the vocabularies of *jihad* and *satyagraha* as nearly equivalent. At least to some extent, his outlook in this respect was shared by prominent Muslim leaders of the time. To quote Muhammad Ali again (speaking to the National Congress in 1923):

> I believe that war is a great evil, but I also believe that there are worse things than war.... When war is forced on Muslims, then as a Muselman and follower of the Last of the Prophets I may not shrink but must give the enemy battle on his own ground.... [But] when persecution ceases, and every man is free to act with the sole motive of securing divine good will, warfare must cease. These are the limits of violence in Islam.[20]

From a broader, world-historical perspective, the most important factor troubling Hindu–Muslim relations was the dispute between Gandhi and Jinnah over basic policy issues. As stated before, Jinnah was a London-trained lawyer with a strong penchant for legal procedures and little or no interest in "heart unity" between different faiths or communities. By contrast, Gandhi sought to cultivate intercommunal harmony and respect as a precondition for the legitimacy and viability of legal procedures and institutions.[21] At least initially, the two leaders strove for the same or a roughly similar goal, namely, India's independence, but they pursued this goal along different paths, which in the end radically diverged. Basically, Gandhi hoped for a unified and legally "secular" (or nondiscriminatory) India whose unity was precisely guaranteed by the strength of intercommunal and interfaith interactions on the societal level. On the other hand,

Jinnah's vision of the future India was predicated mainly on a procedural maxim that can be described as a "separate-but-equal" formula.

This difference in policies brings to the fore more recessed but crucial contrasts involving different views of modernity, and especially different conceptions of a modern liberal political regime. Both sides departed in their own ways from the "mainstream" paradigm of such a regime. For Gandhi, modern liberal institutions were useful for generating a sense of equal citizenship; however, because of a deep-seated distrust of centralized bureaucracies, he aimed to supplement and correct "top-down" legal procedures with "bottom-up" democratic mobilization and intercommunal engagement. Jinnah's departures from the mainline paradigm were even more pronounced—and deeply puzzling. Although he supported the modern conception of the "state" as a contractual artifact, his "separate-but-equal" formula led him to conflate his liberal proceduralism with deeply noncontractual premises and assumptions: premises anchoring the state in "essentialized" modes of religion and nationhood. Thus, a liberal-secular leader became in the end the founder of an Islamic or proto-Islamic country.[22]

The conflict between Gandhi and Jinnah can be pursued through several decades prior to independence, but for now, the briefest sketch must suffice. In the early negotiations with the British regarding representative institutions, the colonial power—with considerable support from Muslims—decided in favor of "separate electorates," which basically divided India along religious and communal lines. The decision was opposed by liberal opinion both in Britain and in India precisely because of its violation of liberal principles (one person, one vote). Bhikku Parekh observes, summarizing the opponents' view, "Under the system of separate electorates, the state reproduced the divisions of society and, rather than impartially arbitrate between them [as modern liberalism demands], became an arena of their conflicts." Moreover, by inscribing religious divisions into the structure of the state, the system "was bound to make Indians abnormally conscious of their differences and prevent them from developing a sense of common citizenship."[23]

Over the years, separate electorates became a standing feature of pre-independence India (with new communal identities steadily being added to the system). Even though it was firmly resisted by the leaders of the National Congress, the electoral arrangement was strongly supported by Jinnah as a device to protect the Muslim minority, a device initially justified on communal-religious grounds and later, more ambitiously, in terms of nationhood. In a letter addressed to Gandhi in 1944, Jinnah stated provocatively: "We maintain that Muslims and Hindus are two major nations by any definition or test of a nation. We are a nation . . . with our distinctive culture and civilization, language and literature, . . . legal laws and moral codes, customs and calendar, history and traditions." Gandhi found it relatively easy to debunk this "two-nation" argument by stressing the many commonalities of language, customs, and historical experiences, and also by pointing to the possible proliferation of Indian "nationalities" (from Sikhs and Parsis to Christians and tribals). There are indications that Jinnah himself did not quite embrace his own argument, except for purely strategic reasons. Once the new state of Pakistan came into being, he abandoned his earlier rhetoric and urged Muslims and Hindus alike to act as "common citizens of the state."[24]

On the eve of India's independence, Gandhi reluctantly and with grave misgivings accepted partition, keenly sensing its dangers and its potential for unleashing massive violence. Despite his deep misgivings about centralized state structures, he also came to accept the need for a formal constitutional order for the country left after partition. On the evening before his assassination, he was actually working on a draft of the new Indian constitution, lending his legal talent to this project. But his heart was not fully in it, and he left the details of "nation-building" to such associates as Nehru and Vallabbhai Patel. What mattered to him more at that point, given the prevailing afflictions, were grassroots initiatives and the fostering of intercommunal solidarity. Shortly before his death, he launched an idea precisely designed to foster such solidarity: the transformation of the National Congress into a *Loka Sevak Sangh*, that is, a national organization for the service of the people or, better, of the servants of the people.

Members of the *Sangh* were to settle in villages and to promote grassroots regeneration. In Parekh's account, they were "to 'awaken' people to their rights, sensitize them to the 'wrongs' done to them, and mediate between them and the official agencies of the state." Acting in this manner, they were "to win over the confidence and trust of the people, build up their strength, and set up a structure of moral authority paralleling the legal authority of the 'official' state."[25] Gandhi during this period did not just formulate ideas or proposals, but exemplified their meaning in his practical conduct. Traveling on foot to distant villages and seeking to calm the fury of intercommunal violence was a concrete demonstration of the idea of *Loka Sevak Sangh*, showing what it meant for an erstwhile leader of the Congress to be a "servant of the people." In this practical testimonial Gandhi was pretty much alone. Sulking and frustrated by events, the former colonial power simply abandoned the subcontinent without providing any military or police protection for the masses of people trying to cross borders in their scramble for new homes. Nor did the man most responsible for the partition, Jinnah, lift a finger in order to douse the flames of communal mayhem. In the words of B. R. Nanda, "If Jinnah had toured East Bengal or West Punjab, he might have helped in stopping the rot." However, such a suggestion would have been "laughed away by the League leader; consummate politician as he was, his political instincts rebelled against fasts and walking tours."[26]

"LIBERAL" STATE AND MULTICULTURALISM

India's struggle for independence is today only a distant memory; however, the issue of intercommunal and interfaith harmony remains as timely and urgent as ever. In this respect, Gandhi's involvement with the "Muslim question" offers numerous lessons for us. The dominant tenor of this involvement was not only open-minded tolerance, but something deeper and more existential: affectionate respect and sympathy. He wrote in his foreword to the *Sayings of Muhammad*: "There will be no lasting peace on earth unless we learn not merely to tolerate but even to respect the other faiths as our own. A reverent study of the sayings of the different teachers of mankind is a step in the direction of such mutual respect."[27] What this means is that interfaith goodwill depends not only on information and acquisition of knowledge, but on a kind of participation in the inner life and spiritual strivings or aspirations of different faiths. Only through such participation, in Gandhi's view, was it possible to foster the emergence of a genuine and peaceful—though highly diversified or multidimensional— community of well-meaning people everywhere, a kind of ethical-spiritual

umma or *Ramarajya.* Margaret Chatterjee aptly states, "It was Gandhi's belief that there was a mysterious connivance at work between the creative
powers in man and the divine forces in the universe. To release, through
cooperation and mutual aid, the positive forces in man was at once to tap
the divine source of energy." She adds, "Religion envisaged as a way of life of
the caring individual who participates in a multi-faith community, striving
non-violently to establish a just society, would be close to the conception of
the founding figures, saints and seers of the different traditions."[28]

Placing the accent on participation in a multifaith community means
to de-emphasize those aspects of religion that tend to divide peoples:
theological dogmas or doctrines and external rituals. In the tradition of
Sufism and *bhakti* devotion—but also in the tradition of Erasmus and
other leaders in the age of Reformation—the core of religiosity here is
found in personal piety and ethical conduct, that is, in *orthopraxis* rather
than *orthodoxy.* This practical aspect of Gandhi's religious outlook is well
highlighted by Sheila McDonough when she writes that he conceived of
religious life as "primarily personal, that is, of the individual using the images which come to him or to her to illuminate a particular situation."
From a Gandhian perspective, religious images and symbols were to be
understood "as catalysts which can stimulate direction and purpose in
specific contexts." Given this purposive orientation (consonant with his
role as a *karmayogin*), McDonough elaborates, there was "a strong element of practicality in Gandhi's make-up which comes out even in his attitude to religious teaching: it is good if it works; otherwise not." Hence, in
his intercommunal or interfaith interactions, his invocation of both
Hindu and Muslim vocabularies was always directed "towards shaping
awareness of the adherents of the two communities in the direction of active involvement in a specific struggle." During his younger years, Gandhi
studied intently the works of the Muslim reformer Shibli Numani, whose
goal was to regenerate Islamic attitudes, especially in India. Among the
heroes singled out in Shibli's writings were such figures as Caliph Umar
and Abu Hanifa, who were characterized by "piety combined with the creative ability to devise new ways in the light of new circumstances." In his
later years, Gandhi often found himself in a situation similar to that experienced by al-Ghazali, who had deplored the potential for corruption and
violence, even among outwardly "religious" people. McDonough states,

"Ghazali and Gandhi had both concluded that personal religious discipline was an essential basis for the sane and healthy transformation of the wider social order." For his part, Gandhi always interpreted fanatical Muslim violence as a "corrupt understanding of Islam," just as Hindu violence was a "corrupt understanding of Hinduism."[29]

Gandhi's attitudes and practices have relevance far beyond the original Indian context. Of crucial significance are his lessons for modern politics, and especially for the workings of a modern "liberal" regime. According to the mainstream construal of such a regime, liberalism denotes an exodus from "tradition," and especially from particular religious traditions, that is, the adoption of a neutral spectator view vis-à-vis all religious, spiritual, and even ethical beliefs and practices. Although "liberating" people (in a way) from traditional constraints, the adoption of this stance is also enormously debilitating for spiritual *orthopraxis* and ethics: removed from the complex agonies of human bonds, neutral liberals are also exiled (or exile themselves) from the challenges of intercommunal or interfaith engagement and from the travails of ethical-spiritual transformation. In this regard, Gandhi's dispute with Jinnah remains deeply instructive. Jinnah—despite his flirtation with Islamic faith and nationhood—preferred to retreat into the realm of legal procedures and formal state structures. Gandhi, by contrast, opted for a grassroots approach seeking to generate goodwill and "heart unity" between different communities. He admonished his fellow workers at one point: "Islam is not a false religion. Let Hindus study it reverently and they will love it even as I do. . . . If Hindus set their house in order, I have not a shadow of doubt that Islam will respond in a manner worthy of its 'liberal' traditions." At the end of his last fast, he again exhorted his assembled associates that they "should understand the meaning of what they read and have equal regard for all religions," as had been his own lifelong practice. By doing so, they would be able "to learn from all" and hence "forget the communal differences and live together in peace and amity."[30]

What looms behind Gandhi's encounter with Jinnah is the broad and difficult question of the relation between the modern "state" apparatus and the complex fabric of civil society with its diverse customs and historical sedimentations. Gandhi did not entirely reject modern state structures; toward the end of his life, he even helped in designing the structures of the new Indian government, but he remained deeply suspicious of centralized state power. It was because of this deep-seated suspicion that he wished to supplement, or juxtapose to, formal state authority with the civil-society–based association or movement of the *Loka Sevak Sangh* entrusted with the task of moral and political awakening and ethical transformation. In his conception, the two institutions of the state and the *Sangh* were to be neither entirely divorced nor conflated, but to function in a differential entwinement. The greatest danger resided in their fusion. In Parekh's presentation, the state by its very nature "wielded enormous legal authority and power"; if it were also operating as an institution invested with moral authority, citizens "would not only feel obliged to obey its laws blindly but also entrust it with the custody of their conscience." Hence, for Gandhi, some tension needed to be preserved to allow for constructive critique. Although he accepted the state as an "essentially *legal* institution," moral and spiritual authority, accruing from "the trust and confidence of the people," belonged in his view to civil-society associations, especially the *Sangh*.[31] Behind the tension between state and society, another tension comes to the fore: that between reason (or mind) and heart, in the sense that the state for Gandhi was chiefly governed by legal rationality, while society was the realm of ethics and goodwill. To this extent one might say that Gandhi's recipe for the divisions of modern life was not only a "heart unity" but a "heart-and-mind" unity. This reading would concur with his statement in *Young India* (1931): "I have come to the fundamental conclusion that if you want something really important to be done, you must not merely satisfy the reason, you must move the heart also."[32]

In our globalizing context today, the idea of a "heart-and-mind" engagement and cooperation among peoples has particular salience. Faced with recurrent interethnic and interreligious conflicts—sometimes styled as "clashes of civilizations"—the world desperately needs a strengthening both of global norms and institutions and of intersocietal or cross-cultural goodwill. At the same time, given the upsurge of neo-colonialism and neo-imperialism in recent times, peoples everywhere need to recall Gandhi's suspicions regarding hegemonic state structures, suspicions based on the proclivity of power structures to foster corruption and to obstruct intercommunal cooperation (sometimes by intensifying communal conflicts). A case in point is the situation on the Indian subcontinent following partition: basically, long-standing intercommunal tensions have been reconstituted and intensified by interstate rivalries, with central state structures often fueling communal strife. Rajmohan Gandhi says that strenuous efforts are needed today to bridge the gaps "that distance Indians from Pakistanis and Bangladeshis," and also those gaps "that will divide India's Hindus from their Muslim counterparts." In order to overcome these divisions, enlightened "statesmanship in the subcontinent's rulers and wisdom in the populace will be required." Returning to recent events in Gujarat, the Mahatma's grandson eloquently pleaded in favor of a renewed "heart-and-mind" engagement and cooperation:

> Huge tasks beckon: lifting from Gujarat the shroud of terror; restoring to Gujarat's Muslims a sense that their lives count and will be protected; . . . bringing some compensation and healing to the thousands damaged by the inferno; recalling Gujarat's Hindus to their tradition of a calm and honest Hinduism, a Hinduism that feels another's sorrow and does not need an enemy for its sustenance; and presenting alternatives to Gujarat's enraged youth, Hindu and Muslim.[33]

CHAPTER SIX

Five Relations Plus One

Confucianism and Public Life

To learn and at proper times to repeat what one has learned,
is that not after all a pleasure? That friends should come
to visit one from afar, is this not after all delightful?

—Confucius, *Analects*

Rudyard Kipling's famous adage about East and West appears obsolete today. In our age of globalization, the two cultural hemispheres not only "meet" but challenge and interpenetrate each other at a steadily accelerating rate. Not implausibly, this process has given rise to anticipations of a global civil society or civic culture, perhaps even of the rudiments of cosmopolis. Yet, despite such "one-world" visions, the interpenetration of hemispheres has not been entirely mutual or a two-way street. In large measure, contemporary globalization is the result of Western initiatives stretching from the Enlightenment to industrialization to the "information revolution." These initiatives, in turn, can be traced to a deeper trait or tendency inhabiting Western culture: the tendency to transgress itself, to prefer distance to proximity, new vistas to habitual ways.[1] In a palpable manner, this tendency has manifested itself historically in a steady sequence of expansions: from Alexander to the conquest of the Americas to later colonialism and imperialism. Seen from this angle, contemporary globalization, at least in part, follows a long-standing pattern. Confined to "Westernization," the ongoing process falls short of proper mutuality and, to this extent, still confirms Kipling's adage about the inability of hemispheres to meet.

Apart from its palpable manifestations, the shortfall surfaces in a number of more recessed cultural and spiritual arenas, including the relations between transcendence and immanence, between universal principles and local customs, between impartiality and concrete engagement. Given the close linkage between globalization and democratization, one cultural arena deserves special attention: the one that has to do with the relation between organized politics and the "life-world," between formal political structures and more informal or personal affairs. In this respect, Western culture has traditionally favored a neat differentiation and even separation: the separation of public from private domains, of uniform legal rules from diversified customs or—in classical terms—of *polis* from *oikos* (household). By contrast, "Eastern" culture—meaning here prominent traditions in South Asia and East Asia—has (on the whole) preferred to think of human life as a complex web of closely intertwined dimensions, a web in which impersonal and personal relations are mingled and fused, and where politics is seen as playing an important but by no means a privileged or autonomous role. Over the centuries, this difference of perspectives has proved to be a serious stumbling block in the mutual understanding between cultures, often fanning hostile recriminations (proving Kipling's thesis). Here I make an effort to explore and, I hope, clarify the difference by focusing on a significant strand in East Asian culture: the legacy of Confucianism. To set the stage for this examination, the opening section recalls prominent features of Western political philosophy from Aristotle to the present, especially features having to do with the distinction between public and private domains. It is against the backdrop of these features that I next profile Confucian classical and neoclassical teachings, with an emphasis on the "five relationships" (with their mingling of political and nonpolitical roles). I end by offering reflections on the prospects of mutual learning and hence of a possible rapprochement or "meeting" between East and West.

WESTERN POLITICAL THOUGHT: POLIS VERSUS NATURE

For many reasons, and especially for reasons of definitional clarity, Aristotle can rightly be considered the founder of Western political philosophy. To be sure, many of his teachings can be traced to earlier precedents, especially to Plato's *Republic* and *Laws*. In these dialogues, we find already an important "dividing line" between passions and philosophical knowledge, a division that gives rise to a pyramidal political structure in which reason or knowledge rules over ordinary dispositions; we also find the idea of a general rule of law superseding more localized customs or practices. Building on such precedents, Aristotle opens his *Politics* with a pyramidal design of human associations in which different households and villages coalesce and culminate in the superior and unique association of the *polis* (city). What links these different associations is their orientation toward "some good"; what distinguishes the *polis* from the rest is that it is "the particular association which is the most sovereign of all and, including all the others, pursues its aim [of the good] most fully and is directed toward the most sovereign of goods." Apart from aiming at the highest good, the *polis* is also distinguished by the fact that it is not simply a "natural" association, prompted by natural impulses, but rather one that—without being unnatural—has a moral and legal basis. Notwithstanding his portrayal of "man" as a "political animal," Aristotle does not exclude the role of deliberate design. Although there is "an immanent impulse in all men towards an association of this [political] type," he writes, "the man who first *constructed* such an association was none the less the greatest of benefactors." What emerges in the *polis* is the novel dimension of justice and lawfulness. For justice, he adds, "belongs to the *polis*"; in fact, justice, "which is the determination of what is just, is an ordering of the political association."[2]

Although admitting a certain continuity between household and *polis*, Aristotle resolutely underscores their difference: "It is a mistake to believe that the 'statesman' [the *politikos* involved in a political association] is the same as the monarch of a kingdom, or the manager of a household, or the master of a number of slaves." Those who hold this mistaken view and assert their similarity maintain that the various roles differ from each other, not with a "difference of kind," but only with a difference of degree or of numbers. Thus, someone who controls a few persons as slaves is said to be a "master"; someone who rules over more people is termed the "manager" of a household; and still someone who governs a multitude is called a "statesman" (*politikos*) or a monarch. This view, Aristotle objects, "abolishes any real difference between a large household and a small *polis*"; and it also "reduces the difference between the *politikos* and the monarch [someone who rules a kingdom like his household] to the mere fact that the latter has sole and uncontrolled authority, while the former exercises his authority in conformity with [publicly established] rules." Such a view "cannot be accepted as correct" because it neglects the "essential" difference between roles and associations. One aspect of this essential divergence was signaled before by the reference to the dimension of justice and lawfulness inherent in the *polis*. Another crucial feature emerges later when Aristotle contrasts the equality prevailing among members of the *polis* with the asymmetrical or unequal character of relations in other associations. A properly constituted *polis*, he says, is "constructed on the principle that its members are equals and peers" and that they should "hold office by turns," a principle that ensures no one is permanently superior or inferior and hence that everyone should conduct public affairs for the benefit of all, in accordance with justice: "Those regimes which foster the common benefit are *right* regimes, judged by the standards of absolute justice," while those privileging "the personal interest of the rulers are *wrong* regimes, or *perversions* of the right kinds."[3]

By contrast to the (relative) equality found in cities, all other human associations are marked by asymmetry or forms of superordination and subordination. This is clearly the case in the household (*oikos*), which is ruled by the "manager," or *pater familias*, and which is made up of three basic relationships: husband and wife, parent and child, and master and slave. To these three relations might be added a fourth: king or monarch in a village that is ruled like a larger household. As Aristotle states, a village is simply "a colony or offshoot from a family," and this is the reason "why each Greek city was originally ruled—as the peoples of the barbarian world still are—by kings," for "households are always monarchically governed by the eldest of kin" and villages likewise. In all these associations or groupings, asymmetry or asymmetrical rulership prevails, which is simply the result of a general principle pervading nature at large. For, leaving aside inanimate matter, Aristotle notes, it is "certainly possible to observe in animate beings the presence of a ruling authority." Thus, the soul rules (or is meant to rule) the body with "the authority of a master," while mind or reason rules over appetite with "the authority of a statesman or a monarch." Now, what holds good in the "inner life" of human beings "holds good outside" also, meaning that the relation of soul to body carries over into the relation of "man to animals"; likewise, the relation of male to female is "naturally that of the superior to the inferior, of the ruling to the ruled." With regard to the management of the household, Aristotle perceives various shadings of rulership. In general terms, the relation of husband to wife is one of unequal partnership, that of parents to children is like the rule of "a king over his subjects," while the relation of manager to slaves is complete mastery. On the other hand, a *politikos* in a city has only "authority over freemen and equals," that is, rules only periodically as *primus inter pares*.[4]

A central part of the *Politics* deals with the character of the *polis* as a "public sphere" inhabited by equal citizens. As Aristotle emphasizes, citizenship is not determined by physical residence or other purely "natural" criteria; nor is it rooted in purely "private" rights, such as the ability to sue or be sued in courts in matters relating to private or personal status (marriage, testation, and the like). Rather, citizenship is anchored in public practices, namely, "sharing in the administration of justice and the holding of public office." As he concedes, this definition applies "particularly and especially to citizens of a democracy," while citizens living under other regimes may only partly fit the description. To accommodate possible variations, the text offers a more general formulation, saying that anyone "who enjoys the right of sharing in deliberative or judicial office [for any period] attains thereby the status of a citizen [*polites*] of his state." Being jointly committed to the goal of justice and lawfulness, citizens in a *polis* are assumed to transgress the narrow limits of private/personal self-interest; to this extent, without sharing ties of kinship, they are linked together by a civic bond or relationship: the bond of friendship (or something close to a friendly disposition). In Aristotle's words, by contrast to people who know only how to rule or how to obey, citizens exhibit a more judicious quality: the "spirit of friendships," which is the proper "temper" of a political community; for where enmity prevails instead of friendship, people "will not even share the same path." Friendship among equals in the city does not entirely obviate or cancel asymmetrical rulership, for the "freedom" of equal citizens is "naturally" superior both to the unfreedom of noncitizens at home and to unfree "barbarians" abroad. Aristotle states somewhat harshly, quoting an earlier poet: "Meet it is that barbarous people should be governed by the Greeks—the assumption being that barbarian and slave are by nature one and the same."[5]

In large measure, subsequent political philosophy in the West is a series of variations on Aristotelian themes. On the whole, the breach between public and private domains, between *polis* and *oikos*, is maintained and even steadily widened, without affecting the basic subordination of the latter under the former. Under the aegis of Aristotle's pupil Alexander, the structure of the *polis* was changed and expanded into a far-flung empire comprising much of the Middle East. Alexander, Ernest Barker writes, embarked on building an empire "in which he should be equally lord of Greeks and Persians," a move that inaugurated "the idea of the equality of all men—urban or rural, Greek or barbarian—in a *cosmopolis*." What Barker does not mention is that this empire still meant the rule of Greeks (or sufficiently assimilated non-Greeks) over large, subordinated populations, while simultaneously bending civic equality to the whim of imperial power. The idea of civic equality in a cosmopolis—or rather, an empire—became later a central tenet of the Stoics, who, according to Plutarch, held that "men should not live their lives in so many civic republics" but "should reckon *all* humans as their fellow-citizens under one order (*cosmos*)," an order coinciding basically with the Roman Empire. During the Christian Middle Ages, this notion of cosmopolis was transformed into the vision of a universal or "catholic" Christendom, but concrete conditions on the ground required many local adjustments. The apex of medieval political thought saw the attempt to combine Aristotle's teachings in the *Politics* with universal Christian aspirations, an attempt at the heart of the work of Thomas Aquinas. Barker says that Thomas's work

> united some of the essential doctrines of the *polis* with the doctrine and practice of cosmopolis. It was through this fusion that there passed into the general thought of the later Middle Ages some of the essential doctrines of the *Politics*—the doctrine that law is the true sovereign, and that governments are servants of the law; the doctrine

that there is a fundamental difference between the lawful monarch and the tyrant who governs by his arbitrary will; the doctrine that there is a right inherent in the people, by virtue of their collective capacity of judgment, to elect their rulers and to call them to account.[6]

The onset of modernity brought a number of significant innovations. Among these, the most important was a deepening of the rift between *polis* and *oikos*, now formulated as the distinction between the political state (commonwealth) and the "state of nature"; a corollary of this change was the bracketing of the former's lingering naturalness in favor of its constructive design under the aegis of the "social contract." Both moves were dramatically inaugurated by Thomas Hobbes. In the very opening pages of his *Leviathan*, and also in *On the Citizen* (*De Cive*), Hobbes takes aim at Aristotle and medieval "schoolmen" following him, and especially at the assumption of the naturalness of politics (captured in the phrase "political animal"), an assumption, he writes, that "though received by most, is yet certainly false and an error proceeding from our too slight contemplation of human nature." Instead of being nature's design, the *polis* or political community for Hobbes is entirely an artifact or artificial construct, which he also calls an "artificial animal"; for by art or design is created "that great Leviathan called a commonwealth or state (in Latin *civitas*) which is but an artificial man" and in which "sovereignty is an artificial soul." The method of construction, however, is by way of contract, through those "pacts and covenants by which the parts of the body politic were at first made, set together and united."[7] Under somewhat changed auspices, Hobbes's initiatives were continued by John Locke, with an opening salvo against naturalness. The waning years of the medieval world had produced various political ambiguities or confusions; prominent among them was the confusion of *polis* and *oikos*, of political rulership and household management. Prototypically, this merger was defended by Robert Filmer, whose *Patriarcha* equated kingship with the role of *pater familias*. Attacking this equation, Locke's *First Treatise* briskly demolished the notion of "paternal government" or "fatherly authority" in politics, guiding his readers back to the more customary way of forming regimes: "by contrivance and the consent of men making use of their reason to unite together into society."[8]

Locke's *Second Treatise* eloquently affirmed the artificiality of the *polis*, its origin in rational design, in a manner that, for all practical purposes, became canonical in modern Western political thought. Taking his cues from Hobbes, Locke underscored the bifurcation of nature and commonwealth, stating that "those who are united into one body, and have a common established law and judicature to appeal to ... are in civil society one with another," whereas "those who have no such common appeal, I mean on earth, are still in the state of nature." The transition from the latter to former condition is the work of deliberate construction, more specifically of a social contract erecting a common government with a shared rule of law. For, Locke insists, being "by nature all free, equal and independent," nobody can be assumed to be naturally subjected to political power except through "his own consent," which is done "by agreeing with other men to join and unite into a community for their comfortable, safe, and peaceable living," and by "putting himself under an obligation to every one of that society to submit to the determination of the majority." In keeping with this basic postulate, later sections of the *Second Treatise* reinforce the distinction between "paternal," "political," and "despotical" power by claiming that the first (of parents over children) is granted by nature, while the second is the result of "voluntary agreement," and the last of subjugation and forfeiture (of rights).[9] In the wake of these teachings, Locke's "liberalism" gave rise to another distinctive feature of modern Western life as compared with classical antiquity: the emergence of a novel "civil society" wedged between *polis* and *oikos*. Congruent with the emphasis on construction and contractual agreement, this society became the driving engine in the development of the market economy (or capitalism) and, concomitantly, in the advancement of modern science, industry, and technology.

This is not the place to recount in detail the story of post-Lockean political thought. Suffice it to say that, although many of Locke's claims have been challenged, including the idea of a "state of nature," the overall structure of his argument has remained largely intact. To illustrate the mixture of continuity and discontinuity, one may wish to glance briefly at a recent political thinker not usually associated with the Lockean legacy: Hannah Arendt. Among her many contributions, Arendt is well known for her vindication of the *vita activa*, or active participation in the "public sphere." Her opening chapter in *The Human Condition* deals precisely with the distinction between *polis* and *oikos*, or what she calls the "public" and the "private" realms. In large measure, this distinction coincides with that between freedom and necessity, or between equal public status and asymmetrical personal relations. The distinctive trait of the "household sphere," she says, is that its members are "driven by their wants and needs," especially the need for survival; hence, "natural community" in the household is "born of necessity." By contrast, the "realm of the *polis*" is the "sphere of freedom," and since ancient times, political thought has taken for granted "that freedom is exclusively located in the political realm" composed of "equals" or peers. An important innovative feature of Arendt's work is her differentiation not only between *polis* and *oikos* (or between "action" and "labor" geared to survival needs), but also between public action and "work" or instrumental design, where the latter term comprises both economic production and the fabrication of technical artifacts. One of her major complaints about modern politics, in fact, is the growing blurring of differences evident in the modern "rise of the social," that is, the progressive colonization of the public sphere first by *homo faber* (or construction) and then by *animal laborans* (or consumerism). In its classical sense, Arendt insists, politics was never a mere adjunct of "society," "a society of the faithful, as in the Middle Ages, or a society of property-owners, as in Locke, ... or a society of producers, as in Marx, or a society of jobholders [consumers], as in our own."[10]

THE CONFUCIAN FIVE RELATIONSHIPS

Arendt's complaint about the blurring of domains might also have been addressed to the East Asian context, particularly the legacy of Confucianism. Asian culture (on the whole) has resisted the neat division or demarcation of domains, preferring to see human and social life instead as a complex web of relationships, as a holistic fabric of elements held together by some kind of inner balance. This difference is particularly important with regard to politics, the public sphere. Asian culture acknowledges the function of politics but has never assigned to politics the commanding height over society that was allotted to it in the Western tradition (even when its supremacy was subordinated to the still more commanding heights of philosophy and theology). In large measure, this Western command structure had to do with the presumed supremacy of reason over passion, of symmetry over asymmetry, of general rules or principles over particular customs or practices. What renders cultural comparison, including the comparative study of political thought, so difficult is the sea change that needs to be negotiated: the fact that one is dealing not with isolated elements but with symbolic "ensembles," or clusters, in other words, with holistic language games that cannot simply be collapsed into each other (without being utterly incommensurable).[11]

In classical Confucian teachings, politics is by no means neglected, but is inserted into a larger ensemble of the "five relationships" (*wu-lun*) of husband and wife, father and son (or parent and child), older sibling and younger sibling, ruler and minister, and friend and friend. All these relationships are at first glance personal relations involving a certain closeness or proximity. The first two dyads (husband/wife and parent/child) correspond to two relations in Aristotle's conception of the *oikos*. Confucian teachings add a third "household" relation (sibling/sibling) not thematized by Aristotle, while entirely omitting the dyad of master and slave, an aspect that will we will take up a bit later. The only "political" relation is that between ruler and minister, but the relation is not elevated above others and certainly not stylized as a "public sphere" in which reason and equal freedom would rule over passions and private asymmetries. The only general (or at least generalizable) relation is that between friend and friend, more precisely between older and younger friend, but the accent is again on proximity rather than broader public engagement (in the Aristotelian sense of public *philia*). Thus, society in the Confucian view seems to be segmented and highly particularized, in contradistinction to the pyramidal structure of Western politics. Moreover, all five relationships are characterized by asymmetry or a degree of superordination and subordination, giving the impression to Western observers of an assortment of quasi-feudal hierarchies. In larger measure, this impression is at the root of the "Orientalist" view of Asian culture as static and confining, predicated on the Western equation of progress and development with growing individual autonomy and rationalization.

Although plausible at first blush, the Orientalist view appears deeply misguided. For one thing, it forces Asian thought into a set of categories not properly germane to it. Although none of the Confucian relationships may be "public," or general, in the Western sense, they also are not simply "private," or particularistic, which is merely the reverse side of the same coin. The tendency to "privatize" or particularize Confucian concepts has been ably criticized by Herbert Fingarette in several of his writings, especially in *Confucius: The Secular as Sacred*. Western students of the *Analects* may be tempted, he says, to place the locus of Confucian conduct in "subjective feelings and attitudes," that is, in private psychological dispositions (in contrast to rational principles). Countering this temptation, Fingarette maintains that the thought expressed in the *Analects* is not at all "based on psychological notions." The point is not that Confucius deliberately meant to exclude reference to "the inner psyche," but rather that the reference "never entered his mind." As an antidote to privatization, Fingarette refers to the role of ceremony or ritual in channeling human conduct, what in the *Analects* is called *li*. Such ceremony, he states, is not simply an external form but a genuine style of life, a style both individual and societal, both personal and impersonal or superpersonal; ultimately it confers meaning and dignity on human life (even a kind of "sacred dignity"). This aspect also points to the profound relationality or transpersonality of human conduct in Confucius's teachings, a quality eloquently expressed in these lines of the *Analects*:

> You want to establish yourself, then seek to establish others. You wish to advance your standing, then advance that of others. From what is near to you to seize the analogy [i.e., to take the neighbor or other as yourself]—this is the way of *jen* [goodness, humaneness].[12]

Most commentators agree that the feature in Confucius's teachings that most resembles a general or public principle is *jen*, the virtue of goodness or humaneness. According to the eminent Chinese expert Wing-tsit Chan, *jen* in fact should be seen as a general virtue, "which is basic, universal, and the source of all specific virtues."[13] Yet, as one must also realize, *jen* is not simply an abstract maxim but always functions in human relationships that are concrete and diversified and shaped, at least in part, by particular customs, ceremonies, or rituals. This complex character of *jen* has been prominently elucidated by Tu Wei-ming, who treats the notion as a "living metaphor," that is, a metaphor for ethical and properly humanized ways of life. "There is no assumption in the *Analects*," he writes, "like the one found in the objectivists' claim that 'all truly reasonable men will always finally agree'" or concur on a general rational principle; rather, it is taken for granted that "reasonable men of diverse personalities will have differing visions of the way" (*tao*) and follow different paths in practicing *jen*. This diversity of paths, however, Tu adds, should not be confused with individual arbitrariness or the pursuit of "projects" suiting private whims. Rather, practicing or cultivating *jen* requires a "continuous process of symbolic exchange through the sharing of communally cherished values with other selves." To the extent that the *Analects* recognize a "self" or selfhood, it is a *relational* self or a "self as center of relationships" rather than an "isolable individual" pursuing random goals; accordingly, cultivation of self or "self-realization" is impossible "except in matrices of human converse" or interaction. To this extent, fostering goodness or humaneness is not a "lonely struggle" or a quest for "inner truth," which would be "isolable from an 'outer' or public realm." Instead of denoting a purely subjective search, *jen* as a basic virtue depends both on self-scrutiny and a "meaningful communal" engagement, which Tu also describes as engagement in a "fiduciary community."[14]

Extending his analysis from the *Analects* to the neo-Confucian period, Tu Wei-ming stresses the continued importance of relationality or transpersonality, despite a steady deepening of inner-directedness coupled with a growing metaphysical universalism (in part due to Buddhist influences). In his view, neo-Confucian thought can best be grasped as a twofold process: "a continuous deepening of one's subjectivity and an uninterrupted broadening of one's sensitivity." Self-cultivation still implies a communal bond, but it now entails a series of tensions and paradoxes. In order to fully plumb its inwardness, the self must simultaneously overcome itself and its self-centered structure. Accordingly, to deepen one's subjectivity requires "an unceasing struggle to eliminate selfish and egoistic desires" while also extending one's sensitivity or receptivity to broadening horizons of the world.

In Tu's words, the neo-Confucian perspective on fostering goodness/humaneness (*jen*) involves "a dynamic interplay between contextualization and decontextualization," which can also be described as "a dialectic of structural limitation and procedural freedom" operative at each stage of the ethical quest. Hence, the self as a "center of relationships" finds itself simultaneously in the grip of an ongoing decentering or displacement, which never cancels, however, the limits of time and place. Just as self-cultivation requires self-overcoming, so cultivation of family and other relations demands a transgression of parochial attachments, such as "nepotism, racism, and chauvinism," and ultimately a transgression of a narrow "anthropocentrism" in the direction of the "mutuality of Heaven and man and the unity of all things" (a mutuality captured succinctly in the famous "Western Inscription" of Chang Tsai in the eleventh century).[15]

From a Western perspective, probably the least appealing aspect of Confucian relationships is their inherent asymmetry or inequality manifest chiefly in the "three bonds" (*san-kang*): the dependency of the son on the father, of the wife on her husband, and of the minister on the ruler. As sociologist Robert Bellah has chidingly remarked, filial piety and subordination in China "became absolutes," with the model of "familial authority" eventually spilling over into political and all other relationships.[16] Responding to this charge, Tu Wei-ming is at pains to disentangle the salient issues. He points out, first of all, that it is misleading to suggest that the father–son, or, more generally, the parent–child relationship "provides a model for the other four." Above all, a common mistake made in interpreting traditional Chinese culture—a mistake encouraged by Orientalist leanings—is the tendency to equate the "political" ruler/minister dyad with the father–son relationship (an equation that would replicate the kind of "parental government" extolled by Robert Filmer). What is neglected in this equation is the difference, acknowledged even in classical Confucianism, between "naturalness" and choice, more specifically between natural, kinship-based "affinity" (*ch'in*) and political "righteousness" (*i*).

Although he concedes a hierarchical element in all five relationships, Tu insists on distinguishing between despotic, whimsical, and self-centered control, on the one hand, and ethical, benevolent, and other-regarding interaction, on the other. In the case of filial piety, widely regarded as the key relation, the father or parent cannot become despotic without forfeiting the "name" or title of parent; hence, "the impression of the father as the socializer, the educator, and thus the authoritarian disciplinarian is superficial, if not mistaken." In terms of Confucian ethics, the father is expected to act "fatherly," so that the son can act in a properly "filial" manner.

Differently put: "The son's filiality is conceived as a response to the father's kindness." For this to happen, the father must "set an example for the son as a loving and respectable person before he can reasonably expect his son to love and respect him."[17]

What needs to be remembered, with regard to all five relationships, is the pervasive role of *jen* (in conjunction with *li*): that is, their insertion into a holistic web geared toward humaneness, humanization, or self-transformation. Without entirely leveling human bonds, this orientation softens or attenuates whatever asymmetry may prevail. Tu says, "The value that underlies the five relations is not dependency but 'reciprocity' (*pao*)," or mutuality. Specifically, the "filiality" of the son or children is reciprocated by the love and "compassion" of the parent, the loyalty of the minister by the justice and "fair-mindedness" of the ruler, and so on. Preeminently, the aspect of mutuality is exemplified in friendship, which represents "a reciprocal relation *par excellence*"; for "it is mutuality rather than dependency that defines 'trust' (*hsin*) between friends." In a quasi-Aristotelian manner, Confucian-style friendship is not oriented toward an extrinsic goal, such as economic gain or social advantage, but rather toward humanity or mutual humanization. In Tu's view, the core of such a relation is captured in the notion of a "fiduciary community," which is predicated not on domination or manipulation but on trust and reciprocal learning. To this extent, the Confucian "way of the friend" (*yu-tao*) is closely connected with the "way of the teacher" (*shih-tao*), for both friendship and the teacher–student relation exist for the sake of personal and transpersonal transformation. The close linkage between friendship and learning or humane transformation is stressed in the very opening lines of the *Analects*: "To learn and at proper times to repeat what one has learned, is that not after all a pleasure? That friends should come to visit one from afar, is this not after all delightful?"[18]

FIVE RELATIONSHIPS PLUS ONE?

What emerges from the preceding discussion is an image of Confucianism, and especially of the five relationships, starkly at odds with Orientalist predilections. Above all, the discussion calls into question the tendency of reducing "political" (ruler–minister) relations to a case of filial piety, in a manner replicating Filmer's model; it also challenges the confusion of relationship with dependency or domination. In a broader vein, this challenge undermines the widespread equation of traditional Asian-style politics with "Oriental despotism." (Here it may also be appropriate to recall the absence of the master/slave dyad in the traditional Confucian canon.) To be sure, recognition of the ethical, transformative qualities of Confucianism does not by itself remove the distance separating the latter from the trajectory of Western political thought. Occasionally, strong cross-cultural sympathies have tempted scholars to deny or at least minimize this cultural distance; eager to overcome East–West barriers, they were occasionally led to champion a kind of global merger or synthesis neglectful of traditional differences. Thus, in several of their writings, David Hall and Roger Ames have underscored the affinities between traditional Chinese thought and modern Western ideas, especially between Confucianism and John Dewey's and Jean-Paul Sartre's teachings. More recently, in *Democracy of the Dead*, they have detected traces of Western democracy latent in traditional Chinese culture, a finding buttressing their argument that "John Dewey's pragmatic vision of democracy" seems "best suited to engage the realities of Chinese social practice and to support the realization of 'Confucian democracy' in China."[19]

Although Hall and Ames are well-meaning and engaging, their argument appears precipitous and unconvincing in many ways. Its main drawback is its effect on cross-cultural interaction, where the assumption of synthesis tends to obviate the need for mutual learning. In this respect, Tu Wei-ming seems more forthright when he candidly acknowledges the shortcomings of traditional Asian ways of life, not for the sake of Orientalizing Asia but in order to place differences on the table for open debate and negotiation. Even while acknowledging its ethical virtues, Tu writes, "we cannot ignore the historical fact that Confucian China was unquestionably a male-dominated society." Throughout the centuries, "the education of the son received much more attention than the education of the daughter, the husband was far more influential than the wife, and the father's authority significantly surpassed that of the mother." Generally speaking, the status of women was deplorable in all stages of their development: in their dependency on the father in youth, on the husband in marriage, and on the son in old age.

In this and many other domains, neo-Confucianism introduced important changes, especially by cultivating a deepened individuality and also a potential universalism. If we take this innovation seriously as "a viable persuasion," Tu states, we must criticize an outmoded Confucian and neo-Confucian ideology "in order to retrieve the deep meaning of its universal humanistic teachings"; even if neo-Confucian thinkers (such as Chu Hsi or Wang Yang-ming) did not adopt a conscious policy of emancipating women, "their legacy speaks loudly in favor of such a tendency." All this does not mean an exit from human relationships in favor of an atomistic individualism. The "authentic approach" for Tu is "neither a passive submission to structural limitations nor a Faustian activation of procedural freedom but a conscientious effort to make the dynamic interaction between them a fruitful dialectic for self-realization."[20]

In our globalizing age, it appears urgent to take up Tu's suggestion and to explore the dynamic interaction not only between individual and community but, more broadly, between East and West or between Confucian teachings and modern Western democracy. To facilitate this exchange, some concessions need to be made on both sides. On the side of Asian or Confucian thought, a helpful concession would be the modification of the traditional five relationships (*wu-lun*) through the addition of a further, more impersonal relation: that between citizen and citizen in a shared public sphere and under a common rule of law. Such a relation necessarily transgresses or cuts through the various "familial" relations and also profoundly modifies the ruler/minister dyad. In some ways, Confucian thought is already partially prepared for this concession by virtue of the neo-Confucian innovations highlighted by Tu Wei-ming: especially the deepening of individual subjectivity and the incipient universalization of the framework of humaneness (*jen*). Further indigenous support for the change can be found in Asian Buddhism, especially the Ch'an (or Zen) variety, which for nearly two millennia existed side by side with Confucian scholarship.

In the tradition of Asian Buddhism, the human self as the "center of [concrete] relationships" tends to be evacuated in favor of a "no-self" (*anatman*) or an "empty," not contextually limited, self (*sunyata*), an evacuation that is at the same time the gateway to liberation and to transcontextual self-realization. In the words of Masao Abe, the renowned scholar of Mahayana Buddhism (especially of Ch'an/Zen teachings), by penetrating to the "negation of negation" or emptiness, "the ground of human subjectivity is transformed from mere [empirical] self to the 'no-self,' which is another term for the true self"; emptiness is thus revealed "at the deepest core or at the bottomless depth" of selfhood. He adds, with a moral-political edge: "In awakening to the true Self, one breaks through the ego and simultaneously overcomes the source of world evil and historical evil [namely, oppression and exploitation], thereby opening up the true path which enlivens both self and others."[21]

Apart from the support of indigenous Asian traditions, the enlargement of Confucian relations is dictated by important social and political developments in our time. Three such currents deserve special mention. One factor is the change of Asian countries from agricultural to incipiently commercial and industrial societies. An important consequence of this change is the rise of a commercial "civil society" in China and other Asian countries, an aspect that is the topic of widespread scholarly discussion both inside and outside of Asia. For present purposes, it must suffice to say that, as a corollary of modernization, social interactions necessarily transgress local exchange relations in the direction of a large-scale, impersonal market, whose impersonality steadily increases with the advances of globalization. The rise of this market, however, brings to the fore motivations of profit-seeking and capital accumulation, which can no longer be contained by the ethics of personal relations thematized in the Confucian canon. It is precisely because of the unleashing of market forces that modern societies—Confucian or otherwise—require the counterweight of a public sphere able to contain or regulate these forces through a common rule of law. Another, equally salient factor is the rise of the modern nation-state: the fact that all Asian societies have been refashioned on the model of Western nation-state structures. With regard to Confucian Asia, this means that traditional segmental or holistic arrangements have been replaced by the pyramidal structure prevalent in Western politics, a change strengthening the hand of governing elites and central bureaucracies. Again, a robust public sphere is required to counterbalance the overbearing and sometimes totalitarian ambitions of nation-state leaders and their officials.[22]

The most important factor speaking in favor of strong "citizen" relations, however, is the character of modern democracy, to the extent that the latter is seen as rule of the people or a regime in which common people are both rulers and ruled. In their capacity as "rulers," common people clearly cannot just relate to particular "ministers," but must cultivate broader, more impersonal relations with each other, which, again, can only happen in a viable public sphere. Much can be learned in this respect from recent discussions of citizenship and democracy in Western literature. As John Pocock observes, commenting on the "ideal" of citizenship from ancient times to the present, active membership in a *polis* is of a special kind: it is a relationship "in which speech takes the place of blood [or kinship], and acts of shared decision take the place of vengeance." Since, in a democratic *polis*, citizens both rule and are ruled, a public sphere is required where "citizens join each other in making decisions" in such a way that each member "respects the authority of the others" and "all join in obeying" the jointly established rule of law.[23]

To be sure, in modern democratic politics, the public sphere can only with difficulty be confined to citizens narrowly defined. Given its emphasis on rational equality (as contrasted with "natural" differences and dependencies), the idea of the public sphere necessarily unsettles or contests ethnic and also nation-state boundaries; its built-in universalizing thrust encourages the progressive amalgamation of civic (or citizens') rights with broader, ultimately cosmopolitan human rights. Norberto Bobbio, the Italian political philosopher, says that one can observe a steady widening or universalizing of public concerns: beginning with the Stoics, it "proceeds through the doctrine of natural law to reach Kantian morals, or a rationalized Christianity, which according to its fundamental maxim means 'to respect the human being as a person.'" Ultimately this universalist trajectory points toward "the establishment of an, albeit ideal, *civitas maxima*, or the city for all," a goal intimated by the Universal Declaration of the Rights of Man and similar initiatives.[24]

Of course, tendencies of this kind do not cancel the simultaneous need for more concrete personal relationships situated in space and time. Precisely the universalizing (and transcendentalizing) bent of Western modernity calls for a counterweight mindful of human finitude and of the welter of differentiated loyalties that structure human life. With regard to citizenship and the public sphere, this need is increasingly recognized by Western political theorists otherwise wedded to a (broadly) liberal tradition. Thus, in Gershon Shafir's perceptive account, the Western conception of citizenship expresses "a desire to create comprehensive membership frameworks capable of replacing the weakened communities of traditional society." Yet, even (and especially) today, "the aspiration to recover small and close-knit communities continues to coexist with the new citizenship frameworks," with some prominent thinkers even calling for differentiated or "multiple citizenships" or at least for a closer attunement of citizenship to communal differences.[25] It is precisely at this point that the Confucian legacy of five relationships is bound to prove its continued importance and salience, especially when the accent is placed on its ethical and transformative qualities. Among these relations, the primary role as a bridge-builder between cultural traditions must be allocated to friendship or the friend–friend relationship, particularly if the latter is allowed to broaden and to penetrate into active public life. Here the genuine possibility of an East–West engagement comes into view: an engagement where both sides can freely learn from each other in a spirit of mutual friendship and sympathy.

PART TWO

Engagement through
Dialogue and Interaction

CHAPTER SEVEN

Self and Other

Gadamer and the Hermeneutics of Difference

To live with the other, as the other of the other—this basic human task
applies to the micro- as well as to the macro-level. Just as each of us learns
to live with the other in the process of individual maturation, a similar learning
experience holds true for larger human communities, for nations and states.

—Hans-Georg Gadamer, *The Legacy of Europe*

Philosophy's relation to the world of lived experience (the life-world) is
complex and controverted. In traditional vocabulary, the issue is whether
philosophy's habitat resides inside or outside the Platonic cave. The issue
has not come to rest in our time. Whereas "analytic" philosophers prefer
to externalize or distance their targets of analysis, Continental thinkers (at
least since Martin Heidegger) refuse the comforts of this spectatorial stance.
Like sensitive seismographs, these thinkers register the subterranean trem-
ors that in our time affect the (once solid) underpinnings of Western culture: the pillars of subjectivity, of the *cogito*, and of rationality seen as
means of mastery over nature. What emerges from these seismographic
soundings is an experience of dislocation or ontological decentering, blurring the boundaries between subject and object, between self and other,
and between humans and nature (the former *res extensa*). As it happens,

this experiential tremor is accompanied in our time by a broader geo-political dislocation: the displacement of Europe from center stage and its insertion into a global welter of competing cultures and countercultures. To be sure, Europe (and the West in general) still forcefully asserts its hegemony, but the self-assurance of this hegemonic position has been irremediably lost or at least placed in jeopardy. Here I seek to explore this double move of dislocation by attending to one particularly prominent and reliable seismograph: the work of Hans-Georg Gadamer. Born in 1900, Gadamer was an astute participant and reflective witness (not just a spectator) throughout our troubled times.

My adopted focus can readily be further justified. Since his early writings on dialogical politics—that is, a politics not dominated by a totalizing ideology—Gadamer's reflections have continuously concentrated on the porous relations between self and other, between reader and text, and between speaker and language; to this extent, his work has served as a beacon for several generations of students now, illuminating the dimly lit landscape of refracted identities and of a selfhood infected with otherness. At the same time, his work resonates deeply with larger global concerns. As the foremost contemporary representative of European humanism, Gadamer has persistently reflected and commented on the tradition of European culture, alerting us both to its intrinsic grandeur and to its tragedy or possible limitations. Thus, I want to argue, Gadamerian hermeneutics is not just a parochial ingredient of Continental thought, but an important building stone in the emerging global city and in a dialogically construed cultural ecumenicism.[1]

I shall proceed from the issue of self–other relations to broader cultural concerns and especially to the topic of cross-cultural dialogue. The opening section takes as its guide a short book titled *Wer bin Ich und wer bist Du?* (*Who Am I and Who Are You?*), which contains Gadamer's comments on the poetry of Paul Celan and, in this connection, probes the interpenetration of self and other and of identity and difference. The discussion of Celan is supported and fleshed out in the first section by references to some of Gadamer's responses to Jacques Derrida, having to do chiefly with the role of dialogue and the "goodwill" in dialogue. The second section shifts attention to the larger cultural arena, taking as its reference point one of Gadamer's more (unjustly) neglected writings, *The Legacy of*

Europe (*Das Erbe Europas*). In the last section, I shall bring out Gadamer's relevance in the ongoing process of hegemonic Westernization and especially for the alternative project of an interactive dialogue—perhaps an agonistic dialogue—among competing cultures.

WHO AM I AND WHO ARE YOU?

Gadamer's work has always revolved around the issue of self–other relations. During the waning years of the Weimar Republic and in the face of fascist totalitarianism, the young Gadamer sketched the contours of a dialogically interactive republic, an image heavily indebted to the legacy of Platonic dialogues (though minus any resort to a "guardian class" possessed of ultimate wisdom). Steering clear of both utilitarian interest aggregation and utopian holism, dialogue in this context was the medium of a community constantly in the process of formation, a process in which both the sense of public life and the selfhood or identity of participants are persistently subject to renegotiation.[2] This view of dialogue was deepened and philosophically corroborated in the postwar years as a result of Gadamer's intensified turn to language and hermeneutical understanding, a turn that at least in part was an outgrowth of his prolonged encounter with Heidegger. A magisterial apex of his mature thinking, *Truth and Method* (1960) presented dialogue as the connecting link between reader and text, between present and past, and between indigenous and alien culture. Still, notwithstanding their rich insights and achievements, Gadamer's writings up to this point continued to be attached to a certain kind of idealism: that is, an outlook where difference was attenuated in favor of a nearly preestablished harmony between self and other and of an eventual "fusion of horizons" between reader and text. A combination of factors and subsequent experiences contributed to a progressive modification of this outlook: foremost among them, the work of the later Heidegger, the influence of French poststructuralism, and exposure to the poetry of Paul Celan. Without in any way trying to rank these factors or to privilege one over the other, I shall start with the latter experience.

In the decade following *Truth and Method*, Gadamer turned repeatedly to a reading of Celan's poetry, offering lectures and writing papers on the topic. His comments were finally collected in *Wer bin Ich and wer bist Du?* (1973). This slender volume offers a probing commentary on Celan's poetic cycle "Crystal of Breath" (*Atemkristall*). The accentuated sense of difference and radical otherness is immediately evident in the preface to the commentary. As Gadamer notes, "Paul Celan's poems reach us—and we miss their point [*wir verfehlen sie*]." This failure or rupture of communication is by no means haphazard; after all, it was Celan himself who described his poetry as a "message in the bottle" (*Flaschenpost*), leaving it entirely up to the reader to decode the meaning of the message and to determine even whether the bottle contains any message at all. In his preface, Gadamer describes himself simply as a recipient of Celan's bottle, and his commentary as "decoding efforts" seeking to decipher "nearly illegible signs." Approaching such bottled or encoded signs, he observes, requires sustained patience, diligence, and attentiveness to the emphatic difference or otherness of the text. Poems locked into a bottle cannot possibly be expected to yield complete transparency or to be amenable to logical resolution. Still, recognition of difference is not equivalent to a counsel of despair. As Gadamer writes, pointing to his own endeavor:

> In presenting the outcome of prolonged attentiveness, this reader believes to have detected "sense" in these dark incunables—not always a univocal sense, and surely not always a "complete" (or completely transparent) meaning. In many instances, he has only deciphered some passages and offered vague hunches how the gaps of his understanding (not of the text) could be mended. Whosoever believes to have already "understood" Celan's poems, this person is not my interlocutor and not the addressee of these pages. Such a person does not know what understanding means in this case.[3]

The "Crystal of Breath" poems discussed in Gadamer's book belong to a larger poetic cycle called "Turning of Breath" (*Atemwende*). These allusions to breath and its turning and crystallization offer a clue to the coded message in the bottle: what the reader encounters here is a peculiarly ruptured communication or a communication through noncommunication. Gadamer observes, "In his later poetry, Paul Celan approaches more and more the breathless stillness of silence in the word turned cryptic cipher."

To make headway into this kind of poetry, the reader must be ready for a journey into alien terrain, where readiness does not mean a specially erudite preparation but simply a willingness to listen to the "breathless stillness" of the word. In this journey, some clues may be provided by the poet himself, but these must be treated with great caution and circumspection. Poetry is not simply the expression of the poet's private feelings or a disclosure of his inner selfhood (or ego); hence, pondering the sense of a poem cannot simply be replaced by psychic empathy. These caveats are particularly important in the case of the cryptic or "hermetic" poetry of Celan, despite the poet's repeated invocation of personal pronouns (such as "I," "thou," "we," and "you"). Notwithstanding this resort to indexicals, Gadamer notes, the actual reference of Celan's pronouns remains in every case "profoundly uncertain." Thus, the term "I" frequently employed in the poems does not simply denote the poet's selfhood seen as something distinct from the "selves" of his readers; rather, the term refers to the self in general, to everybody or "every one of us." Yet, even this formulation is still precarious, because the self of everyone can likewise not be stabilized or pinpointed with certainty, given its embroilment with a "thou," or other. As used by Celan, the term "thou," or "you," means, or can mean, anybody: the reader, a friend or neighbor, or perhaps "that closest and most distant thou which is God." According to Gadamer, the precise target of the address "cannot be determined"; in fact, "the thou is an 'I' just as much and as little as the I is a self (or ego)."[4]

These comments are exemplified in the first poem of Celan's cycle, which starts immediately with pronouns: "You may readily / Welcome me with snow." Subsequent lines of the poem allude to the lushness of summer days and to the restless pace of a life lived "shoulder to shoulder" with the exuberant growth of nature. It is against the backdrop of summer's exuberance that the beginning of the poem welcomes the stillness of snow, but it does so with personal pronouns. Who or what is meant by the opening "You" of the poem?, Gadamer asks, and responds, "Nothing more specific or determinate than the Other or otherness itself which, after a summer of restless striving, is expected to grant welcome relief." Likewise, the "I" invoked in these lines is not simply the poet's selfhood but any being longing for winter and silence, perhaps even for the withdrawn reticence of death. "What is expressed in these lines is the readiness to accept otherness—whatever it may be," Gadamer states. It is important to note that the appeal to winter and snow involves not merely a reference to a change of seasons or an outward cycle of nature; rather, the appeal is manifest in the poem itself, in its subdued brevity and reticent sparseness. To this extent, the lines instantiate poignantly the turning and crystallization of breath. The stillness of the verses is, Gadamer writes,

> the same stillness which prevails at the turning of breath, at the near-inaudible moment of the renewed inhalation of breath. For this is what "*Atemwende*" signifies: the experience of the noiseless, motionless gap between inhaling and exhaling. I would wish to add that Celan connects this turning of breath or this moment of breath reversal not only with a posture of motionless reticence, but also with that subdued kind of hope which is implicit in every reversal or conversion [*Umkehr*].[5]

This element of latent hope, however, does not in any way detract from the stark sobriety and hermetic nonexpressiveness of Celan's poems. This nonexpressiveness also undercuts the prospect of semantic transparency based on interpsychic empathy. Gadamer adds: "The distinction between me and you, between the self of the poet and that of his readers miscarries." To the question "Who am I and who are you?" Celan's poetry responds "by leaving the question open."[6]

Gadamer's comments on the remainder of Celan's poems are richly nuanced and completely resist summary synopsis in the present context. At the end of his step-by-step exegesis, Gadamer appends an "Epilogue," which usefully highlights the most salient points of his commentary. A central point concerns the character of poetic exegesis, especially of cryptically encoded texts, such as Celan's message in the bottle. According to Gadamer, the interpreter in this case has to proceed in a diligent but cautious manner, avoiding the temptations of both complete appropriation and renunciation. Since Celan's verses hover precariously between speech and silence, disclosure and concealment, exegesis likewise has to steer a middle course between understanding and nonunderstanding, by offering a careful account that yet leaves blank spaces intact. For Gadamer, the endeavor of understanding cannot simply be abandoned, notwithstanding the poet's reticence. It is not sufficient merely to register the failure or rupture of understanding; rather, what is needed is an attempt to look for possible points of entry and then to inquire in which manner and how far understanding may be able to penetrate. The goal of this interpretive endeavor, however, should not be mistaken: the point is not to render transparent what is (and must remain) concealed, but rather to comprehend and respect the complex interlacing of transparency and nontransparency in poetic texts. He says in his epilogue:

> The objective is *not* to discern or pinpoint the univocity of the poet's intent; not by any means. Nor is it a matter of determining the univocity of the "meaning" expressed in the poem itself. Rather what is involved is attentiveness to the ambiguity, multivocity and indeterminacy unleashed by the poetic text—a multivocity which does not furnish a blank check to the license of the reader, but rather constitutes the very target of the hermeneutical struggle demanded by the text.[7]

In its stress on interpretive perseverance, Gadamer's postscript reflects something like a generic disposition or a "goodwill" to understanding, that is, a disinclination to let rupture or estrangement have the last word. Instead of celebrating the incommensurability of "language games" or "phrase families" (to borrow terms coined by Wittgenstein and Lyotard), Gadamer's account accentuates the open-endedness and at least partial interpenetration of languages and discourses. In lieu of a radical segregation of texts and readers, his hermeneutics tends to underscore their embeddedness in a common world, even though this world is not so much a "universe" as a "pluriverse" or a multifaceted fabric of heterogeneous elements. Above all, the epilogue does not grant to poets the refuge of a total exile. Such an exile, in Gadamer's view, would transform the poet's text into the object of an esoteric cult or of academic expertise. For these and other reasons, he considers "sound" the general maxim that poetry should be treated not as a "learned cryptogram for experts" but rather as a text destined for the "members of a language community sharing a common world," a world inhabited by "poets and readers and listeners alike." Operating in such a multifaceted context, "understanding" (*Verstehen*) cannot mean a process of psychic empathy or a direct grasp of subjective intentionality; given the diversity of outlooks and idioms, exegesis is bound to exhibit the character of struggle, proceeding along the pathway not so much of a preestablished consensus but of something like an "agonistic dialogue." Like every other hermeneutical effort, poetic exegesis has to respect first of all the integrity of the text; that is, it must be attentive to the "said" (and also the "unsaid") of poetic discourse. To this extent, it is possible to speak of the pure "textuality" of poems quite independently of the poet's particular motivations. Yet, textuality forms part of a broader fabric—the "text" of the world—where readers (successfully or unsuccessfully) seek understanding. To the queries of these readers, the poem responds, even in its cryptic reticence:

> Like every word in a dialogue, the poem too has the character of a response or rejoinder [*Gegenwort*], a rejoinder which intimates also what is not said but what is part of the anticipated sense triggered by the poem—triggered perhaps only in order to be disappointed as expectation. This is true particularly of contemporary lyrical poetry like that of Celan.[8]

Depending on the reader's questions or expectations, a poem will respond differently, that is, in different registers or on diverse levels of sense and significance. Contemporary poetry requires readers to be in a way multilingual or open to a diversity of idioms and discursive modalities. Celan himself noted at one point that his poems permit "different possible starting points" of interpretation, thus allowing a movement between levels of meaning (and nonmeaning). This allowance, Gadamer is quick to add, should not be equated with randomness or a disjointedness of the text itself. Here again, Celan's own testimony that his poems do not exhibit chasms or rigid disjunctures is pertinent. Gadamer observes that, although it constitutes a complex pluriverse, Celan's poetry displays an inner coherence and integrity, often accomplished through linguistic abbreviation, condensation, and even omission. To this extent, his poems resemble not so much a labyrinth or a magician's box as a polished crystal (a "breath crystal") refracting light in multiple ways: "What distinguishes a good poem from a stunning magical trick is the fact that its inner precision becomes all the more evident the more deeply one enters into its structure and its modes of efficacy." This aspect has been duly recognized by contemporary "structuralist" analysis, but, by clinging solely to semiotic elements, structuralism fails to correlate linguistic coherence with the broader semantic world-context, including the context of readers' expectations. Only attentiveness to this broader context can give room to the poem's semantic plurivocity. Poems, in Gadamer's view, are not simply self-contained art-objects but acquire their proper status only through dialogical exchange with readers. What a poem is offering or intimating, he writes, every reader "has to supplement from his/her own experience. This is what 'understanding' a poem means."[9]

Supplementation of this kind, he adds, does not denote a lapse into private idiosyncrasy or arbitrary constructions, a lapse that would ignore the otherness of the text and its intrinsic demands. Hermeneutics from this angle is not a synonym for subjectivism and willful appropriation, but for a sustained, dialogical learning process. Subjective impressions, Gadamer insists, are "no interpretation at all"; they are, rather, "a betrayal of exegesis as such." The common source of exegetic failure resides in unwillingness (or lack of goodwill) to face up to the text's appeal, including its possibly encoded message in the bottle; such unwillingness surfaces in the imposition of extrinsic frameworks or criteria and, more generally, in the obstinate clinging to private feelings: "This kind of understanding remains captive to subjectivism." Preferable to this type of approach is recognition of the radical otherness of the text and the simple admission of nonunderstanding; in the case of Celan's poetry, the latter admission may actually very often be a sign of "interpretive honesty." Yet, for Gadamer, nonunderstanding cannot in turn be elevated into a general goal or maxim, which, in practice, would constitute a recipe for a relaxation of interpretive effort. Textual recalcitrance cannot dispense with the rigors of the "hermeneutical circle," the constant alternation between inquiry and textual response. To be sure, hermeneutical endeavor does not yield an "objective" meaning or the invariant "truth" of a poem; both the diversity of readers' expectations and the multivocity of the text itself militate against such a final completion of understanding. Yet, diversity of access and semantic levels also does not add up to a simple triumph of relativism, which could readily be a motto of subjective self-indulgence. He notes in carefully blending textual demands with exegetic latitude:

It is not contradictory to accept in one case different possible interpretations which all resonate with the sense of the poetic text, and in
other instances to consider one kind of interpretation more precise
and hence more "correct." Different things are involved here (and
need to be considered): on the one hand, the process of approximation toward "correctness" which is the aim of every interpretation;
and on the other, the convergence and equivalence of levels of understanding which all may be "correct" in their way.[10]

The move toward (what I have called) an agonal or agonistic dialogue—a mode of exegesis honoring both the otherness of the text and
the endeavor of understanding—was intensified in Gadamer's later
work, especially in some writings resulting from the "Gadamer–Derrida
encounter" of 1981. In an open "Letter to Dallmayr" published a few years
after that encounter, Gadamer defended himself vigorously against charges
of a certain idealist or metaphysical penchant that had been leveled against
him by Derrida and others. "I too affirm," he asserted at the time, "that understanding is always understanding-differently [*Andersverstehen*]." What is
stirred up or brought to the fore when a word reaches another person, or a
text its reader, can never be stabilized "in a rigid identity" or consensual harmony. Rather, encountering a word or a text means always a certain stepping outside oneself, though without relinquishing one's questions and anticipations. Thus, understanding does not simply amount to consensual
convergence or an effort "to repeat something after the other," but rather
implies a willingness to enter the border zone or interstices between self and
other, hence placing oneself before the open "court" of dialogue and mutual
questioning. It was in this light that one also had to assess the meaning
of terms such as "self-consciousness" and "self-understanding," expressions that had been used extensively in *Truth and Method* and that had
become a target of criticism (because of their presumed preoccupation
with subjectivity). According to Gadamer's "Letter to Dallmayr," the terms
were not meant to refer to any kind of narrow self-centeredness, but rather
to a Socratic process of self-reflection and self-questioning, a reflection
bound to undermine precisely the assumption of a stable identity or rigid
self-certainty. Resuming the central motif of his earlier Celan interpretation, Gadamer profiled more sharply the trajectory of his own work.
Hermeneutics, he noted (agreeing at least partly with Derrida), involves

a decentering, but not an erasure, of selfhood and semantic meaning: "For who we are is something unfulfillable, an ever new undertaking and an ever new defeat."[11]

This line of argument was still further expanded in an essay written a few years later, "Hermeneutics and Logocentrism." Here again Gadamer countered accusations charging his work with harboring a crypto-idealism and, more specifically, a "logocentrism" hostile to the recognition of difference and bent on incorporating and submerging otherness into the vortex of selfhood. As advanced by Derrida and other recent French thinkers, the accusation had a certain intuitive appeal—its rupturing of self-enclosure—but was ultimately misguided. For, in postulating a radical otherness or alterity, "deconstruction" of hermeneutics frustrated precisely the concrete encounter or engagement of self and other. Gadamer states:

> Now Derrida would object by saying that understanding always turns into appropriation and so involves a denial of otherness. Yet, it seems to me that to assume that such identification occurs within understanding is to impute a position which is indeed idealistic and "logocentric"—but one which we had already left behind after World War I in our revisions and criticisms of idealism. . . . Theologians like Karl Barth and Rudolf Bultmann, the Jewish critique of idealism by Franz Rosenzweig and Martin Buber, as well as Catholic writers like Theodor Haeckel and Ferdinand Ebner served to shape the climate in which our thinking moved at the time.[12]

Notions like the "fusion of horizons" discussed in *Truth and Method*, he added, should not be taken in the sense of a complete merger or a Hegelian synthesis, but in that of an engaged dialogical encounter: "I am not referring to an abiding or identifiable 'oneness,' but just to what happens in conversation as it proceeds." Dialogical encounter was perhaps less indebted to Hegelian dialectic than to the Socratic method of self-inquiry through interrogation and mutual contestation. According to "Hermeneutics and Logocentrism," it is in Socrates that we find an idea or a clue "from which one must start and from which I too have started out as I sought to reach an understanding of and with Derrida." This clue is that "one must seek to understand the other" even at the risk of self-critique and self-decentering, which entails that "one has to believe that one could be in the wrong." Regarding the accent on "*différance*," Derridean decon-struction contained a valuable insight, but one that was entirely germane to hermeneutics properly understood: "Difference exists within identity; otherwise, identity would not be identity. Thought contains deferral and distance; otherwise, thought would not be thought."[13]

THE LEGACY OF EUROPE

Viewed as an agonal engagement, Gadamerian hermeneutics is relevant not just to textual exegesis in the narrow sense, but it radiates deeply into the broad arena of social and political concerns. Just as his early essays on a dialogical republic were addressed to the political scene of the Weimar (and later fascist) era, so his later writings on hermeneutical understand-ing are pertinent to our emerging "global city," that is, to an incipient world order marked by a contestation among cultures and a growing re-sistance to one-sided Western hegemony. As it happens, Gadamer has not been an idly detached spectator of the agonies and transformations of our present age; repeatedly, as befits a "humanist" raised in the classical mold, he has voiced his philosophically seasoned views on the dilemmas and fu-ture prospects of humankind in the evolving global setting. Here I take as a road marker a study published barely a decade after the encounter with Derrida, *Das Erbe Europas* (*The Legacy of Europe*) (1989), in which Gada-mer revealed himself to be a concerned and conscientious citizen of Eu-rope, but of a properly chastised and "decentered" Europe. Although he pinpoints and commemorates the distinctive accomplishments of Europe, Gadamer at no point endorses a supremacist outlook, and certainly not the stance of "Eurocentrism," which has been the target of much world-wide criticism and resentment. Instead of accentuating Western advances in science and technology, he underscores the internal heterogeneity and diversity of traditions that constitute or shape European culture. It is this intrinsic multiplicity, this unity in and through difference, that for Gada-mer marks the genuine "legacy of Europe," a legacy that may serve as an exemplar also to non-Western societies and to an impending ecumenical world-culture.

Gadamer's decentered perspective is clearly evident in the opening chapter, "The Multiplicity of Europe: Legacy and Prospect." In the first lines, he presents himself not as a neutral onlooker but as a reflectively engaged participant in the unfolding events of our century: "I have lived through this tumultuous epoch from my childhood on, and hence I may count as a witness," not as someone claiming a specialist's expertise but as a philosopher seeking to come to terms with real-life experiences. One of the central experiences of our century for Gadamer is the dislocation of Europe from center stage and its insertion into a global network of interactions:

> The epoch of the two World Wars has magnified and projected everything into global dimensions. In politics, the issue is no longer the balance of powers in Europe, that old cornerstone of diplomacy which was intelligible to everyone. Rather, what is at stake today is a global balance or equilibrium, that is, the question of the possible co-existence of immense power constellations.[14]

This profound transformation affects the status and role of Europe in the world today, assigning to it a much-reduced position in comparison with the past. As Europeans, Gadamer adds, "we are no longer *chez nous* [among ourselves] on our small, divided, rich and diversified continent"; rather, we are intimately inserted and implicated in "world events." Being embroiled in world events, Europe is also haunted and overshadowed by the global threats or dangers facing humanity today, especially the threats of nuclear catastrophe and ecological disaster. For Gadamer, this is the current sociopolitical reality from which thinking has to start: "Europe is intimately enmeshed in the contemporary world crisis—a crisis for which no one can offer a ready-made solution."[15]

What role can and should Europe assume in this precarious situation? Tackling this question requires some reflection on the meaning and distinctive significance of Europe as it is manifest in the long trajectory of its history. Following in the footsteps of Husserl and Heidegger, Gadamer locates the distinctive trademark of Europe in the penchant for philosophy, a philosophy that from the beginning has been drawn less to meditation than to inquiry and thus bears some intrinsic affinity with science in the broad sense. In our European culture, Gadamer notes, philosophy "from its inception has been linked with scientific investigation"; this, in fact, is "the novelty or novel feature which profiles and binds Europe together." Over the course of many centuries, the scientific aspect of philosophizing came to extricate itself from the broader fabric of European culture, a process that then served as the springboard for the ascendancy of Western science and technology to global hegemony. Yet, for Gadamer, this is only part of the story. Even though friendly to scientific inquiry, philosophy in the West was traditionally also connected with metaphysics, art, literature, the humanities, and theology. In the premodern era, these features formed part of the prevailing cultural framework, a framework whose ingredients were not fused in a bland synthesis but stood side by side in often conflictual relationships. To cite Gadamer again: in Europe, culture and philosophy took shape in a manner that "gave rise to the sharpest tensions and antagonisms between the diverse dimensions of intellectual activity." Still, given the original conception of philosophical inquiry, the decisive issue in European culture, an issue eventually marking Europe's position in the world, was bound to be the relation between philosophy and science or between science and the other ingredients of the cultural fabric.[16]

The ascendancy of empirical science in both the European and the global context was a product of the modern epoch, particularly of the dismissal of classical and medieval teleology in favor of the cognitive and technical mastery of nature. Instead of being a participant in a broader cultural discourse, science emerged as the dominant idiom because of the scientist's ability to distance the entire surrounding world into a pliant target of analysis and thus to act as a general overseer (or overlord). The modern epoch, Gadamer comments, heralds a historical period in which human reason is able "to transform nature into artificial objects and to reshape the entire world into one giant workshop of industrial production." The reaction of traditional philosophy to this upsurge of science was initially purely defensive; practitioners often retreated into a simple "underlaborer" position, a stance limiting reflection to the refinement of conceptual tools and epistemic techniques needed for scientific inquiry. This retreat was particularly widespread in the nineteenth century, during the heyday of positivism. In the meantime, however, the situation has dramatically changed. In view of the crisis potential of our age, a potential triggered in part by the triumph of technology, the issue is no longer simply to assist science, but to reflect anew on the relation of science to other dimensions of culture, both in Europe and in the global arena. According to Gadamer, a major credit for the changed outlook in the European setting goes to phenomenology and hermeneutics as inaugurated by Husserl and Heidegger. Particularly crucial in this context is Husserl's notion of the "life-world," a notion that thematizes the broad backdrop of lived cultural experience from which science itself arises and without which its vocabulary would be unintelligible. The writings of Heidegger and his successors further concretized the notion by linking it with human "praxis" and the basic "worldliness" of human existence. What comes into view from this vantage is the intrinsic situatedness of human life, signaled by such features as "temporality, finitude, projection, remembrance, forgetfulness and being forgotten."[17]

Worldly situatedness challenges the prerogative of distantiation, or at least the presumption of the spectator or overseer to possess a privileged or the only correct slant on reality. Pursuing the insights of phenomenology and hermeneutics, contemporary philosophy is attentive to the contextuality of human experience, its embeddedness both in historically grown culture and in the natural environment, no longer seen merely as extended matter. Gadamer states forcefully: "Nature can no longer be viewed as a simple object of exploitation; rather, in all its manifestations it must be experienced as our partner, that is, as the 'other' sharing our habitat." Seen as our partner, nature is intimately entwined with us; far from denoting a radical externality, nature is "our" otherness or the "other of ourselves" (*das Andere unserer selbst*). And, in fact, Gadamer asks, is there a genuine otherness that would not be the other of ourselves? This consideration is particularly important in the domain of human coexistence, that is, of intersubjective and cross-cultural "co-being" in a shared world, where the issue is neither to distance the other into the indifference of externality nor to absorb or appropriate otherness in an imperialist gesture. On the cross-cultural level, this aspect of self–other entwinement has been one of the profound historical experiences of the European continent, which brings into view the peculiar cultural pertinence of Europe or of the "legacy of Europe" in our time, above and beyond the ongoing Westernization of the globe under the auspices of European science. For Gadamer, it is chiefly the multiplicity (or multiculturalism) of Europe that harbors the Continent's legacy and promise for the world:

To live with the other, as the other of the other—this basic human task applies to the micro- as well as to the macro-level. Just as each of us learns to live with the other in the process of individual maturation, a similar learning experience holds for larger human communities, for nations and states. And here it may be one of the special advantages of Europe that—more than elsewhere—her inhabitants have been able or were compelled to learn how to live with others, even if the others are very different.[18]

The multiplicity of Europe, in Gadamer's view, is evident or has been evident in the diversity of national (and subnational) historical trajectories, in the heterogeneity of literary and religious traditions, and, above all, in the rich profusion of vernacular languages. In the face of ongoing efforts aimed at European unification, this multiplicity for Gadamer cannot and should not be expunged. From a global cultural perspective, the unification of Europe, especially in terms of a geopolitical power constellation, is of relatively minor significance. Unification would be a particularly dubious goal if it entailed the standardization of culture and language at the expense of historical vernacular idioms. According to Gadamer, the deeper significance of Europe resides in its multicultural and multilingual character, in the historical "cohabitation with otherness in a narrow space." Experienced as a constant struggle and challenge among European peoples, this cohabitation implies a lesson for humanity at large, for an evolving ecumenical world culture. The emphasis on indigenous traditions and vernacular idioms may seem to run counter to the prospect of a self–other entwinement or a genuine co-being with otherness. Indeed, concern with cultural distinctness may harbor the danger of a retreat into parochialism or ethnocentrism, but this retreat is not compelling. Gadamer points out that the role of local traditions is a feature endemic to hermeneutics or to the "hermeneutical circle," with its emphasis on "prejudices" or prejudgments seen as the corrigible but indispensable starting points of understanding. In exegesis, just as in any other form of disciplined inquiry, there must be room for critical alertness to prevent the sedimentation of preconceived ideas. Yet, Gadamer concludes,

> where the goal is not mastery or control, we are liable to experience the otherness of the other precisely against the backdrop of our own

prejudgments. The highest and most elevated aim that we can strive for is to partake in the other, to share the other's alterity. Thus, it may not be too bold to draw as the final political consequence of these deliberations the lesson that the future survival of humankind may depend on our readiness not only to utilize our resources of power and (technical) efficiency but to pause in front of the other's otherness—the otherness of nature as well as that of the historically grown cultures of peoples and states; in this way we may learn to experience otherness and human others as the "other of ourselves" in order to partake in one another.[19]

In *The Legacy of Europe*, the discussion of Europe's global significance is continued and fleshed out further in a chapter titled "The Future of European *Geisteswissenschaften*," which takes its departure again from the traditional distinctive mark of Europe: the attachment to philosophy and scientific inquiry. According to Gadamer, this attachment to inquiry has given shape to the European continent throughout the course of its historical development; particularly in the modern era, scientific reason has been a determining force in European civilization and, therefrom, in the rest of the world. Yet, as Gadamer again emphasizes, Europe's cultural or intellectual outlook has not been uniformly scientific, but rather diffracted from the beginning into a variety of facets, including (next to science) metaphysics, art, literature, and religion. This diffraction was intensified in modernity by the rise of empirical natural science and the radical Cartesian bifurcation of mind and extended matter. What emerged as a result of this bifurcation was a new and dramatic tension within the framework of European culture, namely, the division between the natural sciences and the cultural or "mental" sciences (*Geisteswissenschaften*), that is, the humanities. In opposition to the "eternal verities" of traditional metaphysics and the universal propositions of modern science, the humanities place the accent on historically grown traditions, the rich nuances of vernacular idioms, and the concrete fabric of the human life-world. Under the influence of nineteenth-century historicism and twentieth-century phenomenology and existentialism, humanistic inquiry is increasingly attentive to such philosophically charged issues as temporality, historicity, and the finitude of human life. To this extent, although they challenge traditional metaphysics, the humanities are heir to Europe's deeper metaphysical concerns.

In Gadamer's words, it is "precisely the humanities" that have "taken over (more or less consciously) the great legacy of ultimate questioning" and that thereby have given to philosophy a new "historical orientation."[20]

In focusing on historical diversity and contingency, the humanities bring into view an aspect of Europe's tradition often ignored in the face of the steady Westernization of the world, a process seemingly bent on the relentless homogenization of the globe. In opposition to this leveling process, the humanities accentuate the multiplicity of Europe, the fact that Europe is a "multilingual fabric" consisting of the most diverse national and cultural traditions. This historical multiplicity has relevance beyond the borders of Europe for global development and the emerging world culture. Gadamer writes:

> What we are witnessing is in truth a global process which has been unleashed by the end of colonialism and the emancipation of the former members of the British Empire [and other empires]. The task encountered is everywhere the same: to forge and solidify indigenous identities in the search for national [and subnational] autonomy. . . . This leads us back to our central theme. What is at stake is the future of Europe and the significance of the humanities for the future role of Europe in the world. The central issue is no longer Europe alone, but the cultural framework produced by the global economy and the worldwide network of communications—and thus the prospect of cultural multiplicity or diversity as emblem of the emerging civilization on our planet.[21]

This issue throws a spotlight on the problem of human and social change and especially on the controverted question of social "development." In contrast to an earlier, simplistic identification of the latter with Westernization, Gadamer notes, the meaning and direction of development or modernization have lost their "univocity" or unambiguous character in our time. This ambiguity does not basically affect the struggle against poverty and for decent standards of living in the "developing" areas, a struggle that often can only be waged with a dose of Western-style science and technology. What remains unsettled is the degree to which scientific and technological advances can be balanced against the need to maintain the integrity and autonomy of indigenous traditions. Gadamer observes that many countries today are engaged in the difficult search for a mode of culture capable of reconciling "their own traditions and the deeply rooted values of their life-world with European-style economic progress"; "large segments of humanity" now face this agonizing issue.[22]

In seeking to balance science and technology against indigenous or native traditions, developing countries implicitly or obliquely pay tribute to the European legacy of the humanities; thus, anticolonialism and opposition to "Eurocentrism" are not necessarily synonymous with the obsolescence or irrelevance of European thought. According to Gadamer's account, attention to local or national life-forms is everywhere in the ascendancy. What preoccupies leading intellectuals in the Third World, he notes, is no longer or not solely the absorption of the European Enlightenment and its offshoots, but rather the question of "how genuine human and social development is possible on the basis of indigenous traditions." This question, however, brings to the fore the teachings of Herder, one of the founders of the European humanities, renowned for his concern with "folk spirit" and his collection of the "voices of peoples in song." Following in Herder's footsteps, humanistic inquiry since its inception has tended to concentrate on the diversity of historical traditions and life-forms, and especially on the role of "culture," seen as the development or unfolding of native endowments. In Gadamer's view, Herder's legacy in the humanities constitutes a bulwark against the relentless standardization of the world, that is, against its one-sided "Westernization" under the auspices of science, industry, and technology. The issue facing humankind today is whether development is going to come to a grinding halt in the utopia/dystopia of a rationalized "world bureaucracy" (*Weltverwaltung*), or whether history "will keep on moving" with its intrinsic tensions, conflicts, and diversified strands. The issue cannot be settled in advance; yet, present-day societies show powerful tendencies supporting the second alternative. Countering the pull of global standardization, our time witnesses a steadily intensifying trend "toward differentiation and the fresh articulation of hitherto hidden distinctions." Opposing the hegemonic claims of some superpowers and cutting across the fragility of traditional nation-states, "we find everywhere a striving for cultural autonomy—a striving peculiarly at odds with prevailing power constellations."[23]

This striving is evident within the confines of Europe, for example, in the conflict between the Flemish and Walloons in Belgium and in the secessionist struggles of the Basques in Spain and the Baltic states in Eastern Europe. The deeper implications of this phenomenon, however, are global in scope and concern the character of the emerging world culture. Europe, no longer the center of the world, now gains a new salience. This salience relates not to the unity or ongoing unification of the Continent, but rather to the rich diversity of historical trajectories. Far from constituting a bland melting pot, Gadamer observes, Europe "exhibits in the smallest space the richest heterogeneity" and a "plurality of linguistic, political, religious, and ethnic traditions which have posed a challenge for many centuries and generations." It is this very heterogeneity in Europe that provides a lesson for the world today, precisely as an antidote to the leveling thrust of technical and industrial uniformity. Gadamer adds that the cultivation of native traditions is by no means incompatible with cross-cultural tolerance, provided that "tolerance" is understood not as the outgrowth of neutral indifference but as the appreciation of otherness from the vantage of one's own life-world (and its prejudgments). It is a "widespread mistake," he writes, to consider tolerance a virtue requiring the renunciation of indigenous life-forms and beliefs; yet, given that otherness implies selfhood as its correlate, tolerance can only proceed from a concrete dialogical (perhaps agonal) engagement between different perspectives and modes of lived experience. To this extent, the diversity of cultures, inside and outside of Europe's borders, is not so much an obstacle as a precondition and enabling warrant for an ecumenical order. Herein, Gadamer concludes, resides the genuine significance of Europe, a properly decentered and chastised Europe, in our contemporary world:

> This appears to me as the most evident mark and the deepest spiritual emblem of European self-consciousness: the ability, in the contest and exchange with different cultures, to preserve the distinctive uniqueness of lived traditions. To support this preserving effort is, in my view, the lasting contribution which the humanities can make not only to the future course of Europe, but to the future of humankind.[24]

INTERACTIVE DIALOGUE

Gadamer's comments on cultural diversity deserve close attention for their poignancy and judiciously weighted character. In a world rent by the competing pulls of Western-style universalism and bellicose modes of ethnocentrism, his accent on cross-cultural engagement opens a vista pointing beyond the dystopias of "melting pot" synthesis and radical fragmentation. In many ways, ecumenical dialogue in Gadamer's sense bears resemblance to the notion of a "lateral universalism" articulated earlier by Maurice Merleau-Ponty (and restated more recently by Seyla Benhabib under the label of "interactive universalism"). Dialogue in Gadamerian hermeneutics does not simply denote assimilation or a consensual "fusion of horizons"; given the ineradicable "otherness" of the other, dialogical relations are bound to be fraught with ambivalence and mis- or nonunderstanding, and often with agonal conflict. Recognition of such tension or agonistics resonates deeply with prominent strands in contemporary Western thought, especially strands indebted to "poststructuralist" and "postmodern" perspectives with their emphasis on discontinuity, rupture, and contestation. This resonance surfaces particularly in contemporary political theory, which is often marked by an intense concern with alterity and the dislocation of political identity. Thus, William Connolly, a leading American political thinker, speaks of the emergence of an "agonistic democracy,"

> a practice that affirms the indispensability of identity for life, disturbs the dogmatization of identity, and folds care for the protean diversity of human life into the strife and interdependence of identity/difference. Agonistic democracy . . . does not exhaust social space; it leaves room for other modalities of attachment and detachment. But it does disrupt consensual ideals of political engagement and aspiration. It insists that one significant way to support human dignity is to cultivate agonistic respect between interlocking and contending constituencies.[25]

To be sure, agonistics needs to be approached cautiously since it may also give rise to mutual repulsion or exclusion and hence to a mode of nonengagement. Still, given prevailing political conditions, the role of agonal struggle cannot be discounted. On both the global and the domestic

levels, contemporary social life bears the imprint of pronounced disparities or asymmetries, especially the asymmetry between hegemonic power
structures and marginalized or "subaltern" groups and cultures. The notion of a dialogical "conversation of mankind" (to borrow Michael Oake-
shott's phrase) cannot provide a warrant for glossing over these contrasts.
In the global arena, hegemonic disparity is the chief grievance fueling
charges of "Eurocentrism," as Gadamer himself keenly realizes. From the
vantage of developing societies, Europe (or the West) is experienced not so
much as an enticing welter of cultural diversity and multiplicity, but rather
as a monolithic structure bent on standardizing the globe under the banner of Western science, technology, and industry. Although it is appealing,
Gadamer's vision of the multifaceted "legacy of Europe" thus has to be
counterbalanced against another type of Western legacy, a heritage epitomized by imperialism, colonialism, and politico-economic spoilage. As it
happens, this second type of legacy has tended to overshadow the relations
between West and non-West in recent centuries, to the point of nearly
obliterating Europe's more benign and humanistic contributions. In "The
New Cultural Politics of Difference," Cornel West draws attention to
the conflicting legacies of Europe, or what he calls the "Age of Europe."
"Between 1492 and 1945," he writes,

> European breakthroughs in oceanic transportation, agricultural pro-
> duction, state-consolidation, bureaucratization, industrialization, ur-
> banization and imperial dominion shaped the makings of the mod-
> ern world. Precious ideals like the dignity of persons (individuality)
> or the popular accountability of institutions (democracy) were un-
> leashed around the world. Powerful critiques of illegitimate authori-
> ties . . . were fanned and fuelled by these precious ideals refined within
> the crucible of the Age of Europe. Yet the discrepancy between ster-
> ling rhetoric and lived reality, glowing principles and actual practices
> loomed large.[26]

Western hegemonic predominance has become a frequent target of
radical critiques in recent times, critiques that often sidestep the ambivalence of the European legacy in favor of a univocal or monolithic verdict. In his *Eurocentrism*, Samir Amin portrays modern Western culture

as a synonym for capitalistic exploitation and technological domination. Whereas premodern Europe, in his view, still constituted part of a larger "tributary culture" attached to Africa and the Near East, post-Renaissance Western society emancipated itself from this religious-metaphysical background in order to gain worldwide politico-economic supremacy. "With the Renaissance," Amin writes, "begins the two-fold radical transformation that shapes the modern world: the crystallization of capitalist society in Europe and the European conquest of the world." Amin argues that by means of capitalism and modern science, Europe was able to acquire an Archimedean standpoint from which it was possible to unhinge indigenous traditions and to pursue the project of global control. In this sense, the Renaissance period marked a "qualitative break" in the history of humankind because, from that time forward, Europeans became conscious of the idea "that the conquest of the world by their civilization is henceforth a possible objective." With slight modification, a similar outlook is manifested in a number of recent studies and publications, studies whose very titles sometimes express already a political and intellectual indictment.[27] Although Western hegemony surely provides ample motivation for such an indictment, further reflection counsels against a summary verdict. One of the hazards involved in summary judgments is the lure of "essentialism," the pitfall of construing modern Western culture exclusively under the rubric of economic control. A close corollary of this hazard is the detrimental effect on cross-cultural encounter. Viewed strictly from the vantage of Eurocentrism, modern Europe no longer is a partner in a cross-cultural dialogue, but an enemy to be defeated or destroyed.

One might add that the attack on Western hegemony finds a parallel in the very domain Gadamer singled out as an antidote to Eurocentrism: the domain of the humanities. Under the effect of both global and domestic challenges, the humanities in recent times have been the arena of intensive debates involving the status of "canonical" texts and their role in the educational curriculum. Proceeding under the banner of "multiculturalism," critics have denounced the traditional human studies for harboring an intrinsic elitism and for being insensitive to cultural, ethnic, and gender differences. Mirroring the hegemonic ambitions of Western culture in general, the humanities are said to exhibit hegemonic preferences in favor of "white male" standards; moreover, practitioners of the human disciplines are indicted for giving aid and comfort to political, economic, and technological modes of domination. Thus, invoking Michel Foucault's notion of "normalization," Paul Bové credits poststructuralist initiatives for highlighting the importance of "hegemonic elements of societal organization" and for focusing attention on "the determining roles played by the institutionalized practices and discourses of the human sciences in the constitution of relations of knowledge and power between individuals and institutions and among individuals." Though he adopts a distinctly British angle, Stuart Hall similarly observes that the contemporary late capitalist crisis "now cuts into and through the humanities from beginning to end," given that prevailing social technologies "have already invaded the humanities, summoning them to the barricades to defend an old project." In Hall's opinion, the basic issue today is whether the "new theoretical techniques" and the new vistas opened up by feminism and black studies and also by postmodernist and poststructuralist debates can be "won over and drawn into an understanding of the larger historical/ political project that now confronts the humanities." He adds somewhat somberly that the notion that the humanities still have the option "to decide whether or not to become social technologies is, in my view, hopelessly utopian."[28]

As in the case of Eurocentrism, there is probably room to doubt a humanist "essentialism" or the narrow identification of human studies with a traditional cultural elite or a prevailing mode of technology. Precisely under the rubric of multiculturalism, efforts can (and should) be made to enhance the cross-cultural diversity of the humanities, in a manner aligning them more closely with Herder's and Gadamer's perspective. Rather than pursuing this issue further, I want to return by way of conclusion to the theme of agonal dialogue or agonal engagement, an engagement that steers a course between fusional identity and exclusivist difference. Applying the theme to contemporary democracy, William Connolly defines a politics of "identity/difference" as a practice that strives to create "more room for difference by calling attention to the contingent, relational character of established identities," while simultaneously seeking to extend "agonistic respect into new corners of life," a respect that, though embracing strife and contest, also recognizes that "one of the democratizing ingredients in strife is the cultivation of care for the ways opponents respond to mysteries of existence." Proceeding from a similar vantage, Iris Young in *Justice and the Politics of Difference* argues against both "melting pot" assimilation and radical segregation of cultural and ethnic groups. In her view, it is an "oppressive meaning of group difference" that defines the latter as "absolute otherness, mutual exclusion, categorical opposition." Such a categorical opposition of groups and cultures, she notes, "essentializes them, repressing the differences within groups," with the result that difference as exclusion "actually denies difference." By contrast, a genuine "politics of difference" aims at an understanding of group diversity as "ambiguous, relational, shifting, without clear borders that keep people straight." Difference from this angle denotes not exclusivity but rather "specificity, variation, heterogeneity," escaping the twin pitfalls of "amorphous unity" and "non-overlapping otherness." Young states:

> Group differences should be conceived as relational rather than defined by substantive categories and attributes. A relational understanding of difference relativizes the previously universal position of privileged groups, which allows only the oppressed to be marked as different.... Difference thus emerges not as a description of the attributes of a group, but as a function of the relations between groups and the interaction of groups with institutions.[29]

To illustrate this relational meaning of difference (even against the backdrop of hegemonic power structures), I want to turn finally to a concrete instance of the correlation of Europe and the non-West, of colonizers and colonized: the example of European rule in India. In "India and Europe: Some Reflections on Self and Other," Nirmal Verma, the noted Indian novelist and poet, has pondered the agonal relations and profound agonies marking the contacts between the two cultures. Verma points out that the influence of Europe on Indian culture was more far-reaching and disturbing than that of earlier invasions or conquests; for Europe's influence affected not only overt social structures but the unconscious underpinnings of traditional ways of life. Far from being confined to "territorial space," he writes, Europe sought "to colonize India's *sense of time*, its present being merely a corruption of the past, its past, though glorious, believed to be dead and gone." In this scheme, Indian temporality could be rescued only if its past were "transformed into European present," that is, recast "in the ideal image of Europe."[30]

This assault on the time frame also involved an attack on traditional identity, for "the idealized image of the European man subverted the Hindu image of his own 'self,' reducing it to a state of 'sub-self'" constantly aspiring toward fulfillment in the European model. As a result of these developments, Indian culture was internally split or torn asunder, looking, like Janus, "toward opposite directions at the same time: toward Europe for knowledge and material progress, and toward its own tradition for moksha and salvation." A similar schism came to afflict European culture or the European psyche as it was exposed to the fissures of the colonized. Despite all its material advancement and prosperity, Verma observes, Europe during the last hundred years came increasingly to be "haunted by a 'wasteland' feeling of inner desolation," thus bearing witness to relational difference: "Was it a nemesis of fate that, through the circuitous path of history, India and Europe had arrived at a point where the face of the colonizer appeared as ravaged and forlorn as that of the colonized?" Regarding the future relations of these cultures, Verma appeals indeed to dialogue, but to a dialogue permeated by agonal respect, reticence, and even silence:

> Two traditions, Indian and European, are seeking a sort of completion in one another, not through a philosophical discourse or mutual cross-questioning, but by creating a "common space" within which the voice of the one evokes a responsive echo in the other, feeling the deprivations of one's own through the longings of the other.... After all the utterances have been made by the anthropologists, historians and philosophers on either side, perhaps time has come for both India and Europe to pause a little, listening to one another in silence, which may be as "sound" a method of discourse as any other.[31]

CHAPTER EIGHT

Border Crossings

Waldenfels on Decentered Dialogue

> Whatever gains its distinction by differentiating itself in
> a specific manner from others and by deviating from a common level,
> does not aim at a mere consensus. Conversely, deviation here does
> not aim at dissensus either, for it signals a genuine mode of differing.
>
> —Bernhard Waldenfels, *German-French Paths of Thought*

Despite its grander ambitions, philosophy also inhabits the world, if only through its ties to ordinary language communities. In contemporary Western philosophy, it is customary to distinguish between "analytical" and "Continental" versions of philosophizing, where the latter version comprises a broad cross-national smorgasbord of ideas ranging from Nietzsche to Martin Heidegger, Jacques Derrida, and Hans-Georg Gadamer. This smorgasbord approach is surprising in light of a central theme in contemporary Continental thought: the theme of "difference" or "otherness," which militates against any facile homogeneity. Clearly, to remain faithful to this theme, it is necessary to descend from panoramic overviews to the level of situated life-worlds, that is, from the spectatorial to the plane of engaged participants. Among contemporary thinkers located on the Continent, no one has been more persistently attentive to cross-national differences than Bernhard Waldenfels, a German philosopher, who, though reared in Husserlian (German-speaking) phenomenology, has held his sights constantly aimed across the border toward French intellectual developments. Several of his key publications have dealt with this crossroads or border crossing. Having presented, in 1983, the main strands of "French phenomenology" to a German audience, Waldenfels more recently has come forward with a larger book on this theme, *German-French Paths of Thought* (*Deutsch-Französische Gedankengänge*), which serves here as a springboard for my discussion.[1]

His title indicates that Waldenfels is concerned with paths or pathways of thought, and not simply with fashion trends or intellectual fads. Exploring pathways of thought requires patience and diligent scrutiny, which is at odds with rapid appropriation and consumption. With a glance across the Atlantic, Waldenfels speaks at one point of ideas that are "rapidly carried to market" and then suffer equally rapid obsolescence. Such rapidity, he notes, fosters forms of "postism" or beyondism, which awkwardly resemble the perennial "revolutionary changes" in consumer goods. Luxuriating particularly in the United States, such postism in his view constitutes a distinct form of "rapid digestion" of European traditions, giving rise to labels such as *post*structuralism, *post*-Marxism, *post*-philosophy, and the like. Waldenfels's nonmarketing approach is evident in his manner of presentation, which throughout remains on a level of high intellectual intensity. Glancing again back across the Atlantic, this approach offers in many ways a refreshing change of pace. To a large extent, American reception of Continental thought has oscillated between bland dismissal and panegyrical praise: demoted (especially by analytical philosophers) to the status of "mere" literature, Continental texts are often celebrated by their partisans in a style befitting mystery cults. Deviating from both types of reception, Waldenfels soberly speaks of the "labor" of thought, and also of the labor involved in transforming inherited forms of thought. Only such labor, he writes, can prevent new intellectual impulses from being reduced to mere "fashion waves."[2]

Faithful to this discriminating approach, Waldenfels's book offers a careful review of leading figures in German–French interactions during recent decades, but without suggesting a bland synthesis or ready fusion of horizons. Remembering Descartes's motto (about having "one foot in one, the other in another country"), Waldenfels accentuates the border between philosophical idioms, but a border that is not impermeable. "The other land," he writes, "is and remains other in irremediable alterity. By planting our feet in one and then another country, we take our position on one side and do not hover neutrally over both. In this way, we are located both *on this side and beyond* the boundary," that is, both "here and elsewhere."[3] With these comments, Waldenfels intimates a border zone that is not a form of convergence but a mode of complex interlacing and dialogue (possibly of an agonal kind): the border zone between self and other, native and foreign. Although focused on German–French relations, this "between zone" in many ways is the red thread weaving itself through successive chapters and signals the broader significance of his book in contemporary Western thought. Here I shall first highlight some major arguments of *German-French Paths of Thought*, especially as they emerge in the treatment of selected thinkers on both sides of the Rhine. Next, I shall sharpen the focus of discussion by concentrating on two thinkers whose relation appears crucial to Waldenfels's own preferred perspective: Maurice Merleau-Ponty and Emmanuel Levinas. By way of conclusion, I shall try to draw together the diverse facets of Waldenfels's book and offer some of my own critical comments.

GERMAN-FRENCH PATHS OF THOUGHT

Waldenfels opens *German-French Paths of Thought* with a number of general considerations meant to serve as "entry points" or guideposts for his presentation. On the whole, these considerations are marked by a cautiously tempered élan. Foremost among the book's entry wedges is the nexus between self and other, sameness and difference. He notes that the relation between self and other—including that between German and French thought—has the character of a dash or "border sign," which can be read both as hyphen and caesura: "If things were not separated, there could be no possible linkage. On the other hand, if things were wholly separated, linkage could not gain a foothold." Relying on a number of authors, including Husserl, Merleau-Ponty, Helmuth Plessner, and Norbert Elias, Waldenfels speaks in this context of a complex form of interlacing, crisscrossing, *enjambement,* and chiasm: "Self and other originate together, and this means (in Hölderlin's words) that one's own being must be learned just as much as the alien." Linkage with the other here is neither an external fate nor a matter of sheer choice, since "one chooses the other as much and as little as one chooses one's own body." In comments like these, Waldenfels clearly distances himself from more extreme views, especially the polar opposites of a placid consensualism and a radical atomism or separatism (favored by some "postmodernists"). This distancing move is a kind of leitmotif Waldenfels carefully sounds in the preface, which I have chosen as the epigraph for this chapter.[4]

The relevance of this distancing leitmotif extends from general self–other relations to the distinct realm of cross-national or cross-cultural interactions. In this respect, Waldenfels's argument pits itself against both a melting-pot type of globalism and a Balkanizing strategy of fragmentation; the pathways of his book move in a philosophical idiom that "refuses the alternative of particularism and universalism" in favor of a nonconvergent style of dialogue or exchange. Such an exchange, he writes, does not involve concurrence but rather a "laboring from two sides where one may perhaps meet in a common field—but a field where points of departure and orientations never coincide." In this regard, he adds, the encounter between peoples and cultures resembles a dialogical exchange "where question and response, speech and counter-speech follow each other without being sublated jointly in a unified *telos.*" Unsurprisingly (to students of phenomenology), he at this point invokes Merleau-Ponty's notion of "lateral universalism" where cross-cultural contact is not imposed by a "universalism from above" but rather emerges from mutual interlacing, questioning, and contestation. In Merleau-Ponty's view, what hovers at or beyond the border of any ethnocentric experience is an untamed or "wild region" that can serve as a subterranean passageway to other cultures. "The blind spot in one's own culture," Waldenfels comments, "opens a third way which is wedded neither to universalism nor an (abstract) culturalism" but that also does not remain glued to the "collective selfhood" or self-centeredness of one's own culture or nation.[5]

The distancing leitmotif is connected with a number of other entry points or guideposts, which include prominently the status of modern reason, the role of subjectivity or subjective agency, and the meaning of history and tradition. Entering the dispute surrounding the "dialectic of Enlightenment," Waldenfels delineates a position located neither squarely inside nor simply outside the confines of modern rationality. Modern Enlightenment culminated in the postulate of a universal reason anchored in a *cogito*, which itself was universalizable (or sublated into reason). Echoing Nietzsche and Theodor Adorno, he finds in this postulate a domineering strand, a sign of the "tyranny of *logos*" or the "dominance of reason," evident in reason's attempt to expurgate everything nonrational or else to appropriate everything into its rational order. For better or worse, Nietzschean suspicion has unmasked the "presumptuousness" of this outlook. In the wake of this unmasking, several strategies have been adopted to cope with modernity's dialectic. One such strategy is the attempt to salvage the "project of Enlightenment" through a further desubstantialization of reason, a move associated chiefly with the work of Jürgen Habermas and recent critical theory. In this move, reason is sublimated into a string of transempirical and transubjective validity claims, but at the price of being reduced to a formalized grid. Another prominent strategy consists in the stark disavowal or "dissolution" of modern reason, a disavowal often choosing the method of radical reversal. Pursuing this method of reversal, Waldenfels writes, one can no doubt "oppose multiplicity to unity and difference to identity," but one neglects how thoroughly a purely "reactive thinking" remains prisoner to the perspective it tries to undermine.[6]

In lieu of the strategies of retrieval and dismissal, Waldenfels opts for the path of a transformation of reason (and its underlying subjectivity):

> I am convinced that much (though not everything) that has happened in French philosophy since the 1930's can be understood as such a transformation and, moreover, that transformative efforts in this sense have been linked more or less closely with phenomenology—even where the latter is combated or transmuted.[7]

To a large extent, efforts of transformation in the French context have been linked with the notion of an embodiment of reason, an approach subsequently further intensified in the direction of an enlargement and dissemination of reason. Taken singly or in combination, efforts of this kind were not equivalent to dismissal. In Waldenfels's view, the endeavor of transformation at no point served as a cloak for "the denial of reason, for irrationalism." Rather, the endeavor signaled a progressive radicalization intent on opening reason to its other (or otherness) and thus to curb its domineering or imperialist ambitions. Reason's transformation also entailed a rethinking of (constitutive) subjectivity and subjective agency. It is in this domain that "postmodern" rhetoric has gained a dubious notoriety, by replacing traditional humanism with antihumanism and by boldly proclaiming the "death of man" or "death of the subject." For Waldenfels, it is important to distill the sensible point of this rhetoric. Expressed in "less mythical language," he states, the notion of the death of man refers to "the end of an anthropocentric outlook which elevates humans in diverse forms to masters and proprietors of all things, including themselves." What recent philosophical developments render untenable is the assumption of a foundational subject (functioning as *subiectum* of the world). However, transgressing the "principle of subjectivity" leaves room for many options, including the "patient transformation of what used to be called 'subject.'"[8]

Coupled with the displacement or decentering of the subject is inevitably a rethinking of history, which can no longer be viewed as the progressive fulfillment of human objectives and purposes. Together with a linear historical *telos*, this rethinking also calls into question the notion of a pristine origin, which simply unfolds in history and which can always be rationally retraced and recuperated. What takes the place of such teleology is neither a blind fatalism nor the sway of an arbitrary whim but a view of history as continuous renewal where purpose and nonpurpose are closely entwined. Relying on important strands in recent French philosophy, Waldenfels speaks in this context of a "primal past" (*Urvergangenheit*) meaning a "past that was never present," and of a "primal history" (*Urgeschichte*) evolving through steady reconstitutions and reworkings. Historical memory from this vantage always implicates a *temps perdu*, and self-recollection a mode of other-recollection. What this means, for Waldenfels, is that historical time is neither "up for grabs" (to be appropriated by futuristic ideologues) nor a comfortable refuge (for traditionalists). Tradition, he says, is not a secure foundation "upon which our collective experiences and ideas could come to rest"; rather, it is something "from which every renewal deviates," though not in the mode of rejection but of a "coherent reworking." Waldenfels returns at this point to his accent on laboring and transformation, seen as antidotes to a bland retrieval or dismissal. Coun-

tering again the vogue of "postism," he critiques the belief in a "free dis-
posal" over time, the assumption that there is "only the alternative between an *insistence* on tradition and a *liberation* from tradition," and not
also the possibility of "a laboring on and reworking of tradition which
opens new pathways."[9]

The guiding themes sounded in his opening pages are fleshed out
and amplified in subsequent chapters, now in close dialogue and confrontation with leading German and French thinkers. Here a few selected
highlights must suffice to indicate the general drift of his argument. The
dialogue opens in the form of two chapters devoted to the founder of modern phenomenology, Edmund Husserl. In contemporary discussions, especially in the ambiance of postmodernism, Husserl is often sidelined as a
simple "subjectivist" or modern rationalist completely obtuse to the "dialectic of Enlightenment" and unaware of the interlacing or *enjambement*
of self and other. Without denying Husserl's modernist side (as founder
of a constitutive and "transcendental" phenomenology), Waldenfels is intent on alerting readers to profound ambivalences in Husserl's project, to
fuzzy border zones where constitution of self and the world is overshadowed or invaded by traces of otherness. The "sober reticence," Waldenfels
says, characterizing Husserl's work ultimately had to come to terms also
with the situation "where the alien appears *as alien.*" At this point, the
"*logos* of phenomenology" had to prove itself as a "*logos* of otherness"
(*Logos des Fremden*). Husserl wrestled with this issue in his deliberations
on intersubjectivity (in *Cartesian Meditations* and elsewhere). Without in
any way resolving the problem, his writings at least pointed to a whole
new field of questions, which subsequently became guideposts for French
phenomenology.[10]

The questions intimated in Husserl's work were pursued with rigor
by several French phenomenologists, usually in the direction of a decentering of intentionality in favor of the "*logos* of otherness." Waldenfels turns
right away to some early writings of Derrida, writings marked by an intense engagement and wrestling with Husserlian "egology" and linguistic
"idealism." Waldenfels notes that these writings demonstrate a philosophical sobriety that belies Derrida's reputation (in some quarters) of literary
frivolity. Contrary to his detractors, Derrida knew and had studied what
he was "deconstructing"; to this extent, he does not belong to "those
adepts of 'postism' who pretend to have gone simply 'beyond.'" In one of

his earliest writings, Derrida took up a suggestion formulated by Husserl himself regarding a "genetic phenomenology," pushing this suggestion to the very boundary of a subjective constitution of meaning, but without abandoning Husserl's vocabulary. The confrontation was deepened and radicalized by Derrida in *Speech and Phenomena*, devoted to a critical step-by-step analysis of Husserl's theory of signs (as found chiefly in *Logical Investigations*). As Derrida tried to show, subjective meaning constitution is closely linked with language, but a language that, contrary to Husserl, is not reducible to transparent speech but always implicated in a structure of significations recalcitrant to intentional semantics. Borrowing in part from Saussurean semiotics, Derrida resolutely embedded *logos* in sign systems, without, however, opting for a bland empiricism. In Waldenfels's words, Derrida

> did not replace Husserl's transcendentalism with a placid worldliness conforming to existing orders through linguistification and socialization. Rather, he discovered in that transcendence an "ultra-transcendental" dimension . . . fostering a "transcendental ferment or unrest."[11]

Waldenfels does not pursue the later development of Derrida's thought, especially his intense encounters with Nietzsche and Levinas. Instead, he turns to a detailed critical examination of the evolving oeuvre of Merleau-Ponty, a topic I postpone to a later point. In terms of detailed scrutiny and attentiveness, the Merleau-Ponty chapters are matched only by those devoted to Levinas, consideration of whom I likewise postpone. Among other French thinkers, more limited attention is given to the works of Cornelius Castoriadis, Francis Jacques, and Jean-François Lyotard, of which the first two are only distantly related to the orbit of Husserlian phenomenology. In the case of Castoriadis, Husserl's legacy is replaced in large measure by Kant's Third Critique, amplified by elements of existentialism and psychoanalysis. The faculty of imagination, thematized in the Third Critique, is elevated by Castoriadis into a power of creation, extending from individual human life to the "imaginary institution" of society. Although he appreciates the dynamic quality of this approach, Waldenfels distances himself from an abstract "creationism," which, by virtue of its emphatic self-constitution, would be obtuse to the demands of otherness and intersubjectivity. In the case of Francis Jacques (relatively unknown in America), phenomenological motives cede pride of place to linguistic analysis, discourse theory, and elements of "transcendental pragmatics" (as articulated by recent Frankfurt theorists). Although applauding Jacques's intersubjective turn, Waldenfels takes exception to his tendency to formalize discourses, a tendency bent on leveling dialogue into a preordained logical formula.[12]

Critical concerns of a different, nearly opposite character surface in the chapter on Lyotard, and also in the discussion of Michel Foucault (to whom a somewhat longer middle section of the book is devoted). In the case of Lyotard, the accent on linguistic phrases and discourse formations leads to the assumption of a radical divergence between phrases, a divergence that resists neutral settlement and only permits integration into a hegemonic discourse. What this means, Waldenfels notes, is that ethical self–other relations are either stranded between discourse formations or else elevated into an abstract "appeal" without content. A more complex philosophical panorama is presented in Foucault's writings, in their evolution from an early "structuralism" to a later, more nuanced (or post-structural) analysis. What Lyotard pinpointed with the labels "phrase" and "phrase families," Foucault's early writings tended to thematize under the rubric of "knowledge formations" (or structures of *episteme*), which, as "hegemonic formations" in a given period, were closely linked with power or domination. Subsequently, at least since Foucault's *Archaeology of Knowledge*, these formations were translated into the vocabulary of "discourses" or discursive statements; still later, discursive structures and prevailing power constellations were amplified by forms of individuation or "subjectivation" in given periods. For Waldenfels, the central question here concerns the relation between structures and especially Foucault's ability to negotiate their difference, an issue that (he argues) was not properly addressed and ultimately consigned to the status of a recessed aporia.[13]

INTERLACING AND SEPARATION

The most extensive discussions in the book deal with the "pathways of thought" of two thinkers who, in different ways, were profoundly shaped by Husserlian phenomenology: Merleau-Ponty and Levinas. In several of his previous writings, Waldenfels had commented in detail on key themes in Merleau-Ponty's work, including the notions of *monde vécu*, intercorporeality, and the "flesh" of the world. By comparison, attention to Levinasian arguments seems to be of somewhat more recent date.[14] The reception of Levinas, especially in the American context, has tended to be fervent, occasionally bordering on a "conversion" experience. Against this background, Waldenfels's rapprochement with Levinas, though intense, appears cautious and circumspect and marked more by respectful engagement than pliant surrender; although replete with signs of appreciation and even admiration, his Levinas chapters are evidence of sustained, sometimes critical interrogation. To a large extent, Waldenfels's own perspective is located somewhere at the crossroads of his two chosen mentors. This search for a "between" path, an *entre-monde*, colors the book's overall presentation of contemporary German-French pathways of thought.[15]

The discussion of Merleau-Ponty is a model of sustained analysis, of a scrutiny that allows texts to speak without granting them doctrinal status. Waldenfels right away focuses on a crucial aspect of Merleau-Ponty's phenomenology, and especially his theory of language: the problem of linguistic "expression" (*Ausdruck*). Following one of Husserl's suggestions, Merleau-Ponty repeatedly calls expression a riddle or "miracle," having to do with the fact that language tries to say "something" that does not speak by itself and that may vanish when captured in expression. In Waldenfels's reading, this riddle or "paradox" of language is closely related to Merleau-Ponty's move beyond intentionality toward the "*logos* of otherness." Once subjective constitution is left behind, expression can no longer be viewed as pure activity or intentional creation, just as little as it equals pure passivity or imitation. The riddle of expression also impinges on the problem of "truth," likewise one of his lifelong preoccupations. Bracketing traditional theories of correspondence and coherence, Merleau-Ponty's writings with growing intensity centered around the notion of a creative truth, or *vérité-à-faire* (truth-in-the-making), where "making" is not a synonym of fabrication and actually is closer to the adequacy of a "fitting" response. This notion of creative truth was exemplified in Merleau-Ponty's interpretation of painting, especially his critique of the linear panorama of classical painting in favor of the embroilment of multiple (and "incompossible") visions in recent art. On the whole, Merleau-Ponty's work emerges in these chapters not as a closed system but as an "interrogative thinking" where questioning always calls the questioner into question.[16]

A similarly attentive approach also characterizes the chapters devoted to Levinas. As in the case of Merleau-Ponty, Waldenfels focuses his discussion on a number of key themes in Levinas's work, particularly the themes of singularity, self-responsibility, and other-responsibility (*Fremdverantwortung*). He emphasizes that singularity for Levinas designates not simply a constitutive subjectivity or an individual uniqueness, but a selfhood formed through self-transcendence toward the other, a transcendence resisting any totalizing homogeneity and resulting at best in an asymmetrical plurality. "Singularity in the plural," Waldenfels says, "arises only through *self-transgression* of one's own, which means that the self's uniqueness is more and other than itself." Viewed in this sense, singularity presupposes not just any difference, but the "concrete difference between own and alien or foreign [*fremd*], between own-ness and foreignness." For Levinas, exposure to otherness carries deeply ethical connotations, in the sense that the alien other approaches us not as a neutral bystander but as someone who calls upon and lays claim to us (*Anspruch*). This claim or demand escapes the lure both of consensual reciprocity and of a temporal synchrony or repetition; the stark edges of divergence are only tempered, but not removed in a broader social context where the "face" of all others requires something like an equal justice (among singulars). Responsiveness to a claim or call, in Levinas's account, entails inescapably an ethical responsibility, first of all in the form of "self-responsibility" (*Selbstverantwortung*). What is involved here, Waldenfels states, is not a subject in the traditional sense but a genuine "respondent" who becomes "who he/she is in the response." Levinas extends this kind of responsiveness to the difficult concept of "other-responsibility," which means not just a shared responsibility but a radical "responsibility for others" where one "substitutes" oneself for others by accepting the role of culprit, hostage, and victim.[17]

The Levinas chapters are rounded out by a section specifically devoted to the relation between Merleau-Ponty and Levinas, under the heading "Interlacing and Separation." According to Waldenfels, both thinkers were deeply indebted to Husserl's legacy, yet both tried to "deconstruct constitutive phenomenology from within," albeit in very different, only partially overlapping ways. The similarities/divergences between the two thinkers are explored in a number of thematic areas, including intercorporeality (illustrated by the handshake), self–other contacts, gender relations, and residual ontology versus "primary" ethics. For Merleau-Ponty, intercorporeality meant basically a kind of "co-perception," a bodily appresentation permitting "other-experience" (*Fremderfahrung*). This view was exemplified in Merleau-Ponty's treatment of the handshake, a treatment stressing the differential relatedness of active and passive-receptive components, of touching and being touched. It is in this area that an initial divergence surfaces, with Levinas charging Merleau-Ponty with promoting a facile harmonization, a privileging of the active-perceptual element. For Levinas, the lure of harmonization can only be banished by the assumption of a radical otherness or foreignness (*Fremdheit*) that exceeds any type of perception or cognition and that resists "being transformed into *phenomena*." Levinas at this point introduces the idea of a "radical separation" of hands and bodies as an antipode to intercorporeality, a separation culminating in the formula of the "nakedness of the alien face" as the origin of a primary ethics.[18]

Divergence also surfaces in the field of gender relations where Merleau-Ponty preferred to speak of a differential relatedness, with male and female being profiled against each other in intercorporeality, while Levinas insisted on the separation of genders even in the "community of sensation." In the discussion of these and related themes, the respective positions of the two thinkers are progressively sharpened and tested against each other, in the mode of reciprocal contestation (*Auseinandersetzung*). In the course of this testing, Waldenfels's own perspective also begins to take shape. In the opening rounds of the confrontation, Waldenfels repeatedly takes the side of Merleau-Ponty, defending him against spurious or ill-considered accusations. On several occasions, he takes exception to a certain "impatience" or summary bluntness in Levinas's approach, which accounts for the fact that his criticisms of Merleau-Ponty often miss their target. In the same vein, Waldenfels protects Merleau-Ponty against charges of fostering a bland coincidence or totalizing synthesis. Such charges, he says, bypass the complexity of Merleau-Ponty's thought by simply privileging the "motif of separation" over the "motif of interlacing," when one has to ask whether the one "can at all be operative without the other."

While acknowledging the emphasis on relatedness in Merleau-Ponty's thought, Waldenfels finds sufficient countervailing evidence making it possible to speak of an "asymmetrical interlacing" that eludes the tentacles both of synthetic holism and atomistic fragmentation, pointing instead to a complex "between-world" (or *entre-monde*). As it happens, these preferential accents noticeably shift in the course of the presentation, yielding in the end nearly the opposite evaluation. Returning to Levinas's reversal of "logocentrism," Waldenfels concedes that phenomenology of almost every kind is unhinged by the alien other's ethical demands. These demands tend to be muted by interlacing of any kind. For Waldenfels, what needs to be acknowledged at this point is the reality of separation and even rupture (*Riss*) between self and other, a rupture that happens from "outside" and that can never be recuperated in any interlacing (of body or meanings).[19]

DECENTERED DIA-LOGUE

Waldenfels evidently pursues a double aim: to give a balanced overview of German–French intellectual pathways, and, more importantly, to articulate through commentary his own preferred perspective. On both counts, he deserves to be applauded and rewarded by a wide audience of readers. To be sure, congruent with his own approach, Waldenfels would not welcome an uncritical audience, which provides me with leeway to add some of my own critical comments. On a somewhat superficial level, readers may question the selectivity and organizational structure of the book. In a text devoted to German–French interactions, one may be surprised to find only two German authors singled out for treatment: Husserl and Nietzsche, whose discussion is tagged on almost as an afterthought at the end. Readers might have expected some chapters on Heidegger and perhaps on one or the other representative of the Frankfurt School. On the French side, the choice of Castoriadis and Francis Jacques appears puzzling, as is the omission of such figures as Sartre and Luce Irigaray (not to mention the later Derrida). Yet, given the overall quality of the book, such matters shrink into minor quibbles.

More significant, in my view, are questions relating to Waldenfels's own perspective on self–other relations. This perspective is subtle and in many ways tensional. At the conclusion of his book, Waldenfels offers some additional comments on his own pathway of thought. Somewhat surprisingly, he speaks of a "birth of philosophy out of the spirit of dialogue." A thinking inquiring into its own ground, we read, "exposes itself to the labor of dialogue," but the latter has to be seen as a "dia-logue" where the gathering principle of "*logos*" is continuously exposed to the hazard of division and dispersal among participants. Efforts to negotiate this intrinsic tension have produced a number of models or formulas in the history of Western philosophy. Prominent among these formulas is the Platonic ideal of dialogue, where sublimation into a shared *telos* is given primacy over the danger of relativizing disjunction.

To effectuate this goal, the Platonic model, which is said to resonate still in Hegel, Husserl, and recent hermeneutics, relied on a series of premises or guideposts, such as "knowledge is recognition," "knowing means participating in a (cosmic) whole," and "dialogue is (a version of) soliloquy." A different model was developed by Kant, who substituted for the Platonic *telos* a "grounding law" pinpointed in "a priori conditions of possibility." With this move, still reverberating in Habermasian discourse ethics and "universal pragmatics," dialogue is transformed into argumentation before an impartial judge, specifically the "tribunal of reason" located ideally in everyone's conscience. Although no longer animated by a substantive purpose, this tribunal replicates the gathering power of *logos* by expunging critique of the adjudicating norms.[20]

For Waldenfels, both models are flawed and inherently vitiated by their necessary (though unacknowledged) incompleteness: just as the unified classical *telos* cannot comprehend or exhaust the (cosmic) whole, the modern conception of a "grounding law" cannot be part of its own rule system. What is basically missing in both formulas is recognition of the decentering of *logos*, and especially of the dis-orderly and innovative character of self–other encounters as evident in genuine "dia-logue." A questioning that proceeds not on the basis of a pregiven order but "inaugurates and transforms such order," Waldenfels says, is not a mere subsumable instance but, rather, a "*key event* (*Schlüsselereignis*) which opens up a discursive field while precluding other possibilities." Seen as part of this inaugural event, dia-logue exceeds coincidence and, in effect, is decentered and dispersed into a "plurality of *logoi*," into a multiplicity of discursive frames that is not so much a peaceful as an "agonistic" (*kämpferisch*) multiplicity where the pursuit of some possibilities excludes or frustrates others. The only way this multiplicity can escape randomness and fragmentation is through the linkage of question and response, and especially through an understanding of response as "responsiveness" and responsibility. Such responsiveness, Waldenfels notes, implies a "reply to the other," which in its uniqueness exceeds the range of repetition and recollection.[21]

What is admirable in these passages is the attempt to formulate a notion of dia-logue—and of self–other relations more generally—that escapes the tentacles both of a totalizing *logos* and of utter divisiveness and isolation. To this extent, Waldenfels's "postmodernism," if this label is at all appropriate, clearly differs from fashionable versions that celebrate randomness for its own sake. Waldenfels's approach, it seems to me, offers indeed a promising way of coming to terms with contemporary multiculturalism and with the challenges facing Western thought in the aftermath of Eurocentrism and Orientalism. The main question I want to raise here is whether his approach does not perhaps accentuate the *dia* over the gathering function of *logos*, or, to put matters in terms of the *agon* between Merleau-Ponty and Levinas, whether he does not at points too much favor Levinasian "separation" over Merleau-Pontyan "interlacing" (including "asymmetrical interlacing").

This weighting of scales seems to me neither required not warranted, even as a (desirable) countermove to a homogenizing reason. Surely there must be a middle path between a logically predictable response (as to the question, what is two plus two?) and a radically disjointed response (which, perhaps "creatively," misses the question). In common parlance, we call this middle path a "fitting" response, characterizing responsiveness as such, while unfitting responses are considered either pointless or else offensive or rude. Waldenfels himself, of course, is quite aware of the pitfalls of sheer disjointedness and, on several occasions, tries to guard against it. Still, the solution offered in the concluding pages, that of a pure "responsiveness" seemingly without content, comes uncomfortably close to the *interrogatio pura* criticized at another point.[22]

Following in large measure Levinasian teachings, Waldenfels ties responsiveness closely, perhaps indissolubly, to the claim or demand of the other that disrupts any placid soliloquy. Here again, questions can be raised regarding the quality and status of this claim, especially its determining, commanding, or merely soliciting character. In America, Levinas's "face of the other" has often been read and greeted in a near-fatalistic fashion. Although offering a much more nuanced account, Waldenfels is not entirely free of this submissiveness, as is evident in his tendency to absolve the other's claim from any reciprocity and thus from any need to justify its rightness or propriety. To the extent that this is the case, the pitfall of an active "creationism," criticized in the work of Castoriadis, is matched by the opposite pitfall of a reactive passivity. Moreover, devoid of semantic meaning, the notion of a radical claim comes uncomfortably close to an ethics of abstract postulates, to which Lyotard is said to succumb. Reluctant to move in this direction, Waldenfels remonstrates: "Pure imperative sentences which command nothing in particular and are addressed to no one in particular, are a practical chimera."[23]

One needs to recognize, of course, that Lyotard's discourse is not identical with that of Levinas. Waldenfels ably shows that Levinas's discourse is of a special or peculiar kind, in the sense that "singularity" carries for him a transitive connotation and that nonreciprocity hence retains a certain perceptual linkage. Nevertheless, precisely in light of this peculiarity, one cannot help being chagrined by a distinctively one-sided Levinasian vocabulary (exteriority, heteronomy, and the like), a vocabulary that in large measure has shaped his reception abroad. At a minimum, one can question the usefulness of this vocabulary, which seems to undercut any transitivity in favor of rigid antithesis. In the same fashion, the opposition between "totality" and "infinity" (or transcendence) seems to replicate traditional two-world formulas that have been rendered dubious at least since Nietzsche. One may readily grant that the "other" is not simply inside or part of the same (or self), but this does necessarily render it "external," provided decentering is taken seriously enough to disclose the self's otherness to itself. Waldenfels repeatedly stresses the embroilment of self and other, inside and outside, but without making this into a problem for Levinas. Philosophy, he says, despite the lure of logocentrism, is always inhabited by "its own otherness" (*Fremdheit*). Elsewhere, again in reaction to Lyotard, he presents "excess" (or transcendence) as not external to what it exceeds, for "the one is *nothing without the other.*[24]

The accent on exteriority is closely linked with another troubling issue: that of force and violence. Clearly, if self and other are radically separated, the other's claim can reach me only in the form of violent irruption or disruption. Following in large measure Levinas's lead, Waldenfels is replete with references to force and violence (*Gewalt*), seen now as complements of self–other disjunction and the contingent selectivity of choices. Thus, his discussion of creative expression underscores its agonistic or "struggling" (*kämpferisch*) character, which always carries with it "elements of violence" or streaks of "violent irruption." This accent is heightened in the Levinas chapters, which document the nearly imperceptible transition from the superiority of the other's claims to an "excess of alien violence." The comparison between Merleau-Ponty and Levinas culminates in the stress on rupture (*Riss*) through which every relatedness is forcefully "exploded, torn asunder." Several comments are in order at this point.

First of all, the undeniable selectivity of choices surely can lead to a different, nearly opposite conclusion: precisely the absence of one correct framework would seem to impose on choosers the need for moderation and self-limitation (including the limitation of violence). As regards "rupture," the term appears meaningless unless it tears apart what belongs together (rather than indifferent elements), not to mention the painfulness of any *Riss*, which seems to call for healing. On a more general level, and quite apart from Waldenfels's treatment, I find disturbing a pervasive "rupturing" tendency in contemporary Continental thought. In an age ravaged by unbelievable and unprecedented violence and brutality, can one be sanguine about the proclivity of many philosophers to muse about the benefits of *Gewalt*?[25]

Mitigating rupture obviously entails implications for ethics and ethical relations. One can readily concur with the Levinasian notion that "obligation happens," meaning that we are "always already" ethically obligated without deliberate choice. Thus, we are inevitably obligated to our parents and siblings (and perhaps to the world at large) from the time of birth, independently of intent. This, however, tells only part of the story. Clearly, understanding the nature of the obligation and meeting it appropriately requires ethical preparation and cultivation on our part. To this extent, acknowledgment of the "happening" of obligation does not at all dispense with the personal cultivation of virtues and the labor of character formation. According to traditional teachings, these virtues include temperance, courage (in the face of oppression), prudence, and justice. Implicit in the notion of prudence (and other more "theoretical" virtues) is a kind of thoughtfulness, which militates against a presumed "primordiality" of ethics beyond philosophical reflection. It is the same kind of thoughtfulness, in my view, that has prompted the collective wisdom of humanity to shun the extremes of self- or other-centeredness in favor of some version of the Golden Rule. It is the same Golden Rule that seems to reverberate in the end also in Waldenfels's view of "asymmetrical interlacing," as culled from Merleau-Ponty. Rather than pursuing my critical queries, I want to conclude with a passage that ably reflects Waldenfels's nuanced perspective at multiple crossroads:

> Interlacing as an asymmetrical linkage of self-transgressing elements precludes both holism and atomism. The non-coincidence of myself with myself and others prevents integration of myself and others into a totalizing whole. . . . Conversely, the non-difference between myself, the world and others militates against a process of isolation where a single being would congeal in its separateness. The double negation implicit in non-coincidence and non-difference preserves single beings from dissolving in the whole, and it preserves the whole from splintering into radical fragmentation. Constituted by this double "no," interlacing diverges from both total fusion and particularistic dispersal.[26]

CHAPTER NINE

Hermeneutics and Intercultural Dialogue

Linking Theory and Practice

The future survival of humankind may depend on our readiness . . .
to pause in front of the other's otherness—the otherness of nature
as well as that of historically grown cultures of peoples and countries.

—Hans-Georg Gadamer

As customarily defined, "hermeneutics" means the theory, or rather the practice or art, of interpretation. In its primary and traditional sense, interpretation means textual interpretation, that is, the encounter between a reader and a text. In this encounter, something has to happen; some work has to be done: the reader needs to discover the meaning of the text, a meaning usually far from self-evident. The difficulty of the work is increased in case of temporal or spatial distance: when the reader wishes to understand a text from another age or in a different language. Yet, to some extent, the difficulty prevails even in the absence of such distance: for example, in reading the letter of a friend. Basically, the problem derives from the peculiarly ambivalent character of interpretation: the reader cannot remain entirely passive, nor must he or she be overly active. The interpreter cannot find the meaning by passively copying or transliterating the text, nor should she willfully foist a meaning on the text, thereby manipulating or coercing it. Hence, the labor is transformative: the reader must bring oneself to the text, but in an open manner such as to allow for a new learning experience to happen. This is why we say (or why leading hermeneuticists say) that interpretation is necessarily interactive or dialogical. This is also why one might say that hermeneutics is an illustration of integral pluralism since difference is both acknowledged and bridged.

The question I want to raise here is whether this meaning of hermeneutics can be transferred from the reading of texts to interhuman relations and especially to the relation between cultures or civilizations. Obviously, cultures are different from written texts. Cultures are complex semantic clusters; following Wittgenstein, we might say that cultures are complex language games, and, more than language games, they are "forms of life" made up of, in addition to written texts, social customs, religious beliefs, rituals, and practices. Moreover, cultures are internally diversified and unfinished, that is, always evolving and on the move. Given this character, some people consider cross- or intercultural hermeneutics impossible or futile. As main reasons for this impossibility, they cite the internal complexity and the incommensurability of semantic clusters or forms of life. This is a weighty objection; carried to an extreme, the objection lends credence to the thesis of a looming "clash" of cultures or civilizations (famously formulated by Samuel Huntington). However, this seems to be an overly pessimistic and debilitating outlook. As in the case of textual interpretation, we might agree that the difficulties are considerable—and proceed nonetheless. My own preference, in any case, is to adopt an experimental approach, the approach of hermeneutical inquiry, and then see how far it will lead us.

This is basically the approach I follow here. I shall proceed in three main steps. First, I discuss the historical development and basic meaning of hermeneutics, as expounded by the leading proponent of modern and contemporary hermeneutics, Hans-Georg Gadamer. Second, I review some possible practical "applications" of the hermeneutical perspective in the social and cultural domains, lifting up for attention certain parallels between hermeneutics and practical philosophy. Third, drawing on the insights of both Gadamer and more overtly political thinkers, I shall elaborate on the specific relevance of hermeneutics for cross-cultural or intercultural understanding and dialogue.

HERMENEUTICS: ITS MEANING AND DEVELOPMENT

Regarding the meaning and development of hermeneutics, Gadamer's magisterial *Truth and Method* (1960) is an indispensable resource. As Gadamer there points out, hermeneutics has followed a complex trajectory and undergone profound transformations in its history: starting from limited, closely circumscribed beginnings, it evolved over time until, in the end, it came to coincide with human life experience as such. In its infancy, hermeneutics was basically a specialized art or method employed in the fields of theology, classical philology, and jurisprudence. Whereas theologians needed to decipher the meaning of scriptures that were removed in time and place, philologians faced the task of capturing the meaning of classical texts in modern idioms; jurists needed to detect the significance of classical law books in postclassical (say, Germanic) societies. At the onset of the modern age, these endeavors were continued and refined by Renaissance humanism and Protestant theology, with scholars in both fields seeking to distill a more original meaning from later corruptions or deformations. A major innovation or change of focus occurred in the Romantic era and especially in the work of Friedrich Schleiermacher. Departing from the earlier use, the latter extended the role of hermeneutics to all literary expressions, while also "psychologizing" the methodology. The task of interpretation, in his view, was to discern the "author's mind" (*mens auctoris*) or the inner spirit or inspiration animating a given work.

This approach was further broadened and given a more robust academic anchorage by the "Historical School" of the nineteenth century, whose chief spokesman was Wilhelm Dilthey. For Dilthey, all of human history had to be approached hermeneutically, which means an effort had to be made—a scholarly disciplined effort—to decipher the meaning of historical events or activities by examining the motivating intentions of historical actors. In Gadamer's words, it was "for the first time Dilthey who consciously took up Romantic hermeneutics and expanded it into a historical method—indeed into an epistemology of the human sciences." For Dilthey, the point was not just that historical sources are encountered as texts, but that "historical reality as such is a text in need of understanding." In this manner, the enterprise of hermeneutics was "transposed to the study of history"; differently put, "hermeneutics emerged as the basis of the study of history," which is a field of vast dimensions.[1] Although they broadened and transformed the role of interpretation, however, Dilthey and the Historical School remained hostage to certain premises that restricted its scope. The main premises obstructing a full flowering were of an epistemological kind: the aspiration of historical study to be recognized as a "science" on a par with the natural sciences. In trying to grasp history scientifically, the historian had to adopt a superior or neutral standpoint, extricating herself from the flow of historical experience. Critiquing this approach, Gadamer observes that historical experience cannot be reduced to a "procedure" or have the "anonymity of a method." Despite Dilthey's best intentions, the "epistemological pull of Cartesianism" proved in the end too strong, preventing him from "integrating into his thought the historicity of historical experience itself."[2]

For Gadamer, the most important event in recent times, the event that basically reshaped the role of hermeneutics, was the shift from epistemology to ontology, a shift associated with the name of Martin Heidegger. What was involved in this shift was the transformation of interpretive understanding from a methodology tailored for academic disciplines into a mode of human existence, of human being-in-the-world. "Under the rubric of a 'hermeneutics of facticity,'" Gadamer states, Heidegger opposed himself not only to the ambitions of historical science but also to the restrictive "eidetic phenomenology" of Husserl, with its distinction between fact and essence. In contrast to the latter, "the contingent and underivable 'facticity' of existence or *Dasein*—and not the epistemic *cogito* as warrant of essential universality—came to represent the ontological yardstick of phenomenological questioning." For Heidegger, interpretive or hermeneutical understanding was not the province of specialized human disciplines (or of a transcendentally construed phenomenology), but it was, rather, a constitutive feature of every human being inserted both in the world and in the movement of temporality. With his thesis that "being itself is time," Gadamer comments, Heidegger called into question the "basic subjectivism of modern philosophy" along with the entire "frame of reference of modern metaphysics which tended to define being as what is present." At the same time, by focusing on the "understanding character" of human *Dasein*, Heideggerian ontology departed from and overcame the "historicist" dilemmas of the Historical School. In comparison with Dilthey, understanding is no longer a mere "methodological con-

cept"; rather, it pinpoints the "original mode of being of human life itself."
Through his "analytic of *Dasein*," in particular, Heidegger revealed "the
projective [not merely present-ist] character of all understanding and conceived the act of understanding itself as a movement of transcendence,
of moving beyond the existent [state of affairs]."[3]

From Heidegger's perspective, interpretive understanding thus is not
so much a methodology as a happening or temporal event, a happening
with possibly transformative consequences for the interpreter. In the case
of textual exegesis, for instance, the text may (and usually does) prove initially recalcitrant to immediate access. In the attempt to gain leverage, the
reader does not approach the text with a "blank slate" (*tabula rasa*) that
would permit passive appropriation; rather, to gain entry, the reader has
to apply to the text a tentative frame of reference, what Heidegger calls a
"pre-understanding" (*Vorurteil*) or a "projected meaning" (*Vorentwurf*).
Gadamer describes the process: "Whoever is trying to understand a text,
always engages in projecting (*Entwerfen*): he/she projects a meaning for the
text as soon as some initial meaning comes to the fore. That initial meaning,
however, emerges only because the text is read with certain expectations
regarding its meaning." Yet, when approached with this "fore-meaning" or
pre-understanding, the text may refuse to yield and prove resistant. This
resistance, in turn, may force the reader to revise his initial assumptions
or presumptions, a revision that can prove wrenching or painful. In revis-
ing initial assumptions, the reader is not required to abandon all critical
reservations or queries; what is demanded is a certain openness to the issues raised in the text and to the possibility that prior assumptions may
have been wrong or lopsided. When reading a text, says Gadamer, "we are
not expected to jettison all our 'fore-meanings' concerning its content. All
that is asked is that we remain open to the intrinsic lesson of the text (or
of another person)." Hence, "a person trying to understand a text must be
prepared to be told something by the text. That is why a hermeneutically
trained person must be, from the start, sensitive and receptive to the text's
alterity or difference [*Andersheit*]."[4]

These comments bring into view a crucial aspect of hermeneutics as
conceived by Heidegger and Gadamer: the dialogical and circular character of understanding. Gadamer, in particular, is famous for his insistence
on the close linkage and even convergence of dialogue and hermeneutical

understanding. "That a historical text is made the object of exegesis means that it puts a question to the interpreter. Hence, interpretation always relates essentially to the question that is posed to the reader," Gadamer says in *Truth and Method*. But every question solicits a response, and thus leads into the thick of dialogue. A genuine dialogue, Gadamer observes, has necessarily the "structure of question and response." To conduct such a dialogue requires that the participants are "attentive to each other" and do not "talk past each other." Above all, dialogue demands a certain modesty and nonaggressiveness, a willingness to listen and a refusal to try to "overpower the other partner." By placing at the center the "weight" of the respective opinions, dialogue is a mode of "experimental testing" (*Erproben*) or inquiry; its fruit is not the triumph of one opinion over another but a mutual learning process in the course of which partners gain a better understanding of both the subject matter and themselves. This feature leads Gadamer to a poignant formulation of the relation between dialogue and hermeneutics, a formulation quintessential for his entire approach:

> What characterizes a dialogue . . . is precisely this: that—in the process of question and answer, in giving and taking, talking at cross purposes and coming to an agreement—dialogical discourse performs that communication of meaning which, with respect to the written tradition, is the task of hermeneutics. Hence, it is more than a metaphor: it is a recollection of what is originally at stake when hermeneutical inquiry is seen as entering into dialogue with a text.[5]

Dialoguing with a text, just as dialoguing with a human partner, is a difficult process fraught with many pitfalls and possible derailments. Occasionally, Gadamerian hermeneutics is accused of, or identified with, a facile consensualism, with a happy blending of views devoid of conflict. To some extent, his *Truth and Method* has encouraged this construal, especially through its notion of a "fusion of horizons." Understanding does not recognize limits but is always "the fusion of these horizons supposedly existing by themselves."[6] Yet, at a closer (and more sympathetic) look, what is involved here is not so much a fusion in the sense of convergence but rather an unlimited openness to horizons, in such a manner that interpretive understanding can never be fully stabilized or completed. This aspect is admirably highlighted by Gadamer at another place when he speaks of the tensional character of all understanding, a tension deriving from the distance or difference between reader and text, between self and other, between present and past. "Hermeneutics," he writes, "must start from the position that a person seeking to understand has a bond with whatever a transmitted text tries to say and thus is connected with the tradition from which the text speaks." At the same time, however, hermeneutical inquiry is aware "that this connection does not have the character of an unquestioned, self-evident consensus (as would be the case in an unbroken stream of tradition)." Hence, the tensional nature of all understanding. "Hermeneutical work," Gadamer adds pointedly, "is based on a polarity between familiarity and strangeness [*Fremdheit*]," but this polarity should not be construed psychologically (with Schleiermacher) but ontologically. "Here is the tension: the play between strangeness and familiarity encountered in tradition is the mid-point between a distantiated object of history and membership in a living tradition. The true locus of hermeneutics is this in-between."[7]

This tensional character also affects the circular quality of interpretation, what is called the "hermeneutical circle." This circle is not a closed sphere permitting only an empty turning "round and round," but an open circle fostering a learning process or a steady amelioration and transformation of understanding. This, in any event, is the construal favored by Heidegger. In approaching a text, the reader projects a "fore-meaning" of the whole, which, however, suffers shipwreck because parts or portions of the text refuse to be integrated. Hence, a new holistic projection is needed, triggering an ongoing adjustment of parts and whole. In Gadamer's description, it was Heidegger who gave to the circle an existential-ontological significance deriving from the constitutive role of understanding for human *Dasein*. Given this constitutive role, the circle for Heidegger cannot achieve closure, but it points toward an infinite completion. "The circle of whole and part is not dissolved [or terminated] in genuine understanding but, on the contrary, is most fully realized," Gadamer says. Seen in this light, the circle is not "formal in nature" but ontological; it is "neither subjective nor objective" but rather pinpoints understanding as "the interplay of the movement of tradition and the movement of the interpreter." The anticipation of meaning that governs the interpreter's understanding of a text is "not an act of subjectivity" but proceeds from "the commonality linking us with the tradition." But this commonality, Gadamer adds, is never finished but in "a constant process of formation (*Bildung*)."[8]

HERMENEUTICS AND PRACTICAL APPLICATION

Hermeneutics is not, and has never been, a purely abstract theory, but is closely linked with lived experience and human conduct. This linkage has been intensified in recent times with the shift from methodology to ontology when understanding comes to be seen as part and parcel of our living and being-in-the-world. Yet, even in earlier times, the linkage was never entirely lacking. We read in *Truth and Method* that an integral part of traditional hermeneutics was the so-called *subtilitas applicandi*, the ability to bring the meaning of a text to bear on a given situation. Thus, it was commonly assumed that a proper understanding of textual meaning involved "something like applying the text" to the situation of the interpreter and reader, that is, to relate that meaning to practical human conduct. Gadamer gives the prominent examples of scriptural and legal/judicial interpretation. Clearly, scriptural exegesis was not just meant to increase theological knowledge but to provide a resource for pastoral preaching, which in turn was designed to mold the lives of the faithful. The same connection prevailed (and prevails) in judicial interpretation, where the judge is asked to discern the relevance of a legal norm in a particular situation or context. "A law," Gadamer comments, "does not just exist as an historical object or entity, but needs to be concretized in its legal validity by being interpreted." Similarly, the gospel does not exist simply as an edifying historical document, but it needs to be approached "in such a way as to disclose its message of salvation." Hence, in order to be properly grasped, a given text—scriptural or legal—needs to be understood "at every moment, in every concrete situation, in a new and different way." As a consequence, "hermeneutical understanding always involves a mode of application."[9]

This linkage with application or practical conduct is greatly intensified in Heidegger's ontological approach. Construed as an interpretive creature, human *Dasein* now is seen to conduct one's entire life under hermeneutical auspices. From the angle of Heidegger's "hermeneutics of facticity," Gadamer writes, understanding is no longer a method through which an inquiring consciousness targets a given object; rather, it means being situated in a temporal happening, in an ongoing "process of tradition" (*Überlieferungsgeschehen*). In fact, "understanding proves to be itself a lived happening" and as such a mode of human conduct, a conduct neither predetermined by fixed rules (presumably beyond interpretation) nor purely whimsical or arbitrary. In this context, to illustrate the sense of "happening," Gadamer invokes the tradition of Aristotle, and especially the legacy of Aristotelian ethics, which is not an ethics of purely cognitive principles (like Kantian morality) or of irrational will power (like "emotivism"), but an ethics of concretely lived *praxis*. On the level of practical application, he writes, Aristotle's ethical analysis offers "a kind of model of the problems of hermeneutics." As in the case of the practice of virtues, hermeneutical application is not merely "an occasional feature or subsequent addition" to the process of understanding, but rather it permeates this process from beginning to end. As in ethical *praxis*, application does not just consist in relating a pregiven general principle to a particular case; the interpreter has to make sense of her situation in light of the broader "process of tradition" (comprising both that situation and the text). Hence, in order to understand a text and its general teaching, the interpreter "must not try to disregard his/her particular hermeneutical situation," but rather must "correlate that text with this situation if understanding is going to be possible at all."[10]

Moving beyond the strictly ethical dimension, *Truth and Method* also comments on some social and political implications of hermeneutical "application," or *praxis*. Gadamer indicates that such an application cannot really happen in a society or political regime where norms or rules of conduct are entirely static and exempt from further interpretation, that is, where there is a ban on creative exegesis and transformation. At the same time, hermeneutics cannot flourish in a society or regime dominated by arbitrary power or by a Hobbesian sovereign. In Gadamer's words, hermeneutics presupposes a dialogical give-and-take occurring in a continuity of tradition: "Where this is not the case—for example, in an absolutist state where the will of the absolute ruler is above the law—hermeneutics cannot exist, since the ruler can abrogate the rules of interpretation." In such a situation, the arbitrary will of the ruler who is *lege solutus*, "not bound by any law," can render decisions without regard for the law and hence without the effort of interpretation.

Hermeneutics, for Gadamer, hence presupposes a constitutional regime (perhaps a democratic constitutional order) that does not rely on arbitrary decisions or willful domination and makes room for the hermeneutical balancing of "whole and parts" and the dialogical inquiry into the conditions of social justice and fairness. "It is part of a properly constituted legal order," he writes, "that the decision of a judge [and the policy of rulers] does not proceed from an arbitrary and unpredictable fiat, but rather from a just weighing up of the whole," or the balancing of all elements involved in a situation. The possibly democratic connotations of this outlook are evident when Gadamer adds that "anyone [i.e., any citizen] is capable of undertaking this just weighing up, provided she has immersed herself in the concrete particular situation" as seen in a broader social context.[11]

Gadamer's comments on application and practical conduct are not limited to *Truth and Method*. About ten years later, he published "Hermeneutics as Practical Philosophy" (1972), which was specifically focused on the relation between hermeneutics and practical philosophy: hermeneutics should not be viewed simply as an abstract theory, but it always implies or implicates a reference to practical conduct. Since its earliest beginnings, hermeneutical inquiry has always claimed "that its reflection on the possibilities, rules and means of interpretation is somehow directly useful or advantageous for lived *praxis*." For this reason, he notes, interpretation has often been treated as an art form or artistic skill (*Kunstlehre*) rather than a routine technique. The essay traces the development of hermeneutics from its roots in scriptural and juridical interpretation to the shifts occasioned by Renaissance humanism, Reformation, and postrevolutionary Romanticism and historicism. The basic sea change in the meaning of hermeneutics is attributed again to the work of Heidegger, to his break with the static (or presentist) metaphysics of the past, and his inscription of understanding into the lived, temporal experience of *Dasein*. "It was Heidegger's great merit," Gadamer says, "to have broken through the aura of self-evidence of the Greek concept of 'being,'" and through the presumed self-evidence of the modern concept of consciousness or "subjectivity," thus paving the way for a new understanding of "being" as a mode of temporal experience and practical conduct. In this context, Gadamer stresses the significance of Heidegger's famous lecture "What Is Metaphysics?," which he treats as an illustration of (what might be called) a "hermeneutics of suspicion." By focusing on the elusive quality of the "being" (the "is") of metaphysics, he writes, the lecture queries "what metaphysics really denotes in contrast to what it claims to be." Understood in this manner, Heidegger's query "acquires the force of a provocation and reveals itself as example of a new conception of interpretation."[12]

By turning to "being" as lived occurrence, Heidegger's work forcefully discloses the intimate linkage between understanding and *praxis*, which had always been implicit in the hermeneutical tradition. As in *Truth and Method*, Heideggerian ontology is correlated with Aristotle's notion of "practical philosophy," but minus the latter's metaphysics of "substances." In Gadamer's account, *praxis* and practical philosophy in the Aristotelian tradition are not the antithesis to "theory" or theoretical thought, but rather intimate a thoughtful conduct. "The semantic field in which the word and concept '*praxis*' have their proper place," he writes, "is not primarily defined by its opposition to theory or as the mere application of a (given) theory." Rather, *praxis* denotes "the mode of conduct of living beings in the broadest sense." Differently phrased, *praxis* means "the actuation of life (*energeia*) of anything alive—anything that displays in some fashion life, a mode or conduct of life (*bios*)."

To be sure, by contrast to animal behavior, human life conduct is distinguished by a certain measure of deliberation and the employment of language and symbols. The most important distinction, however, prevails between practical conduct and mere instrumental fabrication or technical production (*poiesis*, *techne*): "Practical philosophy is determined by the line drawn between the practical insight of a freely choosing person, on the one hand, and the acquired skill of an expert (which Aristotle names *techne*), on the other." Hence, practical philosophy has to do "not with readily learnable crafts and skills" but rather "with what is fitting for an individual as citizen and what constitutes his/her civic virtue (*arête*)." At this point, the connection between *praxis* and hermeneutics emerges clearly into view. To quote a crucial passage:

> The knowledge that guides action is essentially called for by the concrete situations in which we need to choose the fitting response [*das Tunliche*]—and no skillful technique can spare us the needed deliberation and decision. As a result, practical philosophy seeking to cultivate this practical ability is neither theoretical science (in the style of

mathematics) nor expert know-how (in the sense of mastering technical processes), but a knowledge of a special kind. [As in the case of the hermeneutical circle] this knowledge must arise from *praxis* and, though moving through various generalizations, must relate itself back to *praxis*.[13]

HERMENEUTICS AND INTERCULTURAL DIALOGUE

From Gadamer's perspective, hermeneutics is related not only to practical conduct in general, but to such conduct in a given time and place. In our time of globalization, when different societies and cultures are pushed closer and closer together, hermeneutical understanding is bound to transcend local contexts and to acquire a cross-cultural or transnational significance. At this point, members of a given society or culture are called upon to interpret not only the modalities of their own tradition but the complex lineaments of initially quite alien texts and life forms. To make headway in this endeavor, individuals and groups have to bring to the encounter their own "fore-meanings" or pre-understandings and then expose them to correction or revision in an interactive (or dialogical) process of give-and-take.

Gadamer has been keenly attentive to these cultural issues in some of his later writings, especially in *The Legacy of Europe* (*Das Erbe Europas*) and on the ongoing process of European unification. For Gadamer, Europe represents (or has ideally represented in the past) a model of that "unity in diversity" characteristic of hermeneutical dialogue where, coming from distinctly different backgrounds, each partner seeks to discern the other's meaning. The deeper philosophical and hermeneutical significance of Europe, he observes, resides not in its presumed "universality" but in its multicultural and multilingual composition, in its historical practice of "cohabitation with otherness in a narrow space." In our time, this cohabitation (though threatened by the problem of national security and immigration) can still provide a lesson for humanity at large, for an evolving ecumenical world culture. "To live with the other," says Gadamer, "as the other of the other—this basic human task applies to the micro- as well as to the macro-level. Just as each of us learns to live with the other in the process of individual maturation, a similar learning process holds true for larger communities, for nations and states."[14]

Just as in the case of hermeneutical dialogue, the point of intercultural encounter is not to reach a bland consensus or uniformity of beliefs but to foster a progressive learning process involving possible transformation. For this to happen, local or indigenous traditions must be neither jettisoned nor congealed (or essentialized). As Gadamer points out, the role of local or indigenous traditions is a feature endemic to the "hermeneutical circle" with its emphasis on fore-meanings or prejudgments, which are seen as corrigible but *not* expendable starting points of understanding. In a similar fashion, participants in cross-cultural encounter are expected neither to erase themselves (in a vain attempt to "go native") nor to appropriate and subjugate the other's difference; rather, the point is to achieve a shared appreciation and recognition of differences (what Heidegger used to call "letting-be").

"Where the goal is not [unilateral] mastery or control, we are liable to experience the otherness of others precisely against the backdrop of our own pre-judgments. The highest and most elevated aim we can strive for in this context is to partake in the other, to share the other's alterity," Gadamer states. The stakes, in this encounter, are high, both for individual societies and for humanity at large. In fact, "the future survival of humankind," he says, may depend on the proper cultivation of cross-cultural understanding and dialogue, more particularly, on "our readiness not to utilize the immense resources of power and technical efficiency [accumulated in some states] but to pause in front of the other's otherness—the otherness of nature as well as that of historically grown cultures of peoples and countries." If we are able to do the latter, a transformative and humanizing learning experience may result: for "we may then learn to experience otherness and human others as the 'other of ourselves' in order to partake in one another [*aneinander teilzugewinnen*]."[15]

Gadamer leaves no doubt that his observations are not narrowly tailored to European integration but relevant for broader global developments. Although it was initially triggered by Western colonialism, social and political ferment now engulfs countries around the world. "What we are witnessing," he writes, "is in truth a global process which has been unleashed by the end of colonialism and the emancipation of the former members" of European empires. The central issue today is no longer Europe but "the cultural changes produced by the global economy and the world-wide network of communications." In this situation, many societies today are engaged in the difficult search for a mode of life capable of reconciling "their own traditions and the deeply rooted values of their life-world with Western-style economic [and technological] progress" or advancement; "large segments of humanity" now are facing this agonizing dilemma.[16]

In an interview with Indian political thinker Thomas Pantham, conducted a few years before his death, Gadamer clearly pinpointed the global significance of hermeneutical understanding. "The human solidarity that I envisage," he stated, "is not a global uniformity but unity in diversity. We must learn to appreciate and tolerate pluralities, multiplicities, cultural differences." He frankly conceded that such appreciation is in short supply and actually undermined by the rampant power politics pursued by military-industrial complexes: "The hegemony or unchallengeable power of any one single nation . . . is dangerous for humanity; it would go against human freedom." Hence, he added, that unity in diversity, which has been a European legacy, must today become a global formula: it must be "extended to the whole world—to include China, India, and also Muslim cultures. Every culture, every people has something distinctive to offer for the solidarity and well-being of humanity."[17]

To flesh out and corroborate Gadamer's perspective, I want to invoke here the testimony of three thinkers friendly to his hermeneutics. The first is the Canadian political philosopher Charles Taylor. Following in Gadamer's footsteps, Taylor, in several of his writings, has underscored the importance of hermeneutical interpretation both for philosophy as such and for the academic practice of the human and social sciences.[18] Moving beyond the confines of textual exegesis, Taylor also has ventured into the domain of intercultural understanding and dialogue, concentrating in particular on the difference between the traditional Western conception of selfhood and the Buddhist notion of "no-self" or "emptiness" of self (*anatta, sunyata*), together with the contrasting social imaginaries deriving from this difference.[19] Significantly, Taylor has also tackled one of the persistent conundrums or charges leveled against hermeneutics: the charge that "understanding everything means condoning everything," such that hermeneutics is left devoid of critical ethical standards. As he has pointed out in some of his essays specifically dealing with intersubjective and intercultural "recognition," understanding others or another culture does not always entail acceptance. What another culture has in its favor is only a "presumption of worth," a presumption calling for attentive study, but capable of being dislodged or defeated through contestation. To be sure, once hermeneutical understanding is seen not as a neutral occurrence, but—with Gadamer and Aristotle—as an ethical *praxis*, understanding is already inhabited by an ethical criterion (and does not need to be supplemented by borrowings from "critical theory," as Paul Ricoeur has sometimes intimated).[20]

The other thinker more indirectly or distantly related to hermeneutics is John Dewey, sometimes called "America's philosopher of democracy." In large measure, Dewey's so-called pragmatism can actually be seen as a practical philosophy displaying distinct affinities with Gadamerian hermeneutics. A central parallel resides in the refusal to divorce thinking from doing, in the effort to link theory and *praxis* under the rubric of lived experience. Together with Gadamer (and Heidegger), Dewey rejected the legacy of Cartesian rationalism focused on the *cogito*, together with its corollary, the "spectator theory of knowledge," which exiles the observer from the context of human being-in-the-world. In opposing that theory, he did not opt for a crude empiricism or positivism but rather insisted that sense data or sensory phenomena are perceived in a semantic frame of significance, a frame provided by language and symbolization (and hence in need of interpretation). Together with Gadamer (and again Heidegger), Dewey did not subscribe to a static metaphysics of essences, but rather preferred a dynamic ontology in which being and temporality converge in an ongoing process of disclosure of possibilities. Most importantly, human life for Dewey was not a solitary venture, but basically formed in the crucible of interhuman "interactions" or "transactions," a crucible closely connected with communication, dialogue, and contestation. As in the case of Gadamer's hermeneutics, social interactions for Dewey were a mode of *praxis* (in the Aristotelian sense) and as such imbued with ethical connotations. This aspect is illustrated in his presentation of society as an ethical community and especially in his depiction of democracy as the "idea" or "ideal" of community life, an idea constantly in the process of improvement or perfection.[21]

In view of my concern here with intercultural understanding, there is another parallel between the two thinkers that deserves to be highlighted. Dewey was at no point a fervent nationalist or a supporter of rigid friend/enemy distinctions (as formulated by Carl Schmitt). This aspect is particularly evident in his "Nationalizing Education," written during a time of war. The essay sharply distinguishes between a benign and a destructive sense of nationalism or patriotism. Too often, he writes, the development of a sense of national unity has been "accompanied by dislike, by hostility, to all without." What has happened is that "skillful politicians and other self-seekers" have known how "to play cleverly upon patriotism and upon ignorance of other peoples, to identify nationalism with latent hatred of other nations." Especially during wartime, many influential people "attempt to foster the growth of an inclusive nationalism by appeal to our fears, our suspicions, our jealousies and our latent hatreds." Such people like to measure patriotism by "our readiness to meet other nations in destructive war rather than our fitness to cooperate with them in constructive tasks of peace."

In contrast to this outlook, Dewey upholds the prospect of a global ecumenism that does not erase local or national loyalties but uses them as a springboard for intercultural cooperation. "We are faced," Dewey states, "by the difficulty of developing the good aspect of nationalism without its evil side: of developing a nationalism which is the friend and not the foe of internationalism," which is a matter "of ideas, of emotions, of intellectual and moral dispositions."[22] As it seems to me, this prospect is not far removed from, and even coincides with, Gadamer's vision of a global "unity in diversity," a unity not imposed by "one single nation," and his plea that "the future survival of humankind" may depend on our willingness to engage dialogically with others on both the personal level and the level of larger human communities and cultures.

By way of further elaboration, I want to turn to a third dialogical and cross-cultural thinker roughly of Gadamer's generation: the French philosopher Maurice Merleau-Ponty. What renders Merleau-Ponty's work particularly important in the present context is his opposition to an idealistic consensualism and his insistence on the linkage between dialogue and embodiment. He continuously emphasized that dialogue is not simply a cerebral process or an abstract "meeting of minds," but it rather involves a concrete existential and bodily engagement among participants. This point is made particularly forcefully in his "Dialogue and the Perception of the Other," contained in *The Prose of the World* (assembled posthumously by his friend Claude Lefort). Distinguishing between a purely abstract, logical algorithm and a concrete encounter between human beings, Merleau-Ponty states boldly: "Alongside the analytic truth espoused by the algorithm and leaving aside the possibility of the algorithm's being detached from the thinking life in which it is born, we affirm a truth of transparency, recovery, and recollection in which we participate—not insofar as we think *the same thing* but insofar as we are, each in his own way, moved and touched by it." This being "moved and touched" in an encounter cannot and should not be understood as a simple intellectual convergence but rather as a kind of mutual embroilment and trespass: "the trespass of oneself upon the other and of the other upon me."[23]

Merleau-Ponty first turns to the "silent relationship with the other," as a prologue to the understanding of speech. In opposition to many writers on intersubjectivity, he considers it "not sufficiently noted that the other is never directly present face to face." In effect, the interlocutor or adversary is "never quite localized: his voice, his gesticulations, his twitches, are only symptoms, a sort of stage effect, a ceremony." Their producer is "so well masked that I am quite surprised when my own responses carry over." What comes to the fore is that the other's "self" is not preconstituted and exists neither before nor somehow behind the voice but rather emerges in the encounter itself, in the inchoate relationship being forged. "The other, in my eyes," Merleau-Ponty writes, "is always on the margin of what I see and hear, he is this side of me, he is beside or behind me, but he is not in that place which my look flattens and empties of any interior." This insight leads him to one of his stunning formulations that are a trademark of his existential phenomenology:

> Myself and the other are like two nearly concentric circles which can be distinguished only by a slight and mysterious slippage. This alliance is perhaps what will enable us to understand the relation to the other that is inconceivable if I try to approach him directly, like a sheer cliff.[24]

In the encounter with another human being, the other is both my partner or accomplice and different from or nonabsorbable by me. "I give birth," Merleau-Ponty writes; "this other is made from my flesh and blood and yet is no longer me. How is that possible?" The solution to the riddle must be found in the realization that the difference I encounter is not only external but internal, that somehow I am myself inhabited by difference. "There is," we read, "a myself which is other, which dwells elsewhere and deprives me of my central location." At this point, the roles of the seeing subject and what is seen are "exchanged and reversed." For Merleau-Ponty, the central issue is to understand "how I can make myself into two, how I can decenter myself" or become decentered—how the experience of the other is always at the same time "a response to myself." Like the other human being, the self is neither a compact entity nor thing; nor is it a self-transparent mind (or *cogito*). From this angle, there can be neither a fixed or stable human "nature" nor a self-contained "identity." In lieu of the atomistic units found in an imaginary "state of nature," all that one finds is a fluid cohabitation in a dwelling place to which none of the partners has privileged access or the unfailing passkey: "It is in the very depths of myself that this strange articulation with the other is fashioned. The mystery of the other is nothing but the mystery of myself." What is intimated here is an identity constituted by noncoincidence, but unable to escape elsewhere (outside the world).[25]

CHAPTER TEN

Justice, Power, and Dialogue

Humanizing Politics

Today at the dawn of the twenty-first century, nothing seems more urgently needed than the emergence of something like a global "public sphere" that, as a part of global civil society, would serve as a kind of public tribunal before which political leaders—from would-be emperors to petty dictators—would be held at least morally and ethically accountable. At a time when many "leaders" seem ready to go berserk and when our world is overshadowed by warfare, terror wars, and indiscriminate killings, some restraint on ferocity needs to be imposed, which, in the absence of a global superstate (beset by its own problems), can only come from the alertness and vigilance of responsible people around the world.

Here I want to reflect in some greater detail on the promises and possibilities opened up by the La Trobe Centre for Dialogue. In particular I want to explore some of the paths leading from the institutional setting, and the "dialogue" pursued in that setting, to broader ramifications in the global arena. Differently stated, I want to investigate certain parallels that exist between dialogue, or certain forms of dialogue, and various international or cross-cultural interactions, and thus sketch a transition "from theory to practice." Specifically, I want to do three things. First, I want to

Delivered at the inauguration of the Centre for Dialogue at La Trobe University, Australia, in 2006.

talk about the meaning and contemporary relevance of dialogue, from a theoretical-philosophical angle and from a political angle. Next, I want to highlight different forms or modalities of dialogue or communicative interaction as they are found in actual intersocietal practices. Third, I wish to put the spotlight on the relationship between dialogue and political power in an effort to show how dialogue can be an antidote to political domination and also to political or economic injustices and hence a resource for the promotion of global justice.

WHY DIALOGUE?

By its very name, the La Trobe Centre is committed to the "dialogue" among civilizations and ultimately among peoples. An initial question that may be asked is this: What is the meaning of this commitment? Or, to what has the Centre committed itself? By common agreement, the meaning of a term is best grasped by its juxtaposition to counterterms that limit or circumscribe it. The relevant counterterm here is "monologue," that is, a situation where only one voice is allowed to talk or where one voice drowns out all others, including perhaps its own inner voice or conscience. Transferred to the political context, monologue corresponds to a policy of unilateralism or to a situation where a hegemonic or imperial power reduces all other agents to irrelevance and silence. Silhouetted against this background, dialogue denotes the communicative interaction between two, several, or many interlocutors where no party can claim to have the first or the last word. Politically this translates into a policy of multilateralism or multilateral cooperation, which is the opposite of any absolutism or empire. This rejection of absolutism and empire is, in turn, a precondition of just peace.

Perhaps a brief glance at etymology may clarify things. As we know, the term "dialogue" comes from the Greek and is composed of two parts: *dia* and *logos*. Without going into needless subtleties, we can say that *logos* in Greek means something like "reason," "meaning," and also (more simply) "language and word." On the other hand, *dia* signifies "moving through" or "moving between." Hence, etymologically, dialogue entails that reason or meaning is not the monopoly of one party but arises out of the communicative intercourse between parties or interlocutors. Differently put, the *logos* here is a shared *logos*, a shared truth that depends crucially on the participation of several or many people or agents. This means, in turn, that dialogue is intrinsically at odds with any kind of cognitive absolutism (or a claim to "apodictic" truth), which does not in any way signal a lapse into "relativism" or arbitrary randomness. The latter decay can only happen if dialogue is equated with empty chatter or chit-chat where participants only "pass the time of day." What protects dialogue from this decay is its constitutive *logos*. Without claiming any monopoly, all participants are nevertheless oriented toward meaning and truth. They do this by remaining carefully attentive to the issue at hand, that is, by jointly seeking to explore or clarify a pressing problem or dilemma. In the political arena, the most pressing issue is justice and just peace.

If this is the general sense of dialogue, we can ask: Are we here not face-to-face with a perennial issue? So why was the La Trobe Centre created recently and why does it have special significance in our time? The simple answer, but one that requires a great deal of unpacking, is that dialogue has been egregiously neglected in modern Western history (and perhaps in the world as a whole). This statement is prone to give rise to misunderstanding. I do not mean to say that Western history and Western thought have always been entirely neglectful of the dialogical dimension. The latter claim, unfortunately, has of late gained prominence and been disseminated under such labels as "logocentrism" and "egocentrism" (without any adequate clarification of the terms *logos* and *ego*). In my view, classical Western thought, and even part of medieval thought, pays tribute to dialogue in exemplary ways. Significantly, Plato wrote dialogues, Aristotle's writings reflect a teacher–pupil interaction, and Cicero pays tribute to both Plato and Aristotle in all his texts. To some extent, the dialogical spirit persisted in the European Middle Ages, a period marked by learned disputations and encounters on a high level of erudition. (Cross-culturally one may also point here to the teacher–student interaction, the *guru-shishya-parampara*, in the Indian tradition, and to the many question-and-answer passages in Confucius's *Analects*.)

A slow movement away from dialogue, however, occurred in the late Middle Ages with the rise of nominalism and scientific empiricism. With this development, a type of knowledge steadily gained center stage that was no longer probable and open to dialogical give-and-take; rather, it aimed to be certain, or apodictic, and hence binding on everyone. Without neglecting the role of the community of scientists, one can say that modern science, especially mathematical science, is inherently monological and oriented toward the goal of universal agreement regarding its findings. This bent of modern science was reinforced by dominant tendencies in modern philosophy, especially by the rationalism of Descartes with its focus on the centrality of the "ego" or singular "I." His well-known formula *ego cogito ergo sum* (I think therefore I am) implied that reality can be known by the thinking individual alone, without any need to refer to or to communicate with other people. Seen from this perspective, the *logos* is not basically a shared *logos* or reason, but one that can be possessed and cultivated by the individual scientist or philosopher alone. In different variations, the Cartesian formula tended to dominate Western thought until the end of the nineteenth century (a story that, in its complexity, cannot be recapitulated here).

As it happened, philosophical developments were paralleled by trends in modern politics that likewise pointed away from dialogical engagement in the direction of unilateral autonomy. Most prominent among these trends was the rise of the modern nation-state endowed with a radical autonomy labeled "state sovereignty." To be sure, throughout history, political communities have always claimed some kind of autonomy, but in a limited or circumscribed sense. In ancient Greece, city-states were surely independent from each other and autonomous, but without denying their embeddedness in a larger Hellenic civilization. Similarly, during the European Middle Ages, national kingdoms or principalities were often fiercely competing with each other, but rarely to the point of rupturing or negating their participation in a larger imperial structure held together by Christian faith. It was only the fragmentation of Christianity in early modernity, and the association of different Christian confessions with independent kingdoms or states, that divided the earlier community and gave way to more radical conceptions of autonomy or sovereignty. To be sure, fragmentation was never complete and efforts were continuously made to reaffirm some kind of unity, under the auspices of a shared enlightened humanism, an advanced industrial civilization, and the like.[1] Yet, the fragility of these attempts was made glaringly evident in the twentieth century with the eruption of two world wars initially instigated by

European nation-states. These events also demonstrated the pitfall of radical autonomy—linked with violent aggression, state sovereignty is liable to destroy not only others but, in the end, itself.

The same twentieth century, however, also brought signs of change, and this again in both the philosophical and political domains. In the former domain, the century is noteworthy particularly for its incipient move from monologue and the Cartesian *cogito* to language and communication, a move frequently captured by the label "linguistic turn." This turn, in due course, led to a reappraisal and reaffirmation of dialogue, coupled with the renewed realization that reason and truth cannot be an individual possession but is necessarily shared with others. In this sharing, language plays a crucial role (where language needs to be taken in a broad sense as comprising a multitude of verbal and nonverbal modes of communication). The philosopher Ludwig Wittgenstein is famous for arguing that truth and meaning only make sense within the confines of a given language game, an argument that has been interpreted in many ways (and not always with sufficient attention to the *logos* of language). The basic building blocks for a theory of dialogue, during the same period, were provided by a number of other European thinkers. Thus, Martin Buber developed his interactive view of human life ("I and Thou"), while Gabriel Marcel formulated a notion of human existence strongly rooted in language and shared embodiment. Perhaps philosophically most significant and influential was Martin Heidegger's portrayal of human existence (*Dasein*), not as an isolated ego but as a mode of being necessarily linked with others through language and "care." Proceeding on this basis, his student Hans-Georg Gadamer articulated a conception of meaning and interpretive understanding based entirely on dialogue and communicative understanding. On a more formal or formalistic level, other theorists of the same period proposed various new conceptual models, such as those of "communicative rationality," of "discourse theory," and the like.[2]

Paralleling these developments, the twentieth century witnessed innovative initiatives in the political arena, initiatives designed to correct, at least in part, the excesses of radical state autonomy. Thus, largely in response to the ravages of the great wars, efforts were made to establish at least the rudiments of shared international structures; first the League of Nations and later the United Nations with its complex array of affiliated agencies. These initiatives on the global level were seconded and supplemented by attempts at regional collaboration and unification. The most prominent example of regional reorganization is the formation of the European Union, a process starting initially from a nucleus of a few states and expanding gradually to comprise the majority of West and East European countries. Significantly, the formation of the EU involves not only the unification of economic markets but extends deeply into political, legal, and cultural domains of life. Although the most well known and most widely discussed, the EU is only one example of regional cooperation. On a more limited scale, similar initiatives can be found in Asia, Africa, and Latin America. Likewise, within the confines of Islamic civilization, the idea of the *umma* (community of all Muslims) has gained renewed appeal, as a corrective to the antagonism of separate (and often artificially created) nation-states. To be sure, the sketched trend is not universally followed or effective; some countries, especially hegemonic countries, tenaciously cling to the old ways of unilateralism. Supported by exceptional wealth and military power, traditional state sovereignty in these cases tendentionally is expanded into a super-Leviathan claiming radical autonomy and blanket immunity from accountability for state actions.

MODES OF CROSS-CULTURAL DIALOGUE

Having sketched some of the reasons for the recent rise to prominence of dialogue, it now seems appropriate to move from general theoretical and historical considerations to actual practice, that is, to the ways in which dialogue is concretely practiced in intersocietal and cross-cultural relations. In this respect, I like to distinguish between at least three modalities: a *pragmatic-utilitarian*, a *moral-universal*, and an *ethical-hermeneutical* form of dialogue or communicative interaction. This tripartition is an adaptation, but also a significant modification of a scheme first proposed by Jürgen Habermas in an essay distinguishing between different types of (what he called) "practical reason."[3] The main difference between my approach and Habermas's scheme has to do with the status of moral-universal discourse, a discourse to which he grants absolute priority, while I treat it as an intermediacy modality needing to be deepened and supplemented by ethical understanding.

The tripartition I propose represents, in a way, an ethical ascent in the sense of a progressive move away from unilateralism and monologue in the direction of growing mutual respect and recognition. The first modality—pragmatic-utilitarian communication—still hovers close to the domain of monologue. Each partner in such communication seeks to advance primarily his or her own interests, his or her own goals and agendas, against the interests of others. Sometimes, the impression prevails as if one simply witnesses an exchange of monologues. What saves pragmatic communication from this kind of exchange (or nonexchange) is the element of bargaining: each party, in seeking to advance its interests, needs to take into account the perceived interests of others, if only in order to better counter, circumvent, frustrate, or defeat the others' interests. For this reason, even a narrowly pragmatic approach needs the medium of dialogue (however closely circumscribed). This kind of communication forms the core and foundation of modern economics and "rational choice" theory, that is, the theory according to which each partner seeks to maximize gains or profits while minimizing losses or expenditures. The narrow curtailment of dialogue in this interaction is demonstrated by the fact that rational choice can be, and frequently is, formalized in a strategic "game" scenario where each participant, without further attentiveness, pursues his or her own strategies on the assumption of the opponents best possible strategies.

Beyond the economic domain, pragmatic communication also plays a large role in modern international or intersocietal political relations. Here, the legacy of the modern nation-state and state sovereignty still exacts its tribute both in the practice of state actors and the conceptions of mainstream scholars. Thus, the so-called realist school of international politics—the dominant Western perspective in this area—takes it for granted that all politics outside the domestic arena is interstate competition where each state actor single-mindedly pursues the "national interest" (often identified with national security) while assuming that other state actors do the same. The difference between the realist scenario and the scenario envisaged by game theory—a difference recognized by most realists—is that interstate politics occurs in variable historical and cultural contexts whose components cannot be neatly formalized or predicted. Hence, a measure of real-life dialogue is accepted as important by most proponents of this perspective. Evidence of pragmatic communication can be found in nearly all traditional interstate interactions, such as trade negotiations, disarmament negotiations, settlements of border disputes, and the like. The most prominent example of such communication, carried forward in continuous, day-to-day interactions, is traditional diplomacy (where the skill of a diplomat can probably be measured by the extent of his or her dialogical skill).

In proceeding to the second modality—moral-universal discourse— we move beyond the level of a narrowly construed self-interest, but only up to a point. The aim of such communicative discourse is to establish general, potentially universal rules of the game or norms of conduct binding on all participants in a given interaction. In order to establish and (at least in principle) follow such norms, participants must be able to transcend their immediate self-interests and to cultivate a "higher" interest in general or universal rules. To be sure, in cultivating this higher perspective, participants do not simply abandon their particular interests. On the contrary, general rules or norms are established precisely for the purpose of allowing participants to pursue their goals with minimal mutual interference or obstruction. For this reason, rules or norms must be sufficiently abstract in order not to thwart or unduly restrict individual initiatives. One speaks here of "rule-governed freedom," and most modern legal or constitutional systems seek to advance this conception. Of course, rules and norms do not exist by themselves but require some form of communicative endorsement, but the latter feature gained prominence only in modernity. Philosophically, moral-universal discourse can look back to a long and venerable tradition stretching from Kantian moral philosophy and modern natural law all the way back to Stoic cosmopolitanism.

Moving again from theory to practice, it is not hard to find rudiments of moral-universal discourse in the international and intersocietal arenas. Thus, basic norms of potentially universal significance can be found in the rules of international law, a legal system whose development can be traced from the ancient *ius gentium* through the golden age of Spanish jurisprudence to the rise of modern international law (inaugurated by Hugo Grotius and others).[4] Again, rules and norms in this area do not exist by themselves, but rely on communicative endorsement. As it happens, the central norms of international law have in late modernity been endorsed or ratified by a large majority of governments and peoples around the world. Among these rules, we find the norms governing warfare (both *ius ad bellum* and *ius in bello*); the norms dealing with war crimes and crimes against humanity; the Geneva Conventions concerning the treatment of prisoners of war; the Universal Declaration of Human Rights; and many others. It belongs to the definition of norms that actual behavior is measured against them; hence norms have (what is called) a mandatory or prescriptive, in Kant's language, a "categorically binding" character. This fact has to be remembered in our time when norms, especially international norms, are often sacrificed on the altar of particular (national) interests. Thus, the rules of the Geneva Conventions are mandatory in all armed conflicts, no matter what terminology particular governments choose to adopt. Likewise, launching an aggressive war is and remains a crime against humanity, and so is the wanton killing of civilian populations. In all these instances, the collective conscience of humanity has reached a certain level below which we do not dare to regress.

To be sure, appealing to the conscience of humanity means to move already a step beyond the level of rules of the game or legal norms of conduct. As everyday experience indicates, rules or norms do not by themselves assure their observance. If resort to force is to be avoided (or minimized), the only alternative is to cultivate and strengthen the conscience of people, that is, the genuine awareness of the ethical quality of all human relations and interactions. This leads me to the third modality: ethical-hermeneutical dialogue. "Ethical" here refers to the "ethos" or shared sense of humanity prevailing among peoples (or groups of people); "hermeneutical" points to the effort to gain better understanding among participants and thereby to enhance mutual respect and recognition. In such dialogue, partners seek to understand and appreciate each other's life stories and cultural backgrounds, including religious or spiritual traditions, storehouses of literary and artistic expressions, and also existential agonies and aspirations. In contrast to the abstract and formal character of general rules and legal norms, ethical-hermeneutical dialogue enters into the "thick" fabric of lived experiences and historical sedimentations. The effort here is not so much to ascend above particular life stories to reach the bird's-eye view of rule governance, but rather to render concrete life-worlds mutually accessible as a touchstone of ethical sensibility. In the language of classical philosophy (from Aristotle and al-Farabi to Confucius and Mencius), dialogue here is oriented toward the "good life," not in the sense of an abstract "ought" but as the pursuit of an aspiration implicit in all life-forms (though able to take very different expressions in different cultures).

Since dialogue on this level speaks to deeper human motivations, leaving behind narrow self-interest, this is really the kind of communication most likely to mold human conduct in the direction of justice and just peace. Hence, there is an urgent need in our time to foster this mode of interaction, not only on the domestic but on the global level. Fortunately, albeit on a limited scale, cross-cultural dialogue in this sense is already practiced today in a variety of forms. Examples would be interfaith dialogues; the Parliament of the World's Religions; the World Social Forum bringing together a multitude of NGOs and grassroots movements; and the embryonic World Public Forum seeking to generate something like a public arena or global "public sphere" where the pressing political issues troubling the globe could be discussed from the vantage of justice and ethical obligations. A by no means negligible role is also played by exchange programs of scholars and students, grassroots diplomacy programs, and the like. Needless to say, much more needs to be done to make cross-cultural ethics a meaningful antidote or corrective to hegemonic ambitions and the tradition of political unilateralism.

DIALOGUE AND POWER

At this point, the question is liable to be raised, especially by political "realists": What good is dialogue in confrontation with power and domination? How can dialogue possibly serve as an antidote to the strategies of the powerful? And here one has to agree, at least initially, that dialogue is no match for power and that power, at least at first glance, holds the trump card. From this fact, "realists" draw the conclusion that power can only be corrected by power and that hence all the efforts of the powerless (or less powerful) should be directed at matching and even outstripping the power wielded by the powerful. But the result can easily be foreseen: the competition for power leads to a steady burgeoning power, which finally culminates in a super-Leviathan, which is of little or no benefit to the powerless. In this context, it is good to remember the comment of Hannah Arendt on the role of violence: "The practice of violence, like all action, changes the world; but the most probable change is to a more violent world."[5]

There is another consideration that realists might usefully ponder: power cannot maintain itself solely through power, especially through armed force. Here the insight of the great diplomat Abbé Talleyrand is relevant: "There are many things one can do with bayonets, except sit on them." This means that power, in the sense of coercive force, may be useful for conquest, but it is completely inadequate for maintaining a regime over time. If a ruler wished to rely on coercive force alone, a soldier or policeman would have to be assigned to every citizen in order to ensure obedience, but then who would police the soldier or policeman? This indicates that every ruler or regime has to rely on a preponderant extent on the approval or goodwill of the citizens, that is, on their sense that the regime is not entirely out of step with their pragmatic, moral, and ethical sensibilities. This need to keep in step is usually called legitimacy, and one can now add that without a general sense of legitimacy, power as coercive force is, in the long run, powerless. Such legitimacy, in turn, is fostered by open communication in its different modes, which brings us back to the role of dialogue as a corrective to and restraint on power.

I would like to add, however, that dialogue can itself be structured in such a way as to include a critique of power and domination. This happens in what I like to call an "agonal" or agonistic dialogue or contestation. In such an agonal situation, participants seek not only to understand and appreciate each other's life forms, but to convey to each other grievances, that is, experiences of exploitation, domination, and persecution, experiences having to do with past or persisting injustices and sufferings. Hence, dialogue here serves directly the goal of a restoration of justice or just peace. Great care must be taken in this context to preserve the dialogical dimension of the encounter. In the absence of such care, there is great danger that the encounter deteriorates into a sheer power play and that the goal of justice is replaced by the desire for revenge and punishment. It is for this reason that I prefer to treat this mode as a subcategory of ethical-hermeneutical dialogue, in order to make sure that the accent is not placed purely on power, on the desire to "get even," the desire to return injustice for injustice by turning the previous victims into victimizers. Seen as an ethical engagement, agonistic contestation is not an end in itself but put in the service of healing and reconciliation.

Turning our attention to the contemporary global arena, we can find several examples of agonal dialogue put into practice. I am referring to the great commissions of inquiry established in various parts of the world at the end of ethnic conflicts and/or political dictatorships: the so-called Truth and Justice or Truth and Reconciliation commissions. The point of these commissions has been basically twofold: to establish a record of past criminal actions and injustices through archival research and the interviewing of large numbers of witnesses; and to initiate and foster a process of social healing so as to prevent the future recurrence of victimization or unjust domination. The two aims are obviously in tension: whereas, in the first goal, agonistic contestation and confrontation assume center stage, the second goal seeks to reduce agonistics for the sake of mutual respect and understanding. Hence, great skill and wisdom are required to preserve the commissions from derailment.

By way of illustration, let me cite some words of Bishop Desmond Tutu, who served as president of the Truth and Reconciliation Commission in South Africa. The words can be found in his *God Has a Dream: A Vision of Hope for Our Time*:

> I saw the power of the gospel when I was serving as chairperson of the Truth and Reconciliation Commission in South Africa. . . . The Commission gave perpetrators of political crimes the opportunity to appeal for amnesty by telling the truth of their actions and an opportunity to ask for forgiveness. . . . As we listened to accounts of truly monstrous deeds of torture and cruelty, it would have been easy to dismiss the perpetrators as monsters because their deeds were truly monstrous. But we are reminded that God's love is not cut off from anyone.[6]

FROM THEORY TO PRACTICE

The series of international institutions, conventions, and commissions mentioned above reveal that the notion of an international legal and ethical order is not merely a nice idea, but that is has taken root in many domains of contemporary international life. For many centuries, philosophers and religious thinkers had speculated about the feasibility of a world parliament or a global "league of nations," but today we have institutions that instantiate or at least approximate the content of these speculations in real-life contexts. Here we encounter another objection raised by political "realists," that is, people wedded to the primacy of power: the objection that theories or theorizing are pointless exercises with little or no relevance for practical political life. In a particularly emphatic manner, this objection takes aim at the supposedly abstract and hopelessly "impractical" character of normative or ethical theorizing. During the nineteenth and twentieth centuries, the distance between normative theory and factual reality, or between "ought" and "is," was erected into a first-order philosophical maxim: every attempt to bridge the distance between norm and fact, or to move from one to the other, was (and continues to be) denounced as a serious mental lapse (labeled "naturalistic fallacy").

No doubt, the relationship between norm and fact, or more broadly between theory and practice, is complex and cannot be reduced to a simple linear derivation. Fortunately, the philosopher Immanuel Kant has lent us a helping hand in this matter with an essay he wrote in 1793, "On the Common Saying: 'This May be True in Theory, but it Does not Apply in Practice.'" Kant took exception to some arguments advanced by a prominent contemporary, the philosopher Moses Mendelssohn. Although himself a child of the Enlightenment, Mendelssohn disagreed with one of the most cherished beliefs of Enlightenment thinkers: the belief in the continuous moral progress of humankind. In his view, enlightened thought was able to generate fine and high-sounding theories or principles, theories that were perhaps beneficial to some individuals here and there, but were of no use to the practical life of humanity at large. For Mendelssohn, it was sheer fantasy to say "that the whole of mankind here on earth must continually progress and become more perfect through the ages." The only thing one could say about human history with some degree of assurance was that, taken as a whole, humanity keeps "moving slowly back and forth" and that, whenever it takes a few steps forward, "it soon relapses twice as quickly into its former state." Seen from this angle, human history thus resembles the fate of Sisyphus, whose practical labors are constantly thwarted or come to naught— no matter how high the ideals or theories animating the struggle.[7]

From Kant's perspective, Mendelssohn's skeptical line of reasoning was unacceptable because it vitiated both the meaning of theory or philosophy and the integrity of practical life. Basically, the skeptic's argument was predicated on a Manichean view of things, which erects a gulf between norm and fact, between thinking and doing. For Kant (still imbued with some classical teachings) this kind of Manicheism was misleading because it distorted the character of both moral reasoning and practical conduct. Although Kant was famous for postulating, in his own moral theory, a series of "categorical imperatives" binding on human conduct, these imperatives were by no means akin to arbitrary or despotic commands imposed from an external source. Rather, these commands derived from reflection on human "nature," on its inherent dispositions and capabilities, including the potential for moral improvement. In Kantian terminology, human beings through the use of reason are able to legislate norms for their own conduct, and hence to subject themselves not to an external despot but to their own better judgment and insight. Seen in this light, theoretically formulated norms and practical conduct are no longer opposites, but closely connected or linked—as in a democratic regime (properly constructed) rulers and ruled are not at loggerheads, but united in the enterprise of self-rule. To be skeptical about this possibility means to be skeptical about human life itself.

This point was forcefully put forward in Kant's essay on theory and practice. "I may be permitted to assume," he writes there, "that, since the human race is constantly progressing in cultural matters (in keeping with its natural purpose), it is also engaged in progressive improvement in relation to the moral end of its existence." Although this progressive movement may at times be interrupted, it will "never be broken off." As Kant submits, Mendelssohn himself must have been imbued with a belief of this kind, seeing that he was indefatigable in trying to teach and educate the younger generation. "The worthy Mendelssohn," we read, "must himself have reckoned on this [improvement], since he zealously endeavored to promote the enlightenment and welfare of the nation to which he belonged. For he could not himself reasonably hope to do this unless others after him continued upon the same path." Hence, moral skepticism—though a shield against an empty utopianism—offers no excuse from the hard work of education and self-transformation. At this point, Kant articulates one of his most important guideposts, valid for all times: the counsel that, irrespective of empirical obstacles or periodic setbacks, the task of ethical improvement (of both the individual and humanity at large) constitutes a moral "duty" (*Pflicht*) that cannot be shirked. "It is quite irrelevant," he writes, "whether any empirical evidence suggests that these plans, which are founded only on hope, may be unsuccessful. For the idea that something which has hitherto been unsuccessful will therefore never be successful does not justify anyone in abandoning even a pragmatic or technical aim. . . . This applies even more to moral aims which, so long as it is not demonstrably impossible to fulfill them, amount to duties."[8] This means that the path leading from theory to practice cannot be arbitrarily disrupted without moral blemish.

It is chiefly in the field of international politics that concrete experience may lead to frustration and skepsis. Kant states: "Nowhere does human nature appear less admirable than in the relationships which exist between peoples. No state is for a moment secure from the others in its independence and its possessions." At another point, he speaks eloquently of "the distress produced by the constant wars in which the states try to subjugate or engulf each other," a distress greatly increased in our time by global wars, "terror wars," and ethnic cleansings. For Kant, there is one redeeming feature, however, in this distress: the calamities and miseries endured by peoples may prompt them, at long last, with or against their express will, to form a peaceful "cosmopolitan constitution" or at least a "lawful federation under a commonly accepted international right." Thus, calamities endured in real life can provide a cue or incentive to human reasoning to reflect on the source of misfortunes and possible ways of correcting or avoiding them. Once the light of reflection illuminates the scene, however, the practical enactment of corrective measures is no longer a merely optional task but an ethical duty whose fulfillment—with the help of "divine providence"—is within reach. Kant again: "The very conflict of inclinations, which is the source of all evil, gives reason a free hand to master them all; it thus gives predominance not to evil, which destroys itself, but to good, which continues to maintain itself once it has been established." Hence, theoretical moral insight and practical conduct can eventually be seen to be in harmony, contradicting the common saying that "this may be true in theory, but it does not apply in practice."[9]

In his subsequent writings, Kant always remained faithful to the notion of a possible harmony between moral insight and practice, or at least the notion that, despite enormous obstacles and constant setbacks, it was possible to reconcile the two through moral effort. It may be true, as some have asserted, that reconciliation for Kant always moved in one direction, from theory to practice (where other thinkers might prefer a more reciprocal, especially dialogical relationship). Yet, Kantian "moralism" always remained tempered by common sense and human sensibility. One of his most famous political tracts is *Perpetual Peace: A Philosophical Sketch* (1796). There, Kant made explicit room for human inclinations, commercial interests, and ambitions, but without abandoning the notion of a cosmopolitan "duty." "The peoples of the earth," he says, "have entered in varying degrees into a universal community, and it has developed to the point where violation of rights in *one* part of the world is felt everywhere." Hence, through travels, commercial interactions, and improved communications, peoples have entered into a condition of "cosmopolitan right" (we might call it a "global civil society"). Thus, Kant adds in a famous formulation: "Nature guarantees perpetual peace by the actual mechanism of human inclinations. And while the likelihood of its being attained is not sufficient to enable us to *prophesy* the future theoretically, it is enough for practical purposes. It makes it our duty to work our way towards this goal, which is more than an empty chimera."[10] To these lines one can add the equally famous statement from the conclusion of *The Metaphysics of Morals* (1797):

> By working towards this end, we may hope to terminate the disastrous practice of war, which up till now has been the main object to which all states, without exception, have accommodated their internal institutions. And even if the fulfillment of this pacific intention were forever to remain a pious hope, we should still not be deceiving ourselves if we made it our maxim to work unceasingly towards it, for it is our duty to do so.[11]

In light of Kant's arguments, it becomes clear that the establishment of the Centre for Dialogue at La Trobe University does not reflect an empty pipe dream, but responds or corresponds to deep-seated human needs or aspirations in our time. Through its manifold activities—sponsoring conferences, engaging in research and teaching—it means to move humanity some steps closer to the accomplishment of a basic moral aim shared by people around the world: the aim of perpetual peace.

CHAPTER ELEVEN

Befriending the Stranger

Beyond the Global Politics of Fear

Do not neglect hospitality to strangers,
for thereby some have entertained angels unawares.

—Letter to the Hebrews 13:1

To take as far as possible every conflict which arises—
and they are bound to arise—out of the atmosphere and medium
of force, of violence as a means of settlement, into that of discussion
and of intelligence is to treat those who disagree—even profoundly—
with us as those from whom we may learn and, in so far, as friends.

—John Dewey, "Creative Democracy—The Task before Us"

Cosmopolitanism has a difficult relationship with borders or boundaries. It cannot completely discard borders or bounded limits without turning into an extraterrestrial enterprise or a mere flight of fancy. But it can also not blithely accept them, preferring instead to treat them as moving horizons. This dilemma is endemic to human living and thinking. Clearly, our thinking, that is, our attempt to understand the world, inevitably proceeds from certain bounded premises, certain taken-for-granted assumptions or frames of significance, whose precise contours, however, remain amorphous and open-ended. Even if, hypothetically, we should be able to fix or determine the initial framework, we would necessarily have to place ourselves beyond in order to see the limit as a limit. When encountering alien or unfamiliar life-forms, our initial assumptions are exposed or subjected to testing, a testing that induces a process of transformation navigating precariously beyond affirmation and negation. Hence, our initial understanding or frame of significance can be neither simply discarded nor stubbornly maintained, which attests to the fact that thinking is not a rummaging in finished doctrines but rather a journey, a peregrination. Beyond thinking, this insight applies also to our acting and concrete living, that is, to our existential being-in-the-world. This is why some writers describe human life as a continuous mode of "border-crossing" and human agents as "*Grenzgänger*," that is, as people crisscrossing multiple borders.[1]

In our world today, border-crossing is under siege, even in danger of being erased. There are two major features marking our present age: the process of globalization and the so-called war on terror. The first process is bent on sidelining, perhaps even eradicating, borders in favor of borderless global markets, borderless financial transactions, and digital global communications. The second feature opens up abysmal borders or cleavages far transcending traditional geopolitical divides: the gulf between terror and counterterror, between "world order" and disorder (or unorder), and ultimately between life and death. As can readily be seen, the war on terror or "terror war" is a strategy affecting not only so-called terrorists but also their opponents and humankind at large. Actually, the phrase "war on terror" is redundant since war itself means the unleashing of terror, with the result that such a war "terrorizes" people on both (or all) sides of the divide. Terror, however, is another expression for intense, overpowering fear. This has as a consequence that terror war, globally pursued, results, not accidentally but inevitably in a global politics of fear (rather than a politics of dialogue and hope), that is, a politics conducted exclusively under the rubric of security versus insecurity, of the rigid border control between "us" and "them."

In the following, I want to examine this ominous development in world politics from a number of angles. First, I want to explore the growing linkage of politics with terror war by tracing its roots ultimately to the friend/enemy distinction. Next, I want to discuss the shortcomings of the terror war syndrome by turning to some prominent critics of this ideology. Finally, I want to examine possible ways pointing beyond this ideology, enlisting for this purpose a number of theologians and intellectuals, to arrive again at the promising notions of "thinking with(out) borders" and political-existential *Grenzgänger*.

THE POLITICS OF FEAR

Thomas Hobbes described himself, in an autobiographical vein, as a child of fear. The reason for his self-description is that, at the time of his birth (in 1588), the mighty Spanish Armada was sailing toward England. One can plausibly argue that fear, or the sense of fear, never left the philosopher and, in fact, came to overshadow his entire work. Hobbes's theory has human beings move from an initial "state of nature" via a social contract to a "civil state," or commonwealth, but fear is present from the beginning to the end. Given that the natural human condition is marked by aggressive selfishness engendering the prospect of a "war of all against all" (*bellum omnium contra omnes*), the dominant and overpowering psychic condition at that stage is the fear of violent death. However, even after people contract with each other and establish a civil state, fear does not come to an end. Now fear is not caused by the aggressive conduct of the contracting agents, but by the awesome power of the sovereign who is above and beyond the contract and rules, not by reason or persuasion, but by political might (*auctoritas non veritas facit legem*). Hence, order and peace in a commonwealth are predicated not on social custom or on the intrinsic virtue of citizens, but on the general fear of sovereign retribution. As Hobbes stated, articulating the perennial watchword of political "realism," words or arguments "without the sword" are empty slogans incapable of securing civic order.[2]

In many ways, the Hobbesian formula of sovereign power became the bedrock of the modern (Western) state; even when softened or outwardly repudiated, its harsher features continue to hover in the background. Although John Locke reformulated the notion of sovereign prerogatives, his approach retained many aspects of the earlier formula: especially the accents on contract and self-centered competition (readily giving rise to violent conflict in crisis periods). From Locke's time forward, this soft version of Hobbesianism served to buttress—overtly or covertly—the agenda of modern liberal politics and public (state-centered) policy. Under the influence of steadily intensifying economic (or class) conflicts and culture wars, the Hobbesian background features moved progressively into the foreground. One of the most prominent spokesmen of neo-Hobbesianism in the twentieth century is the German legal and political theorist Carl Schmitt. Taking Hobbes as his mentor, Schmitt deliberately center-stages the primacy of sovereign power over all forms of public deliberation or civic cohesion. He states famously at the very start of *Political Theology*, "Sovereign is the one who decides on the case of the exception." The state of exception is not an ordinary condition manageable by ordinary procedures; rather, it is an "exceptional" or extranormal state, one that opens up an abyss or breach where only sovereign power can secure order. Although abnormal, the exceptional state for Schmitt is not marginal, but penetrates deeply into the very fabric of politics or political life by pinpointing a decisive divide or division: the division between friend and enemy, between "us" and "them," between inside and outside. He writes in *The Concept of the Political* that the very meaning of "the political" must be found in a "specific political distinction," namely, the division or difference "between friend and enemy." This distinction, he adds, denotes "the utmost degree of intensity of a union or separation, of an association or dissociation" (where union applies to friends and separation to enemies).[3]

For Schmitt, the friend/enemy distinction was not just a rhetorical formula but a criterion of war and peace in the sense that (according to his repeated statements) the enemy is someone who can be killed. Thus, in the guise of legal-conceptual language, the Hobbesian fear factor powerfully returns: fear of the sovereign and fear of violent death. Without any familiarity with the textual sources, many prominent political leaders in our time have appropriated the Schmittian formula for their own purposes. According to then U.S. senator Joseph Lieberman, the United States in the twenty-first century lives in an "either/or" world and cannot achieve its objectives "by being inoffensive." What many well-meaning observers tend to brush aside or forget is a basic feature of international reality today: "the difference between America's friends and America's enemies."[4] In the wake of these pronouncements, the Hobbesian fear factor reasserted itself, with unmitigated intensity, in the linkage of enmity and warfare. In the aftermath of 9/11, traditional warfare was supplemented and deepened by the spread of seemingly unlimited "terror wars," by the upsurge of a Manichaean division of the world into friends and enemies, into supporters of Western-style "freedom" and devotees of an infernal "axis of evil."

For present purposes, a crucial implication of the Schmittian formula is its erection of a basic divide or unbreachable boundary. At the site of the friend/enemy distinction, border-crossings and the role of *Grenzgänger* are deemed to be impossible or impermissible. In the face of enmity, borders are meant to be solidified, fortified, and militarized. From this results a peculiar feature of our presumably globalizing and ultimately "borderless" world: the return to fences, checkpoints, detention centers, and dividing walls. Just a few decades after the dismantling of the infamous Berlin Wall—inaugurating or accompanying the demise of the Cold War—we witness today the ominous resurgence of dividing barriers: the fence between the United States and Mexico, the gulf between Europe and North Africa, and the wall between Israel and Palestine. By themselves, the barriers are only physical constructs, but their presence testifies to deep-seated motivations: the prevalence of fear and distrust, the desire to exclude the unfamiliar or alien, and the obsession with being free from immigrant intrusions. Another term for fear is "phobia," and the world today is inundated with phobias, among which "Islamophobia" probably tops the list. More than in other phobias, Islamophobia is closely connected with violence and the (Hobbesian) fear of violent death, which today means fear of "terror." In this respect, though unsettling traditional (national) boundaries, Islamophobia opens up new borders or fissures of horror on both domestic and global levels. Against this background, the frequently voiced question of "How can a nice boy from Brooklyn become a terrorist?" reveals a deep and unsettling shift in the friend/enemy formula.

In less dramatic form, the fear of Islamic strangers comes to the fore in the battles over the wearing of veils or burqas and the building of minarets, which recently have agonized many European countries. A more amorphous, but no less widespread type of fear today is "xenophobia," which in many cases has the character of an economic phobia, fear over the loss of job security from the influx of migrant workers or immigrants. Almost everywhere in the West today, one finds an insistence—among both right-wing and left-wing political movements—on new immigrant legislation and a tightening of border controls. A prominent example in this area is a new law enacted in the state of Arizona that allows police to investigate the legal or illegal immigrant status of suspicious people, a law that not unexpectedly has led to widespread protests and demonstrations. In the context of Europe, recent surveys and analyses have shown that major sources of exclusion or distrust are primarily economic, and no longer (or not exclusively) cultural and religious. Albena Azmanova, one prominent researcher, states: "In contrast to the old version in which hostility to foreigners was cast in terms of the protection of cultural and political sovereignty (national chauvinism), the foundation of xenophobia is now often economic. It is related to the perceived threats to socio-economic well-being, especially job loss, brought about by the open border policies of globalization." This development obviously has profound implications for the conception of borders and the prospect of border-crossings. Azmanova adds: " 'Closed border' attitudes are grounded on the emerging culture of individual responsibility for economic survival which has redefined the legitimacy relationship between public authority and citizens in recent years. The more individuals [have to] accept responsibility for their own economic well-being in a context of economic uncertainty, the more they are averse to otherness—as they see the other as [hostile] competitor, rather than as a 'significant' other."[5]

COUNTERING TERROR WARS

Although they are unprecedented in their scope and intensity, today's terror wars have distant precursors in the religious wars of seventeenth-century Europe. Hobbes's congenital fear was based on the approach of the Armada, that is, Spain's military attempt to extend its Catholic empire, an attempt that was only a prelude to the devastating religious conflicts of subsequent decades (and also to the English Civil War between Royalists and Puritans). These conflicts exacted a horrendous price in terms of human lives and civil culture, but somehow a sense of decency survived. In the midst of bloody conflagrations and displays of terror, a few European intellectuals stood out as mediators and models of political restraint. One was Erasmus, who did not cease to urge moderation on all contending religious parties and also on the conflictual relations between Europe and the "Turks."[6] Another major figure was Michel de Montaigne, who experienced and reacted to the bitter feud between French Catholics and Huguenots. Both Erasmus and Montaigne sought to mitigate and, if possible, resolve the prevailing enmity—the friend/enemy polarity—without necessarily endorsing a bland compromise neglectful of just aspirations. In the words of social theorist Bryan Turner, Montaigne presented an argument "that gave priority to *humanité* as the basis for mercy and sympathy because *humanité* moderates vengeance and resentment." Properly applied, Montaigne's ethics—stressing "forgiveness, clemency, talking it out rather than fighting it through"—was able to "make men behave more humanely to one another, perhaps lead his countrymen out of their civil war, and restore conditions of justice."[7]

In our own time, do we still have moderating mediators of this kind? Can we still find public intellectuals attuned to, and living up to, the tradition of Erasmus and Montaigne? To be sure, there are some outstanding religious leaders, such as the Dalai Lama and Bishop Tutu, willing and able to resist the prevailing politics of fear (I shall return to this point a bit later). When we look elsewhere, however, the situation is more bleak. Faced with the accelerating terror wars after 9/11, members of the academy in the West have for the most part maintained silence, even deafening silence. Preoccupied with careers within professional borders, academic philosophers and literary intellectuals have by and large been unwilling, or else unable, to challenge the predominance of the Schmittian formula. The task itself, to be sure, is challenging and daunting, mainly because of the globalization of that formula. Basically, in contrast to earlier, mainly domestic conflicts, terrors wars in our time have both a national and a transnational or global character; as such, they hover uneasily between domestic and international warfare and, more precisely, between civil war and interstate war. Whereas, in modern times, interstate wars have precariously been regulated by international norms, nonstate conflicts are typically subject to police control, a control that comes to an end in outright civil war (including global civil war), which then inaugurates a state of total normlessness and savagery spawning intense fear of violent death.

Given the complexity of terror wars, few intellectuals have stepped into this arena in a properly humanist spirit; a major exception (in my view) is the international relations scholar Richard Falk. In *The Great Terror War*, published at the onset of the invasion of Iraq (2003), Falk lucidly pinpointed the character of the newly emerging friend/enemy division. "Unlike most past radical movements that were embedded in a specific society whose ruling structure was being challenged," he writes, "al-Qaeda exemplifies the organizational form of the current era of globalization: a network that can operate anywhere and everywhere, and yet is definitely situated nowhere," that is, a network "without an address." Falk in this context introduces the term "megaterrorism" to characterize the elusiveness of the new warfare with respect to normative limits, and especially with regard to the borders between civilians and combatants. "Megaterrorism," he notes, "is violence against civilian targets that achieves significant levels of substantive as well as symbolic harm, causing damage on a scale once associated with large-scale military attacks under state auspices, and thus threatening the target society in a warlike manner that gives rise to a defensive urgency to strike back as effectively as possible." Conceived under the rubric of "terror war" or war against "terrorism," this "defensive urgency" takes on the same amorphous character that marks the network launching the 9/11 attack. Hence, Falk notes in a critical vein, the generalizing of terrorism "misdirects the American-led response, weakening the commitment to struggle specifically against the al-Qaeda network, while distracting the needed energies from an appropriately conceived 'war.'"[8]

What particularly troubles Falk is the fact that the broad rhetoric of terror war or war against terrorism extends or generalizes the resort to violence, while weakening or blurring the distinction between state actors and nonstate actors, that is, between interstate and civil war. "I believe," states Falk, "that the over-generalized American approach to the megaterrorist challenge is dangerously serving to exempt state violence and policies from being regarded *as* terrorism—even when their violence is deliberately directed at civilian society." This exemption allows governments everywhere "to rely on large-scale violence against their own and other civilian populations, and to avoid the stigma of terrorism, while at the same time tending to taint all *reactive* violence from oppressed peoples . . .

as terrorism." For Falk, the only chance to make headway in the present politics of fear is to restrict the focus to very specific targets, rather than extending it to global networks, and thereby to rein in the danger of indiscriminate global mayhem or war on civilian populations. By proceeding in this manner, the traditional normative standards applicable (however loosely) to interstate warfare are bound to be strengthened, while the normlessness of civil strife can, we hope, be curbed. On the other hand, terror warfare is liable to be a "lost" or a losing strategy through an overindulgence in violence, and also by treating attacks "in isolation from their social, political, and cultural contexts." The likelihood of failure is prone to be increased by unilateralism and the relentless pursuit of global hegemonic designs, a pursuit "pushing the world into a new phase of strategic [friend-enemy] rivalry" while being undertaken "behind the smokescreen of the war on global terror."[9]

Yet, Falk does not entirely reject a military response to terrorist attacks, as long as the politics of fear is not allowed to trump or obliterate the politics of hope and global cooperation. Faced with the threat of megaterrorism, he writes, "the rationale for *limited* war seems to me persuasive, provided the focus on al-Qaeda is not superseded by more expanded war aims—which lamentably seems to be happening as a matter of deliberate choice by American political leaders" (during the George W. Bush administration and later). As a student of global politics, Falk finds our world precariously lodged at the cusp between two paradigms: the "Westphalian" paradigm based on military state power and an (emerging) paradigm of global interdependence. "We find ourselves in a situation," he states, "that *both* calls for reliance on war to achieve tolerable levels of security . . . and [for] an emphasis upon the minimization of disruptive violence and a receptivity to post-Westphalian alternatives."[10] In the meantime, since 2003, the paradigm of military warfare has continued, simply shifting its accent from Iraq to Afghanistan (and possibly Iran). Despite the ongoing relocation of geographical focus, however, a basic feature of terror wars has remained unchanged: the intermingling of state war and civil war, that is, of violence against armed forces and against civilian populations. In the case of Afghanistan, the use of unmanned "drones" illustrates in a particularly dramatic fashion the confluence of combatants and noncombatants. Although they are, we are told, ostensibly directed at terrorist cells, drone

attacks in many cases have resulted in a bloodbath of entire civilian families and village clans. Outrage and resentment are the inevitable result.
Falk states in subsequent publications that large numbers of people in the
Islamic world are prone to end up with the conclusion that their "sufferings and grievances" do not count and are "the result of the abusive ways
in which America uses its power and wealth in the world."[11]

Falk is not the only prominent international relations expert willing
to examine and challenge global terror wars. Among some others in this
field, I want to single out especially Joseph Nye, author of such well-known
books as *The Paradox of American Power* and *Soft Power*; I also mention
some writings of Andrew Linklater.[12] Their voices have been ably seconded and reinforced by the renowned Malaysian student of global politics Chandra Muzaffar. In a book penned after the invasion of Iraq, and
after the reelection of George W. Bush, the U.S. president guiding that invasion, Muzaffar reflected on the deeper sources or motivations of these
events. "Fear," he comments, "had probably a great deal to do with [Bush's]
electoral triumph." In the aftermath of 9/11, the U.S. public's "overwhelming concern" was with "security," which is thought to provide a bulwark
against the onslaught of terror. At the end of the day, this concern with
security, in Muzaffar's view, was "more important to voters" than all the
problems surrounding the war in Iraq, including the pretended weapons
of mass destruction, the burgeoning military budget, Abu Ghraib, and the
rest. Fear of terror and the resulting concern with security provided the
West with the rationale, or, better, the excuse, to extend its military reach or
hegemony throughout the Middle East and around the globe. Like Falk
and others observe, Muzaffar does not attribute the politics of fear exclusively to 9/11, but he lists a number of other contributing factors, including "the quest for identity, the upsurge of ethnic consciousness, political
antagonisms and animosities, and economic instability and upheaval."[13]

BEYOND THE POLITICS OF FEAR

When searching for a more just and peaceful global order, as an alternative to the politics of fear, attention shifts almost inevitably to religious-
spiritual and to moral or ethical resources and traditions. Both Falk and

Muzaffar are eloquent in invoking and articulating these resources. Addressing the "growing evidence of geopolitical hubris" evident in the militarization of the globe, Falk stresses the counterstrategy of geopolitical self-limitation and interdependence nurtured by a sense of religious and ethical "humility." Humility, he says, in this setting would mean "adopting the narrowest war aims possible, identifying limits, seeking closure, and exploring alternatives to war-based security politics," alternatives designed to "promote and sustain the well-being of all peoples on the planet." In his turn, Muzaffar finds the "root cause" of the ills of our time in the neglect of spiritual and ethical legacies or teachings that could provide a remedy to the fear-inspired focus on security. "The question we have to ask at this point," he writes, "is this: should we—as inhabitants of the planet Earth—not look for the metaphysical causes, the spiritual cures for the ailments that afflict us?" Indeed, has the time not come for modern people "to develop a deeper understanding of what really lies behind the colossal challenges of our age," and thereby to garner glimpses of a more peaceful, less fear-inspired global politics?[14]

When consulting the scriptures or traditions invoked by Falk and Muzaffar, we are not at a loss. All the spiritual and ethical teachings emphasize an alternative to self-centered fear and security: the alternative of self-transcendence, self-opening, and border-crossing. In the so-called Abrahamic traditions, the key teachings are found in Deuteronomy and Leviticus, in passages stressing the two commandments (which in the end are one) to love or open ourselves to God with all our being, and to love our fellow beings in the same way (Deut. 6:5; Lev. 19:18). The teaching was taken over almost verbatim by Jesus when he identified the core of religious faith with the enactment of these two modes of love (Matt. 22:37–40; Luke 10:27–28; Mark 12:29–31). However, Jesus added to this dual plea a new, and hitherto unheard-of commandment—"love your enemies" (Matt. 5:44; Luke 6:27).

By all accounts, this is the plea most disturbing and even unacceptable to international "realists" preoccupied solely with fear and security. In *The Concept of the Political*, Carl Schmitt seeks to circumvent Jesus's commandment, by employing a deft form of verbal casuistry, namely, the distinction between private and public enemy (*inimicus* and *hostis*): "An enemy exists only when, at least potentially, one fighting collectivity of people confronts a similar collectivity. The enemy is solely the public enemy" and not "the private adversary." In Schmitt's construal of Christ's exhortation, "no mention is made of the political enemy," with the result that, against the latter, warfare and killing remain altogether legitimate and permissible. As it happens, of course, no such private/public distinction is made anywhere in the Gospels.[15]

Several religious leaders in our time have stepped forward critiquing or denouncing the dominant focus on fear and terror wars;[16] fortunately, their pleas have not been isolated or ignored. Following 9/11, a number of Christian theologians and religious scholars have pondered the challenge posed by megaterrorism and megafear, reflections collected in *Strike Terror No More: Theology, Ethics, and the New War.* As can readily be seen, for theologians and Christian believers, fear and especially the fear of violent death cannot have the central status it tends to have for nonbelievers or agnostics; above all, fear cannot provide a ready-made license for counterfear or counterterror. Seen in the light of biblical teachings, death no longer possesses final authority but is inserted into a redemptive story and the vision of "final days." In the words of theologian Stanley Hauerwas, Christians as a community are "shaped by the practice of baptism that reminds us there are far worse things that can happen to us than dying." Unfortunately, the indiscriminate leveling of Christians into the secular American "way of life" is an indication "that the Christian 'we' of baptism has been submerged in the American fear of death." In the wake of 9/11, what Christians can and should do, in Hauerwas's view, is to escape from fear and terror in favor of an alternative possibility and pathway. For, what Christians have learned and can show to others, he writes, is "that the worst thing that can happen to us is not death, but dying for the wrong thing." After all, Christians have been instructed, by their Lord's example, "that we must prepare for death exactly because we refuse to kill in the name of survival."[17]

For theologians such as Hauerwas and others, the main point is not simply to resist the fear syndrome, but to lay the groundwork for another scenario where fear would give way to trust, cooperation, and redemptive care. At this juncture, the instructions of Deuteronomy and Leviticus and also Jesus's new commandment are of crucial importance. In a section in *Strike Terror No More* titled "Do Christians Have Anything Distinctive to

Say?," John J. Cobb Jr. turns precisely to these teachings for support. In the face of our dark horizons, he comments, it cannot be the proper Christian response to resort to "us-versus-them" formulas and to endorse policies "that harm them for our gain." Especially in situations of danger when fear is trying to overwhelm us, it is crucial to remember and enact the biblical instructions and, above all, Jesus's new commandment. This does not mean that we condone or approve of terrorism or fail to bring terrorists to justice, if possible, but it *does* mean that we do not simply retaliate and repay terror with terror, enmity with torture and Abu Ghraib. In a similar vein, Walter Wink pleads for the exercise of nonviolence, at least to the greatest possible extent, as an alternative to blind retaliation or revenge. "The church," he writes, "is called to nonviolence—not in order to preserve its purity, but to express its fidelity. . . . The gospel is not in the least concerned with our anxiety to *be* right; it wants to see *right done*." He adds that nonviolence of this kind, in the final analysis, is "not a matter of legalism but of discipleship. It is the way God has chosen to overthrow evil in the world."[18]

In remonstrating against terror wars (including counterterrorism), theologians can find assistance, apart from biblical passages, also in ethical-philosophical teachings of the past, including the traditional theory of "just war." Thus, John Milbank aptly points to the compatibility, within certain limits, between biblical faith and classical philosophical insights: "Both empty secular power and arbitrary theocratic power, in their secret complicity, show us no way forward." Rather, what we need to reconsider is the "Platonic-Aristotelian" legacy and its resonance in all three monotheistic religions. "We should ponder ways," he states, "in which this legacy may provide us with a certain common vision and practice, while at the same time respecting social and cultural spaces for existing difference." In this manner, we might glimpse how "human wisdom can imitate, imperfectly but truly, something of an eternal order of justice." Appealing explicitly to the "just war" tradition, Max Stackhouse reminds us first of all that "God wants everyone to live in peace and to be nonviolent toward the neighbor near and far." Recognizing that among imperfect human beings, violence sometimes has erupted and continues to erupt in history, just war theory lays down normative principles designed precisely to keep violence in check. First, resort to violent means (*ius ad bellum*) must be for defensive reasons only, undertaken as a last resort (after all alternatives have been exhausted), and guided by a legitimate authority (not a bunch of mercenaries). Second, during warfare (*ius in bello*), care must be taken to distinguish between combatants and civilians, to use only proportionate force, and to treat enemies "as human." Finally, the entire course of war must be oriented toward its end, that is, conducted in such a way as to render possible final reconciliation and a just peace.[19]

To be sure, the struggle against the politics of fear cannot be left to theologians and religious leaders alone. There are major tasks left for political leaders and policymakers, tasks such as reforming the United Nations, strengthening regional organizations, building new cross-cutting alliances, and reducing the stockpiles of nuclear weapons and other armaments. Given that the focus on terror and counterterror is ultimately destructive of peace and democracy, it is also important to consult political theorists and philosophers on this point. In this context, it is fruitful to remember the work of the Baron Montesquieu, which in the modern Western tradition constitutes the perfect antidote to the fear paradigm of Hobbes. In *The Spirit of Laws*, Montesquieu pinpointed the underlying motivation or "spirit" of different political regimes. Tellingly, his work associated the motive of fear with tyranny or despotism, while democracy or a republican regime was necessarily linked for him with the spirit of "love," more specifically the "love for equality" (or equal dignity) among all citizens or participants. In Montesquieu's view, such love cannot be legislated or imposed by political force, but it is a civic virtue that needs to be cultivated through an ethics of openness and generosity toward fellow beings.[20] John Dewey would have fully agreed with him in this respect. Democracy for Dewey was not a finished product but an ongoing process requiring the constant openness of participants to new learning experiences, new border-crossings, and the diligent cultivation of ethical sensibilities capable of fostering the common good. Accordingly, he called democracy "a form of moral and spiritual association."[21]

All this does not imply a neglect of fear and of the danger of violence and terror wars, but an insistence on vigilance to keep this danger at bay or at a minimum, and to prevent it from crowding out the prospect of cooperation and peace. In this regard, Dewey was clearly more than a "realist," adopting the perspective of (what one may call) a "utopian realist" or a "realistic idealist" willing to "befriend" strangers and even enemies. He wrote in one of his famous texts on democracy (in the spirit of both Montesquieu and Gandhi):

> To take as far as possible every conflict which arises—and they are bound to arise—out of the atmosphere and medium of force, of violence as a means of settlement, into that of discussion and of intelligence is to treat those who disagree—even profoundly—with us as those from whom we may learn and, insofar, as friends.[22]

CHAPTER TWELVE

Dialogue among Faiths

The Dignity of Religious Difference

If the nobility of (modern liberal) secularism resides in its quest to enable multiple faiths to exist on the same public space, its shallowness resides in the hubris of its distinction between private faith and (neutral) public reason.

—William E. Connolly, *Pluralism*

In the teeth of its modern despisers, religion has made a comeback in our time. Now, religion can mean many things. In my view, it means, or should mean, the awakening of a profound longing, the probing of a depth dimension of human existence. But I realize there are other meanings. What Gilles Kepel has called the "revenge of God" has also surfaced or resurfaced in our time: in the form of the ill-will and vengefulness between religious communities and their leaders.[1] The litany of contemporary religious clashes, or conflicts in good part spawned by religious motives, is long and depressing. Christians are pitted against Muslims in Africa and the Balkans; Jews against Palestinians in the Middle East; Hindus against Muslims in India and Kashmir; Hindus against Buddhists in Sri Lanka; Confucianists against Muslims in China. And, of course, we cannot forget the long and bloody conflict between Catholics and Protestants in Northern Ireland. Not a very uplifting scenario! Is there an alternative?

Can a religious faith coexist peacefully with other religious faiths? More ambitiously phrased, Can religious faith respect and even cherish religious diversity? This is the question I want to examine here.

A ZERO-SUM GAME?

The question often asked regarding interfaith dialogue, especially a dialogue animated by mutual respect and generosity, is whether mutual recognition is not purchased at too steep a price: the price of the shallowness or lukewarmness of one's own faith commitment. Does entering into, and navigating in, the "pluriverse" of faith traditions not necessarily erode the firmness of one's own convictions and possibly lead to alienation from traditional faith practices? It seems to me that this question is predicated on a perceived antimony between two kinds of relationships, namely, a "vertical" and a "horizontal" (lateral) relationship, where "vertical" refers to the human–God and "horizontal" to human–human relationship. In terms of this antinomy, only the vertical relation is often considered to be "properly religious," while interhuman relations are treated as "merely" secular, worldly, and possibly even harmful to religious faith. Construed in a strictly binary fashion, the governing assumption of this view is that of a zero-sum game where the winnings of one side are the losses of the other side.

On occasion, the dichotomy between vertical and horizontal relations is equated with the distinction between revelation and human reasoning or philosophy, with the former bearing the stamp of asymmetry. Thus, Leo Strauss, without aligning himself with Jewish orthodoxy, has resolutely stressed the asymmetry governing religious faith in opposition to reason. He noted in a lecture titled "Reason and Revelation" (presented in 1948 at Hartford Theological Seminary) that a basic conflict or dichotomy prevails between human reasoning and revelation, between the freedom of questioning claimed by philosophy and the obedience to divine sovereign authority demanded by revelation: "To the philosophic view that man's happiness consists in free investigation or insight, the Bible opposes the view that man's happiness consists in obedience to God."[2] On these premises, as it appears, no bridge can be built between freedom and obedience,

between human inquiry and faith. But we know that Jewish faith, even orthodox faith, cannot be restricted to this absolute asymmetry. To show
the possibility of bridge-building, it suffices to point to the Hasidic tradition and especially to Martin Buber's accent on the "I–Thou" relationship
(where horizontal and vertical dimensions seem to permeate each other).[3]

By all accounts, the clash between relations appears to be most acute in
the context of Islam. In large measure, the dilemma is particularly severe
because of the status of the central text, the Qur'an. Whereas the Hebrew
Bible and the Christian Gospels are agreed to have been written by piously
inspired human beings, orthodox Muslims tend to regard the Qur'an as
God's directly revealed word, and hence in no way as a human product
(certainly not the product of Prophet Muhammad). Whereas the Hebrew
Bible and the Christian Gospels are acknowledged to be historically situated texts and hence amenable to historical interpretation (possibly to
"higher criticism"), the Qur'an for most orthodox believers is transtemporal and even transmundane, and thus outside the realm of contingency, including the contingency of historical interpretation or philosophical re-
construction. Unsurprisingly, the clash between radical orthodoxy and
nonorthodoxy in Islam is profound, with nonorthodoxy frequently being
labeled as heterodoxy, if not a slide into apostasy (*kafir*) or pagan ignorance (*jahiliyya*).

As in the case of Judaism, however, the situation is not one-dimen-
sional. In the broader "house of Islam" (*dar-al-Islam*), we find a long het-
erodox or barely orthodox tradition that stresses the nearly horizontal
love of God for humanity over the absolute sovereignty or heteronomy of
God. A prime example is the richly variegated legacy of popular Sufism.
As one should also note, there are long-standing efforts among Muslim
theologians to break the stranglehold of orthodox "literalism" and to
open Islamic faith to the demands of historical interpretation and understanding. A leading contemporary protagonist of these efforts is the Iran-
ian philosopher Abdulkarim Soroush, whose basic agenda has been to
differentiate between an invariant core of faith (especially the doctrine of
tawhid that "there is no God but God") and the concrete historical, social,
and political contexts in which Islamic faith is bound to find variable expression. Given the upsurge of orthodox "fundamentalism" in many parts
of the Islamic world, the work of Soroush and his peers is intensely con-
troversial and often socially marginalized or ostracized.[4]

In less acute form, the tension or antagonism between relations can be found in all or most religions around the world. Within the confines of the "Abrahamic" tradition, Christianity seems to be least vulnerable to the conflict between vertical and horizontal dimensions. The reason is the central position of Christ, who theologically is considered to be both God and human being, thus establishing a bridge between immanent and transcendent domains. Despite this emphasis on balance and reconciliation, however, the tension between immanence and transcendence has not been absent in Christianity. Especially the rise of modern secularism in the West has prompted many believers, typically those with orthodox leanings, to suspect concern with interhuman relations as being tainted with worldliness, "liberal" progressivism, and agnosticism.[5] The issue that surfaces here is whether faith is at all amenable to dialogue or whether the latter involves necessarily a betrayal, an issue too weighty to be neglected or brushed aside.

INTERFAITH DIALOGUE CONTESTED

With admirable clarity and precision, the German Protestant theologian Jürgen Moltmann has formulated the problem or, better, the dilemma of interfaith dialogue. As he points out, in our age of globalization, it is difficult and perhaps impossible for believers to remain confined in their own traditional circles or communities. Moreover, the attempt to remain so confined carries with it the danger of ossification that results from the stale repetition of beliefs. On the other hand, however, opening communities up to interaction does not necessarily entail religious renewal. "No one," Moltmann states bluntly, "has ever become a Christian or a Jew or a Muslim or a Hindu or a Buddhist through interfaith dialogue." The problem is that such dialogue between communities can have a "tranquillizing effect," in the sense that participants "converse or are simply 'nice' to each other" while basically leaving each other and the prevailing status quo "in peace." The chief danger is that religions become simply items in the modern "supermarket economy," served up inoffensively in the cafeteria of beliefs.[6]

Moltmann does not disparage interfaith tolerance and mutual respect wherever they are found; in modern multifaith societies, such qualities are surely preferable to intolerance and disrespect. What troubles him is a certain linguistic closure, a self-confinement of conversation akin to the self-confinement of sectarian creeds. "If peaceful coexistence is the goal of dialogue," he writes, "then in contrast to the religious disputations [of earlier ages], dialogue has no higher goal than itself: dialogue is the goal of dialogue." A corollary of this confinement is the tendency to privilege consensualism or conformism over contestation, a tendency bracketing the truth claims of revelation. Reporting on his own experiences in this area, Moltmann notes that so-called interfaith dialogues often turn into "discussions between Christian theologians in the presence of astonished and silent Rabbis, Swamis or Buddhist monks. 'Of course, you can ask us anything at all,' they say—and see that as their contribution to dialogue."[7]

For Moltmann, the basic issue is how to keep the faith dimension—we might say, the vertical dimension of faith—alive in interhuman dialogue, without succumbing to missionary zeal or the endeavor of unilateral conversion and domination. From a Christian angle, what one has to grant to other faith traditions is their own aspiration toward salvation, liberation, or *moksha*, an aspiration that manifests itself in different forms. Moltmann prefers to use for these goals the terms "blessedness" and "eternal life"; one might also speak (with Aristotle) of "flourishing" or "fulfillment." "The mission to which God sends men and women," he writes, "means inviting *all* human beings, the religious and the non-religious, to life, to the affirmation of life, to the protection of life, to shared life, and to eternal life." Hence, everything that ministers to life in other religions or faith traditions must be deemed "good" and sanctified.[8]

Outside some radical Augustinian strands, recent Catholic theology on the whole has endorsed a position not far removed from that of Moltmann. A clear example is Karl Rahner, who, in this respect, takes his lead from a judicious mode of bridge-building: the Thomistic blending of grace and nature. As described by a fellow theologian, Rahner's position can be summarized as follows: "People can be saved whether or not they are related to the Catholic Church or consciously accept Jesus Christ." Insisting on a still stronger form of lateral pluralism, theologian Hans Küng has famously (and provocatively) stated: "God saves Hindus as Hindus, not as anonymous Christians." Probably one of the leading thinkers wrestling with the issue of religious pluralism and revelation is the American theologian John Cobb Jr. Strongly committed to religious ecumenism and interfaith dialogue, but also strongly opposed to "do-it-yourself" relativism, Cobb has endeavored to reconcile competing dimensions largely along Moltmann's lines: "My central thesis here is that, for Christianity to be and to remain to the end one among others, does not involve its relativization in the destructive sense. . . . It does not relativize the process of creative transformation by which it lives and which it knows as Christ."[9]

THE ONE AND THE MANY

Perhaps it is helpful to look at the relationship between faith and faiths briefly from a strictly philosophical or theoretical perspective. In the philosophical tradition, the quest for truth in its vertical and lateral senses is usually discussed as the conundrum of "the one and the many," or else of "absolutism" versus "relativism." Absolutism here means that truth is one and can be known absolutely or with certainty. Denial of this absolute claim is termed relativism involving the denial of the oneness of truth, a denial entailing the randomness, and ultimately, the dismissal of truth as such. Is there an exit from this conundrum? Can there be a persistent pursuit of truth coupled with the acceptance of a variety of approaches to truth? Differently phrased, Can truth be pursued through dialogue? The prime example of this possibility stands at the very threshold of Western philosophy: the dialogues of Plato. In these dialogues, Socrates does not proclaim a univocal doctrine of truth, but through questions and answers, through trial and error, he seeks to clear a path for the pursuit of truth for people from different backgrounds.[10]

The conundrum of the one and the many, or of absolutism and relativism, carries over into the domain of political or practical philosophy. Here the dilemma is usually phrased in terms of the relation between the "common good" shared by all members of a community and the variety of concrete or distinct goods as perceived by particular individuals or segments of the society. Dangers clearly lurk on all sides. If the common good is erected into a uniform doctrine or ideology, the peril of totalitarianism arises together with its accessories of mind control, brainwashing, and repression of dissent. On the other hand, if goodness is identified with particular self-interest or desire, social life is abandoned to egomania, and ultimately, the struggle of warlords (in a Hobbesian "state of nature"). The question here becomes, How do you reconcile the common good with a variety of interpretations? Differently put, How do you preserve the horizon of goodness in the midst of diversity?

In a series of writings, political theorist William Connolly has clearly perceived and pinpointed the issue. In *Pluralism*, he champions what he calls a "deep" or "expansive" social, cultural, and religious pluralism, but without endorsing a simple multiplication and possible clash of self-interests. In his presentation, pluralism does not mean the mere "plurality" or juxtaposition of different orientations, all coldly indifferent and possibly hostile to each other. Rather, its "depth" character involves a deep mutual engagement, what he calls a "receptive generosity" between different agents. Such generosity, however, is not merely a biological trait but an ethical or civic disposition or virtue, a disposition disclosing at least a latent orientation to the horizon of goodness. Among the plethora of social differences, Connolly pays special attention to the issue of religious diversity and the related problem of interfaith relations. Although strongly opposed to any kind of religious "establishment" or any dogmatic imposition of faith, he also criticizes the mere juxtaposition of beliefs as seen from the supposedly neutral standpoint of the modern secular state. He observes, in a striking formulation, that liberal defenders of the so-called neutral state pretend to identify "a forum entirely *above* faith through which to regulate diverse faiths" while entirely ignoring "faith practices themselves." Hence, he adds, "if the nobility of [modern liberal] secularism resides in its quest to enable multiple faiths to exist on the same public space, its shallowness resides in the hubris of its distinction between private faith and [neutral] public reason."[11]

Connolly recognizes that the idea of "deep" or "expansive" pluralism gains its acute significance precisely in the context of our globalizing, pluricultural, and multireligious world. "The most urgent need today," he observes, "is to mix presumptively generous sensibilities into a variety of theistic and nontheistic creeds, sensibilities attuned to the contemporary need to transfigure relations of antagonism between faiths into relations of agonistic respect." The point here is not to obliterate different faith traditions in a bland universalism but to forge "a positive *ethos* of public engagement between alternative faiths."[12] In issuing this plea, Connolly's argument is ably seconded by a number of voices coming from a variety of religious traditions. A prominent exemplar of lived religious practice is Jonathan Sacks, widely renowned as a religious leader, public intellectual, and peacemaker. Although he is intensely involved in interfaith relations, Sacks is not a shallow believer; he is an "orthodox" Jew and, in fact, the chief rabbi of the United Hebrew Congregations of Britain and the Commonwealth. A prolific writer, he is most widely known for *The Dignity of Difference* (2002). Subtitled *How to Avoid the Clash of Civilizations*, the book makes a seminal contribution to interfaith harmony and, through it, to global peace.[13]

Basically, *The Dignity of Difference* celebrates a "deep" or "expansive" kind of pluralism (to use Connolly's terms); in several respects, however, it moves beyond the level of simple mutual recognition or (what Connolly calls) "agonistic respect." In a stunning formulation, Sacks articulates an idea that belongs to the core of (what I have called) a "religion of service."[14] Faith communities, he writes, "should encourage its members to do an act of service or kindness to someone or some group of another faith or ethnicity—to extend a hand of help, in other words, *across* the boundaries of difference and thus turn communities outward instead of inward." As a believing Jew, Sacks invites members of other faith traditions to join him in prayer; but prayer needs to be linked with action and practical engagement on behalf of the marginalized and persecuted. In this respect, his text is again exemplary by counseling not mindless activism but engagement in response to a summons or call. "I believe," Sacks states, "that God is summoning us to a new act of listening" today, involving above all caring attentiveness to some of the side effects of globalization: "Its inequities, its consumerism and exploitation, its failure to address widespread poverty and disease, its juggernaut insensitivity to local traditions and cultures, and the spiritual poverty that can go hand in hand with material wealth."[15]

CONCLUSION

To be sure, the task of ecumenical friendship is formidable and tends to be challenged or blocked by numerous obstacles, some of them of a religious origin. The very idea of interfaith dialogue, still falling short of interfaith service, is contested today by many religious fundamentalists, including Christian fundamentalists. The latter might recall with benefit the legacy of St. Paul, the founder or cofounder of the early Christian church. As we know, it was mainly Paul who extended the Christian fellowship beyond the initial Jewish community laterally (or horizontally) to the "gentiles" in their many ethnic, tribal, or national settings. Although he was initially resisted by the leaders in Jerusalem, Paul's broader, genuinely "catholic" (or cosmopolitan) orientation ultimately prevailed. We should note that this "catholic" orientation involved not only the missionary expansion of Christian faith to previous nonbelievers, but also—and perhaps more importantly—the accommodation and peaceful symbiosis of Christians with non-Christians (at least on the limited scale of "just" borrowing). The basic idea was to extend Christian fellowship to people everywhere, or, more ambitiously phrased, to apply Christ's commandment to "love your fellow beings" rigorously by befriending in love all people whether Christian or non-Christian. In this way, I believe, Paul anticipated, at least in a limited way, the religious goal or maxim to cherish the dignity of difference.

Epilogue

Peace in the Horizons of Difference

In this book I have discussed dialogue in many contexts and from many angles. Above all, I have underscored the importance of dialogue seen as the engagement with others in horizons of difference. Why this thematic focus? What is the reason for this stress on dialogical engagement with others?

For some people, dialogue is just a means to an end, a means to reach something else. One hears it said: "You dialogue in order to gain some other benefit." For instance, business partners dialogue with each other in order to have better commercial success, to make more money, in order to increase profit. Likewise, politicians or statesmen may dialogue in order to have greater political or geopolitical advantages. We also find in many other areas of life that dialogue is used as a means to reach another end.

By contrast to this means/end formula, I want to claim that dialogue is an end in itself, that it is worthwhile in itself, and not in the sense that we just dialogue about dialogue. Some people (with whom I again disagree) say that all you do is just talk, you dialogue about dialogue. But that is mistaken. We dialogue, or should dialogue with others, about real things, about real concerns, real issues, sometimes life and death issues. These issues are at the heart of dialogue, because they involve what it means to be "human" for all participants or partners. By teaching us about humanity, there is something in dialogue deeply educational and transformative.

If we seriously dialogue with somebody else, not just chatting about the weather, something happens to the participants. In a certain way, we are changed: we are being humanized, or we become more human in dialoguing. The intrinsic goal of dialogue thus has something to do with goodness. Our goodness is increased, we are no longer selfish, enclosed in our selfishness, but we are elevated to a higher level, which one might call the level of humaneness.

Aristotle said that we play the flute not to achieve something else—playing the flute is intrinsically valuable. In the same way, I would say that dialogue has an intrinsic ethical value by transforming us into more educated and human beings. To that extent, we can also say that dialogue has a political value. If we are able to transform political antagonists or contestants into people who are more sensitive to each other, more responsive to each other's aspirations and inclinations, then there is the possibility of promoting through dialogue something like justice and peace.

We live today in a world that is not very hospitable to this kind of dialogue. We live in many ways in a very grim context full of disputes and festering hostilities. If we just think of the present scenario in Syria, the problems of the Middle East, Iran. In all those areas and elsewhere, there is a great potential of conflict, and ultimately, warfare. I am of the generation that still experienced the last great war: World War II. So my enduring ambition is to reduce the likelihood of a repetition.

The dangers of catastrophes are all around us: environmental catastrophes but especially nuclear catastrophes. Whatever I can do to combat these dangers, I want to do, and dialogical engagement is a good and promising path, especially in the midst of horizons of differences. Dialogue does not seek to dominate others, does not inflict a certain dominant ideology or worldview on others; it aims to promote mutual respect and understanding. And through this mutual understanding, some way of living together may be possible, some *symbiosis*, some peace with justice.

At this point, let me return to the cover picture of the present volume. Let me again stress that in genuine love, we are cherishing not only the beloved but everything "around her," as Marc Chagall says. Thus genuine love fosters our engagement with each other, with humanity, with nature and the divine. Is this not a good and promising itinerary for all human beings capable of loving?

NOTES

Introduction

1. Merleau-Ponty describes the distinction: "When one is living in what Péguy called an historical *period*, in which political man is content to administer a regime or an established law, one can hope for a history without violence. When one has the misfortune or luck to live in an *epoch* where the traditional ground of a nation or society crumbles, then one is in a time when 'man' must reconstruct human relations"; see Maurice Merleau-Ponty, *Humanism and Terror*, trans. John O'Neill (Boston: Beacon Press, 1969), xvii.

2. See Charles Taylor, *Sources of the Self: The Making of Moderns Identity* (Cambridge, MA: Harvard University Press, 1989). When we speak of a centered or binary paradigm, Taylor and I refer to a dominant structure. To be sure, there have been important deviations from this paradigm. I would certainly count among these nonconformists Nicholas of Cusa, Meister Eckhart, and Baron Montesquieu.

3. From a different angle, this gulf or noncoincidence has been captured by the Spanish sociologist Manuel Castells, *Rupture: The Crisis of Liberal Democracy* (Cambridge: Polity Press, 2019). For Castells, what we are witnessing today in the West is not a normal evolution or continuation of past antagonisms, but a historic rupture of the institutional relationship between "the governing elites and the governed," between inherited formal structures and peoples' actual life experience. Whereas Castells focuses mainly on the political domain, I expand the "rupture" to the integral spectrum of existential life and practices.

4. See Edmund Husserl, *Cartesian Meditations: An Introduction to Phenomenology*, trans. Derion Cairns (1931; The Hauge: Nijhoff, 1960); Husserl, *The Crisis of European Sciences and Transcendental Phenomenology*, trans. David Carr (1936; Evanston, IL: Northwestern University Press, 1970); David Carr, "Husserl's Problematic Concept of the Life-World," in *Husserl, Expressions and Appraisals*, ed. F. A. Ellison and J. R. McCormick (Notre Dame, IN: University of Notre Dame Press, 1977), 202–12.

5. See Martin Heidegger, *Being and Time*, trans. John Macquarrie and Edward Robinson (New York: Harper and Row, 1962); Heidegger, *Identity and Difference*

(New York: Harper Torchbooks, 1978); Heidegger, *Letter on Humanism*, in *Martin Heidegger: Basic Writings*, ed. David F. Krell (New York: Harper & Row, 1977), 189–242; Maurice Merleau-Ponty, *Sense and Non-Sense*, trans. Hubert L. Dreyfus and Patricia A. Dreyfus (Evanston, IL: Northwestern University Press, 1964); Merleau-Ponty, *The Visible and the Invisible, Followed by Working Notes* (Evanston, IL: Northwestern University Press, 1968); Jacques Derrida, *Writing and Difference*, trans. Alan Bass (Chicago: University of Chicago Press, 1975); Derrida, *The Other Heading*, trans. Pascale-Anne Brault and Michael B. Naas (Bloomington: Indiana University Press, 1992); Simone Weil, *Gravity and Grace*, trans. Emma Crawford and Mario von der Ruhr (New York: Routledge and Kegan Paul, 2004); Weil, *Oppression and Liberty*, trans. Arthur Wills and John Petrie (New York: Routledge and Kegan Paul, 2001). Some thinkers prefer the term "transversality." Compare Fred Dallmayr, "Transversal Liaisons: Calvin Schrag on Selfhood," in *Calvin O. Schrag and the Task of Philosophy after Postmodernity*, ed. Martin J. Matustik and William L. McBride (Evanston, IL: Northwestern University Press, 2002), 129–51.

6. Jacques Maritain, "Integral Humanism and the Crisis of Modern Times," *The Review of Politics* 1 (January 1939): 12–13, 16.

7. Ibid., 8.

8. Ibid., 7, 16. See also Fred Dallmayr, *For a New and "Other" Humanism* (Mauritius: Lambert Academic Publishing, 2019).

9. Jacques Maritain, *Integral Humanism: Temporal and Spiritual Problems of a New Christendom*, trans. Joseph W. Evans (Notre Dame, IN: University of Notre Dame Press, 1973), 93, 119.

10. Maritain, *Integral Humanism*, 173, 201. See also Fred Dallmayr, *The Promise of Democracy: Political Agency and Transformation* (Albany: SUNY Press, 2010); Dallmayr, *Democracy to Come: Politics as Relational Praxis* (New York: Oxford University Press, 2017); and Dallmayr, *Post-Liberalism: Recovering a Shared World* (New York: Oxford University Press, 2019).

11. Compare on these points Will Kymlicka, *Multicultural Citizenship* (Oxford: Clarendon, 1995); Majtaba Mahdavi and W. Andy Knight, eds., *Towards the Dignity of Difference* (Farnham: Ashgate 2012); and Talal Asad, *Secular Translations: Nation-State, Modern Self, and Calculative Reason* (New York: Columbia University Press, 2018).

12. See Peter C. Phan, *Being Religious Interreligiously: Asian Perspectives of Interfaith Dialogue* (Maryknoll, NY: Orbis Books, 2004), 60. Compare also Anselm K. Min, *The Solidarity of Others World: Postmodern Theology after Postmodernism* (New York: T&T Clark International, 2004); and Vinay Lal, ed., *Plural Worlds, Multiple Selves: Ashis Nandy and the Post-Columbian Future* (Ann Arbor, MI: McNaughton & German, 1995–96).

13. Compare Fred Dallmayr, "What Is *Swaraj*? Lessons from Gandhi," in *Gandhi, Freedom and Self-Rule*, ed. Anthony J. Parel (Lanham, MD: Lexington Books, 2000), 103–18.

CHAPTER ONE. After Babel

1. The meaning of the Latin terms are, in sequence, "man the toolmaker," "the speaker," "the inquirer," and "the symbolizer." On the last term, compare, e.g., Edward H. Henderson, "Homo Symbolicus: A Definition of Man," *Man and World* 4 (1971): 131–50.

2. Plato, *Republic*, bk. 2, 369c–375a; see Eric H. Warmington and Philip G. Rouse, eds., *Great Dialogues of Plato* (New York: New American Library, 1956), 165–71.

3. In Aristotle's words: "A pilot will judge a rudder better than a ship builder; in the same way, the diner—not the cook—will be the best judge of a feast" (*Politics* 1282a8). See also his statements: "The end and purpose of a *polis* is the good life [*eu zen*], and the institutions of social life are means to that end" (*Politics* 1280b32); "We may therefore lay down that all associations aim at some good; and we may also hold that the particular association which is the most sovereign and includes all the rest, will pursue this aim above all and will thus be directed toward the highest of all goods" (*Politics* 1252a). The first point regarding the uniformity or homogeneity of Plato's imagined city was also noted by Aristotle, who, in his critical comments, goes so far as to say that "a city which becomes more and more unitary eventually ceases to a *polis* at all" (*Politics* 1261a). Compare *The Politics of Aristotle*, trans. Ernest Barker (Oxford: Clarendon, 1946), 1, 40, 120, 126; and Fred Dallmayr, *In Search of the Good Life: Some Exemplary Voices* (Lexington: University Press of Kentucky, 2007).

4. Economic Policy Institute, "The State of Working in America," as reported by Harold Meyerson, "In the Taxing Debate, Find Out Where the Money Is," *South Bend Tribune*, April 22, 2011. Relying on data from the U.S. Commerce Department, Meyerson also points to the increasing tendency of "outsourcing" labor: "U.S. multinationals eliminated the positions of 2.9 million American employees during the past decade, while adding 2.4 million in other lands." Compare in this context also Larry M. Bartels, *Unequal Democracy: The Political Economy of the New Gilded Age* (Princeton, NJ: Princeton University Press, 2008), and Joe Soss, Jacob S. Hacker, and Suzanne Mettler, eds., *Remaking America: Democracy and Public Policy in an Age of Inequality* (New York: Russell Sage Foundation, 2007).

5. Aristotle, *Politics* 1295a24, 1295b29; Barker, trans., *The Politics of Aristotle*, 180, 182. See Fred Dallmayr, *Post-Liberalism: Recovering a Shared World* (New York: Oxford University Press, 2019), 45–66.

6. See United Nations, *Human Development Report 1999* (Oxford: Oxford University Press, 1999); World Bank, *World Development Report 2000* (Oxford: Oxford University Press, 2000); also Richard Falk, *Predatory Globalization: A Critique* (Cambridge: Polity Press, 1999); and Fred Dallmayr, "Globalization and Inequality: A Plea for Global Justice," in *Dialogue among Civilizations: Some Exemplary Voices* (New York: Palgrave Macmillan, 2002), 67–84.

7. Human Development Report 2010, *The Real Wealth of Nations: Pathways to Human Development, 20th Anniversary Edition,* https://read.un-ilibrary.org /economic-and-social-development/human-development-report-2010_e5a0500a -en#page1.

8. See Human Development Report 2010, http://hdr.undp.org/en/reports /global/hdr2010 (Summary and Overview). For additional literature on the grim effects of unregulated financial capitalism, see, e.g., Richard D. Wolff, *Capitalism Hits the Fan: The Global Economic Meltdown and What to Do About It* (Northampton, MA: Olive Branch Press, 2011); Angus Sibley, *The "Poisoned Spring" of Economic Libertarianism* (Washington, DC: Pax Romana, 2011); and for some remedies, see Gar Alperovitz, *America beyond Capitalism: Reclaiming Our Wealth, Our Liberty, and Our Democracy* (Hoboken, NJ: Wiley, 2005); and Herman E. Daley and John B. Cobb, Jr., *For the Common Good: Redirecting the Economy toward Community, the Environment, and a Sustainable Future,* 2nd ed. (Boston: Beacon Press, 1994).

9. Human Development Report 2010. The report in this context pays tribute to Karl Polanyi's "brilliant exposition more than sixty years ago of the myth of the self-regulating market—the idea that markets could exist in a political and institutional vacuum. Generally, markets are very bad at ensuring the provision of public goods, such as security, stability, health, and education. . . . Without complementary societal and state action, markets can be weak on environmental sustainability, creating the conditions for environmental degradation, even for such disasters as mud flows in Java and oil spills in the Gulf of Mexico." Compare Karl Polanyi, *The Great Transformation: The Political and Economic Origins of Our Time* (1944; Boston: Beacon Press, 1957).

10. Jonathan Sacks, *The Dignity of Difference: How to Avoid the Clash of Civilizations* (London: Continuum, 2002), 113–16. Referring to Human Development Reports and other available data, Sacks states, "By the end of the millennium, the top fifth of the world's population had 86% of the world's GDP while the bottom fifth had just 1%. The assets of the world's three richest billionaires were more than the combined wealth of the 600 million inhabitants of the least developed countries" (29). These and similar findings support his complaint that global capitalism represents a system of "immense power" whose effects in terms of maldistribution constitute "a scar on the face of humanity" (15, 28). Compare also Fred Dallmayr, "The Dignity of Difference: A Salute to Jonathan Sacks," in *Small Wonder: Global Power and Its Discontents* (Lanham, MD: Rowman & Littlefield, 2005), 209–17.

11. Sacks, *The Dignity of Difference,* 32, 78. Compare also Alasdair MacIntyre, *After Virtue: A Study in Moral Theory,* 2nd ed. (Notre Dame, IN: University of Notre Dame Press, 1984), and Fred Dallmayr and Edward Demenchonok, eds., *A World Beyond Global Disorder: The Courage of Hope* (Newcastle upon Tyne: Cambridge Scholars Press, 2017).

12. See Sacks, *The Dignity of Difference,* 136, 140–41; Martha Nussbaum, *Not For Profit: Why Democracy Needs the Humanities* (Princeton, NJ: Princeton Univer-

sity Press, 2010), 44–46. Compare also Nussbaum, *Cultivating Humanity: A Classical Defense of Reform in Liberal Education* (Cambridge, MA: Harvard University Press, 1997); and Fred Dallmayr, *In Search of the Good Life: A Pedagogy for Troubled Times* (Lexington: University Press of Kentucky, 2007).

13. Sacks, *The Dignity of Difference*, 17–18, 21.

14. Aristotle, *Politics* 1274b32; Barker, trans., *The Politics of Aristotle*, 93.

15. Iris Marion Young, "Polity and Group Difference: A Critique of the Ideal of Universal Citizenship," in *Theorizing Citizenship*, ed. Ronald Beiner (Albany: SUNY Press, 1995), 175–76, 181–84. Compare also Young, *Justice and the Politics of Difference* (Princeton, NJ: Princeton University Press, 1990).

16. Charles Taylor, "Why Democracy Needs Patriotism," in Martha Nussbaum, *For Love of Country?*, ed. Joshua Cohen (Boston: Beacon Press, 1996), 121.

17. See Richard Falk, "An Emergent Matrix of Citizenship: Complex, Uneven, and Fluid," in *Global Citizenship: A Critical Introduction*, ed. Nigel Dower and John Williams (New York: Routledge, 2002), 27–28; also Christian van den Anker, "Global Justice, Global Institutions and Global Citizenship," in ibid., 167–68.

18. Richard Falk, "The World Order between Inter-State Law and the Law of Humanity: The Role of Civil Society Institutions," in *Cosmopolitan Democracy: An Agenda for a New World Order*, ed. Daniele Archibugi and David Held (Cambridge: Polity Press, 1995), 163–79.

19. David Held, "Democracy and the New International Order," in Archibugi and Held, eds., *Cosmopolitan Democracy*, 111, 116. See also Held, *Cosmopolitanism: Ideals and Realities* (Cambridge: Polity Press, 2010).

20. Immanuel Kant, *Perpetual Peace: A Philosophical Sketch*, in *Kant's Political Writings*, ed. Hans Reiss (Cambridge: Cambridge University Press, 1970), 93–130.

21. In Sacks's words: "We are not in sight of a global contract whereby nation-states agree to sacrifice part of their sovereignty to create a form of world governance. There is, however, an alternative, namely a global *covenant*. Covenants are more foundational than contracts. . . . Covenants are beginnings, acts of moral engagement. . . . There is at least a starting point for a global covenant in which the nations of the world collectively express their commitment not only to human rights but also to human responsibilities, and not merely a political, but also an economic, environmental, moral and cultural conception of the common good, constructed on the twin foundations of shared humanity and respect for diversity" (Sacks, *The Dignity of Difference*, 205–6).

CHAPTER TWO. Continuity and Historical Change

1. For an elaboration of this point, see Fred Dallmayr, "Religion and the World: The Quest for Justice and Peace," in *Integral Pluralism: Beyond Culture Wars* (Lexington: University of Press of Kentucky, 2010), 85–101.

2. See in this context Fred Dallmayr, "A Pedagogy of the Heart: Saint Bona-venture's Spiritual Itinerary," in *In Search of the Good Life: A Pedagogy for Troubled Times* (Lexington: University Press of Kentucky, 2007), 23–39; Dallmayr, "Wise Ig-norance: Nicolaus of Cusa's Search for Truth," *In Search of the Good Life*, 58–79; and Dallmayr, "Nature and Spirit: Schelling," in *Return to Nature: An Ecological Counterhistory* (Lexington: University Press of Kentucky, 2011), 11–32. I am not sure to which extent what is called "transcendental Thomism" escapes the lure of possessive rationalism.

3. See Fred Dallmayr, "Rule of, by, and for the People: For an Apophatic Democracy," in *Democracy to Come: Politics as Relational Praxis* (New York: Oxford University Press, 2017), 22–41; and Dallmayr, "Apophatic Community: Yannaras on Relational Being," *Comparative Philosophy* 10 (2019): 3–17.

4. See, especially, Fred Dallmayr, *The Other Heidegger* (Ithaca, NY: Cornell University Press, 1993); Dallmayr, *Between Freiburg and Frankfurt: Toward a Criti-cal Ontology* (Amherst: University of Massachusetts Press, 1991); Dallmayr, "Hei-degger on *Macht* and *Machenschaft*," *Continental Philosophy Review* 34 (2001): 247–67; Dallmayr, "Letting-Be Politically: Heidegger on Freedom and Solidarity," in *Freedom and Solidarity: Toward New Beginnings* (Lexington: University Press of Kentucky, 2016), 39–64.

5. See Martin Heidegger, *Breiträge zur Philosophie (Vom Ereignis)*, in *Gesam-tausgabe*, Vol. 65 (Frankfurt am Main: Klostermann, 1989); and Heidegger, *Das Ereignis*, in *Gesamtausgabe*, Vol. 71 (Frankfurt am Main: Klostermann, 2009).

6. Compare, e.g., John Caputo, *Heidegger and Aquinas: An Essay on Over-coming Metaphysics* (New York: Fordham University Press, 1982); also John F. X. Knasar, "A Heideggerian Critique of Aquinas and a Gilsonian Reply," *The Thomist* 58 (1994): 15–39; Robert E. Wood, "Aquinas and Heidegger: Personal Esse, Truth and Imagination," in *Postmodernism and Christian Philosophy*, ed. Roman T. Cia-palo (Notre Dame, IN: Jacques Maritain Center, 1997), 268–80.

7. Basically, for Heidegger, God is not an object, not even the biggest, most powerful, and most adorable object. Compare in this context John Macquarrie, *Hei-degger and Christianity* (London: Continuum, 1999); Benjamin Vedder, *Heidegger's Philosophy of Religion* (Pittsburgh, PA: Duquesne University Press, 2006); Richard Kearney, *The God Who May Be: A Hermeneutics of Religion* (Bloomington: Indiana University Press, 2001); John Caputo, "Heidegger and Theology," in *The Cambridge Companion to Heidegger*, ed. Charles B. Guignon (Cambridge: Cambridge Univer-sity Press, 2006), 326–44; and Martin Heidegger, *The Phenomenology of Religious Life* (Bloomington: Indiana University Press, 2004): "The love of God to human be-ings is what is fundamental not theoretical knowledge" (71).

8. See Jacques Maritain, "Integral Humanism and the Crisis of Modern Times," *The Review of Politics* 1 (1939): 1, 8, 15, 16.

9. See Raimon Panikkar, *The Rhythm of Being: The Gifford Lectures* (Mary-knoll, NY: Orbis Books, 2010). As Paul F. Knitter states in the title of one of his

works: Knitter, *Without Buddha I Could Not Be a Christian* (London: Oneworld Publications, 2009). I have explored the attractiveness of Buddhism and Asian thought for some Western theologians (especially Paul Tillich, Raimon Panikkar, and Thomas Merton) in Fred Dallmayr, *Spiritual Guides: Pathfinders in the Desert* (Notre Dame, IN: University of Notre Press, 2017).

10. His comments reach greater depth when he writes that "racism is existentially bound to demonic para-theism. Because in its reaction against individualism and its thirst for communion, it seeks this communion in human animality which, separated from the spirit, is no more than a biological inferno" (Maritain, "Integral Humanism and the Crisis of Modern Times," 9–11, 17).

11. Maritain, "Integral Humanism and the Crisis of Modern Times," 2, 7. For a while, Jacques Derrida was leaning toward a radical antihumanism. See Derrida, "The Ends of Man," in *Margins of Philosophy*, trans. Alain Bass (Chicago: University of Chicago Press, 1983), 111–36. Compare also Michel Foucault, *The Order of Things: An Archaeology of the Human Sciences* (New York: Random House, 1970).

12. Martin Heidegger, "Letter on Humanism," in *Martin Heidegger: Basic Writings*, ed. David F. Krell (New York: Harper & Row, 1977), 193–242. See also Emmanuel Levinas, *Humanism of the Other*, trans. Nidra Poller (1972; Urbana: University of Illinois Press, 2003); and Karl Barth, *The Humanity of God*, trans. John N. Thomas and Thomas Wieser (Atlanta: John Knox Press, 1960).

13. See Charles Taylor, *Sources of the Self: The Making of Modern Identity* (Cambridge, MA: Harvard University Press, 1989); Taylor, *The Malaise of Modernity* (Concord, ON: Anansi, 1991); and Taylor, *A Secular Age* (Cambridge, MA: Harvard University Press, 2007).

14. See Fred Dallmayr, "Humanizing Humanity: For a Post-Secular Humanism," in *Against Apocalypse: Recovering Humanity's Wholeness* (Lanham, MD: Lexington Books, 2016), 75–86; Dallmayr, "Who Are We Now? For an 'Other' Humanism," in *The Promise of Democracy: Political Agency and Transformation* (Albany: State University of New York Press, 2010), 135–54; Dallmayr, "Humanizing Humanity: Education for World Citizenship," in *Being in the World: Dialogue and Cosmopolis* (Lexington: University Press of Kentucky, 2013), 59–71.

15. Compare Fred Dallmayr, "Post-Secular Faith: Toward a Religion of Service," *Revista de Ciencia Politica* 28 (2008): 3–15; Dallmayr, "Rethinking Secularism (with Raimon Panikkar)," *The Review of Politics* 61 (1999): 715–35.

16. On "postliberalism," see, especially, John Gray, *Post-liberalism: Studies in Political Thought* (London: Routledge, 1993); Ruth Abbey, "Charles Taylor as a Postliberal Theorist of Politics," in *Perspectives on the Philosophy of Charles Taylor*, ed. Arto Laitinen and Nicholas H. Smith (Helsinki: Societas Philosophica Fennica, 2002), 149–61; John Milbank and Adrian Pabst, *The Politics of Virtue: Post-Liberalism and the Human Future* (London: Rowman & Littlefield International, 2016); and Fred Dallmayr, *Post-Liberalism: Recovering a Shared World* (New York: Oxford University Press, 2019).

17. Maritain, "Integral Humanism and the Crisis of Our Time," 7–8, 15–16.

18. Jacques Maritain, *Integral Humanism: Temporal and Spiritual Problems of a New Christendom*, trans. Joseph W. Evans (Notre Dame, IN: University of Notre Dame Press, 1973), 28, 93.

19. Maritain, *Integral Humanism*, 118–23.

20. In Maritain's words: "I hold that while awaiting the 'beyond history' in which the kingdom of God will be accomplished in the glory of full manifestation, the Church is already the kingdom of God in the order called *spiritual* and in the state of pilgrimage and crucifixion, and that the world, the order called *temporal*, this world enclosed in history, is a divided and religious domain—at once of God, of man, and of the Prince of this world" (Maritain, *Integral Humanism*, 120). This formulation puts some pressure on Panikkar's notion of "sacred secularity," which is discussed in chapter 3.

21. Maritain, *Integral Humanism*, 133.

22. Ibid., 172–73. The stress on "minimal unity" shows that Maritain was as far removed from being a reactionary medievalist as he was from being a supporter of the extreme French nationalism of the Action Française of Charles Maurras. On the latter point, see, especially, Bernard E. Doering, *Jacques Maritain and the French Catholic Intellectuals* (Notre Dame, IN: University of Notre Dame Press, 1983), 6–36.

23. Maritain, *Integral Humanism*, 201.

24. Jacques Maritain, *Christianity and Democracy; and the Rights of Man and the Natural Law*, trans. Doris C. Anton (San Francisco: Ignatius Press, 2011), 41, 99–100.

CHAPTER THREE.   Sacred Secularity and Prophetism

1. See, especially, Raimon Panikkar, *Worship and Secular Man* (Maryknoll, NY: Orbis Books, 1973.

2. See, especially, Raimon Panikkar, *The Cosmotheandric Experience*, ed. Scott Eastham (Maryknoll, NY: Orbis Books, 1993).

3. See Raimon Panikkar, *The Rhythm of Being: The Gifford Lectures* (Maryknoll, NY: Orbis Books, 2010). Compare also Fred Dallmayr, "A Secular Age? Reflections on Taylor and Panikkar," in *Being in the World: Dialogue and Cosmopolis* (Lexington: University Press of Kentucky, 2015), 119–50. On the "ek-static" character of human existence, see especially Martin Heidegger, "Letter on Humanism" (1946), in *Heidegger: Basic Writings*, ed. David F. Krell (New York: Harper & Row, 1977), 203–7.

4. Panikkar, *Cultural Disarmament: The Way to Peace*, trans. Robert R. Barr (Louisville, KY: Westminster John Knox Press, 1995), 22–23, 83, 88–94. For the statement "the desert grows" see Friedrich Nietzsche, *Thus Spoke Zarathustra*, in *The Portable Nietzsche*, ed. Walter Kaufmann (New York: Viking Press, 1968), 417.

5. Panikkar, *Cultural Disarmament*, 65. See Dante, *Inferno* 3.5–6. For Heidegger's invocation of Hölderlin's phrase, compare Martin Heidegger, "The Question Concerning Technology," in Krell, ed., *Heidegger: Basic Writings*, 310, 316.

6. For the reference to fullness, or *pleroma*, see Raimon Panikkar, *The Intra-Religious Dialogue* (New York: Paulist Press, 1978) 82. Regarding the ultimate anchoring of hope or promise in reality or some sense of "being," compare his statements: "Peace can only be a harmony of the very reality in which we share when we find ourselves in a situation of receptiveness by virtue of not having placed obstacles in the way of the rhythm of reality, of the Spirit, of the ultimate structure of the universe"; "In the last analysis, only that which *is* [ontologically] enables us to measure, think, judge *what* is. What *has to be* is subordinate to that which *is*. But this *is*, understood as synonymous with *being*, also means *becoming* and '*oughting*' *to be*" (see Pannikar, *Cultural Disarmament*, 10, 14).

7. Panikkar, *Cultural Disarmament*, 91. See also Paul Knitter, "Cosmic Confidence or Preferential Option?," in *The Intercultural Challenge of Raimon Panikkar*, ed. Joseph Prabhu (Maryknoll, NY: Orbis Books, 1996), 187, 189, 195. In a critical vein, Knitter invokes the suspicion of David Tracy that holistic pluralism can easily lead to the temptation "to enjoy the pleasure of difference without ever committing oneself to any particular vision of resistance or hope"; see Tracy, *Plurality and Ambiguity: Hermeneutics, Religion, Hope* (New York: Harper & Row, 1987), 90.

8. Raimon Panikkar, "A Self-Critical Dialogue," in Prabhu, ed., *The Intercultural Challenge of Raimon Panikkar*, 276–77, 281–83. He adds: "The Vedic notion *rta* or cosmic order may be a homeomorphic equivalent of what we are saying" (281).

9. Raimon Panikkar, *Blessed Simplicity: The Monk as Universal Archetype* (New York: Seabury Press, 1982), 10–12, 14.

10. Ibid., 98. Compare also Fred Dallmayr, *Mindfulness and Letting-Be: On Engaged Thinking and Acting* (Lanham, MD: Lexington Books, 2014).

11. Panikkar, *Blessed Simplicity*, 16.

CHAPTER FOUR. Apophatic Community

1. Martin Heidegger, *Aufenthalte* (Frankfurt am Main: Klostermann, 1989), 6. The letter of July 16, 1957, was written to Erhart Kästner; see *Martin Heidegger—Erhart Kästner Briefwechsel*, ed. H.W. Petzet (Frankfurt am Main: Klostermann, 1986), no. 7.

2. See Christos Yannaras, *On the Absence and Unknowability of God: Heidegger and the Areopagite*, trans. Hazalamtos Ventis (London: T&T Clark International, 2005), 17.

3. Ibid., 21. See also Martin Heidegger, "Der Europaeische Nihilismus", in *Nietzsche*, 2nd ed. (Pfullingen: Neske 1961), 2:31–256, and for an English translation:

Nietzsche, Nihilism, ed. David F. Krell (San Francisco: Harper & Row, 1987), "European Nihilism," 4:3–250.

4. Yannaras, *On the Absence,* 22–24.

5. Ibid., 25–27, 30, 32–34. Yannaras adds (a bit rashly): "The logical conclusion of the 'monism of the subject,' inflicted on European philosophy by Descartes [and his followers], is not God, but the absolutized subject itself, the 'superman' (*Übermensch*)" (24).

6. Ibid., 28–29.

7. Ibid., 65–67, 69. See also Pseudo-Dionysius, *On the Divine Names,* 1.1, in Migne, *Patrologia Graeca,* vol. 3, 588B; and Maximus, *Scholia on the Divine Names,* in Migne, *Patrologia Graeca,* vol. 4, 256A. On Dionysius, see Andrew Louth, *Denys the Areopagite* (London: Continuum, 2001).

8. Yannaras, *On the Absence,* 51, 72. See also Heidegger, *Identität und Differenz* (Pfullingen: Neske, 1957), 65.

9. Yannaras, *On the Absence,* 71.

10. Ibid., 84–86, 104–7. He adds, summing up his findings: "The whole ecclesial life of the Greek East is articulated around the axis and aim of apophatic and erotic knowledge of God. Iconography and hymnology make accessible to the senses this theology of beauty, with the art of referential transition to the 'archetype' of personal immediacy with what is celebrated in icons and hymns" (109). Compare in this context also Christos Yannaras, *Elements of Faith: An Introduction to Orthodox Theology,* trans. Keith Schram (Edinburgh: T&T Clark, 1991).

11. Andrew Louth, "Introduction," in Yannaras, *On the Absence,* 7. See also Christos Yannaras, *Person and Eros,* trans. Norman Russell (Brookline, MA: Holy Cross Orthodox Press, 2007), 5; Malcolm Bradshaw, review of *I elevtheria tou ithous,* by Christos Yannaras, *Eastern Churches Review* 5, no. 2 (1973): 205.

12. Yannaras, *Person and Eros,* 6–8.

13. Ibid., 9–11.

14. Ibid., 17–19.

15. Ibid., 19–20.

16. The text contains a longer section titled "The Fall and Nothingness," but it does not reach the level of Heideggerian "nihilation." This is evident in passages such as the following: "Nothingness constitutes a *personal* potentiality of existence because it is the denial of the mode of existence which the person alone can attain (or refuse to attain). It is the opposite of *Kenosis.* . . . Sin is the moral content of nothingness as an existential fact, the measure of the annihilation of existential fulfillment. . . . Nothingness hence may be defined in the end not as a concept but as a moral reality, a confirmation of the existential truth of the person, the ability of a human being to say No to God—nullifying but not annihilating the truth of his or her personal existence" (see Yannaras, *Person and Eros,* 273, 292–93).

17. Yannaras, *Person and Eros,* 118–22.

18. Christos Yannaras, *The Freedom of Morality,* trans. Elizabeth Briere (Chestwood, NY: St. Vladimir's Seminary Press, 1996), 14–15, 20–21, 23. Yannaras observes

sternly: "Any systematic pursuit of 'improvement' in man through his own individual will and effort, of taming his nature through his own powers, is condemned by nature itself. Man on his own cannot cease to be what he 'naturally' is. . . . This is also why every anthropocentric, autonomous morality ends up as a fruitless insistence on an utterly inadequate human self-sufficiency, an expression of man's fall" (114).

19. Ibid., 30–31, 37, 52–53.

20. See Christos Yannaras, *The Church in Post-Communist Europe* (Berkeley, CA: Inter-Orthodox Press, 2003), 21–30.

21. Christos Yannaras, *Postmodern Metaphysics*, trans. Norman Russell (Brookline, MA: Holy Cross Orthodox Press, 2004), 1–2.

22. Hostility to Western-style modernity is not limited to non-Western countries. One can find similar denunciations also in the West. One may recall here the "antimodernist" doctrine in the Catholic Church in the early part of the last century. Compare also Allan Bloom, *The Closing of the American Mind* (New York: Simon and Schuster, 1987), and Patrick Deneen, *Why Liberalism Failed* (New Haven, CT: Yale University Press, 2018).

23. Daniel Payne, *The Revival of Political Hesychasm in Contemporary Orthodox Thought: The Political Hesychasm of John S. Romanides and Christos Yannaras* (Lanham, MD: Lexington Books, 2011), 252–53.

24. The classic text in this domain is Max Horkheimer and Theodor W. Adorno, *Dialectic of Enlightenment*, trans. John Cumming (New York: Seabury Press, 1972).

25. See Miroslav Volf, *Exclusion and Embrace: A Theological Exploration of Identity, Otherness and Reconciliation* (Nashville, TN: Abingdon Press, 1996).

26. Payne, *The Revival of Political Hesychasm in Contemporary Orthodox Thought*, 263. Compare also Fred Dallmayr, "Rule of, by and for the People: For an Apophatic Democracy," in *Democracy to Come: Politics as Relational Praxis* (New York: Oxford University Press, 2017), 22–41; and Dallmayr, *Gemeinschaft und Differenz: Wege in die Zukunft* (Freiburg-im-Breisgau: Verlag Karl Abber, 2018).

27. Christos Yannaras, "Apophatik und politisches Handeln," in *Gottes Zukunft—Zukunft der Welt: Festschrift für Jürgen Moltmann zum 60. Geburtstag*, ed. Hermann Deuser et al. (Munich: Kaiser Verlag, 1986), 374.

CHAPTER FIVE.   A Heart and Mind Unity

1. Rajmohan Gandhi, "Understanding Gujarat," *Just Commentary* 2, no. 5 (2002): 7; reprinted from *The Hindu*, March 12, 2002. The reference to Rama was prompted by the fact that the train attacked near Ahmedabad was returning from Ayodhya, the supposed hometown of Lord Rama and the site of a planned temple in his honor (involving the destruction of a Muslim mosque on the same site). The last phrase is itself a "healing" phrase since the name of Rama is used in conjunction with "almighty" and "compassionate," which are epithets of Allah.

2. Margaret Chatterjee, *Gandhi's Religious Thought* (Notre Dame, IN: University of Notre Dame Press, 1983), 120. Chatterjee quotes C. F. Andrews's opinion that Gandhi was "a saint of action rather than of contemplation" (1), a view that probably underestimates the reflective quality of Gandhi's writings and utterances.

3. Muhammad Mujeeb, *The Indian Muslims* (London: Allen & Unwin, 1967), 167.

4. Mohandas K. Gandhi, *An Autobiography, or The Story of My Experiments with Truth*, trans. Mahadev Desai (Ahmedabad: Navajivan Publishing House, 1927), 28. See also Sheila McDonough, *Gandhi's Responses to Islam* (New Delhi: Printworld, 1994), 5, 7, 12.

5. *The Collected Works of Mahatma Gandhi* (Delhi: Government of India, 1967), 2:72.

6. McDonough, *Gandhi's Responses to Islam*, 21. She adds: "Gandhi often used Muslim and Hindu imagery in this way because his fundamental assertion was that the symbols from the two religious traditions both made sense in the immediate context of the suffering of the Indians in South Africa. . . . Gandhi believed that the essential struggle of Muhammad's lifetime, the struggle to create a new form of civilization, could be equated with the mystical struggle of [Lord] Rama against Ravana as portrayed in the epic, the *Ramayana* . . . . In this respect, Gandhi was a follower of the *bhakti* and *Sufi* traditions in which the importance of religious symbols lies in the illumination the symbols may awake in the hearts of believers" (27). See also S. Abid Husain, *Gandhiji and Communal Unity* (Bombay: Orient Longmans, 1969), 57.

7. McDonough writes: "Gandhi hoped to win the support of these Muslims by himself joining the *Khilafat* movement, and becoming one of its organizers. He did not get much strong support from the other Hindu leaders in India for this activity" (see McDonough, *Gandhi's Responses to Islam*, 42). She also mentions that he used again vocabulary from both religions to promote his efforts (46–48). Thus he invoked the martyrdom of Hasan and Husain, the grandsons of the Prophet, as equivalents to the Hindu notion of *tapascharya*, meaning the power of self-suffering and self-purification. On another occasion, he compared the Indian struggle for independence from England with the Prophet's exodus (*hijra*) from Mecca to Medina.

8. McDonough, *Gandhi's Responses to Islam*, 49–55. See also *The Collected Works of Mahatma Gandhi*, 19:153.

9. Assessing the long-range significance of the *Khilafat* movement, Gail Minault remarks: "The national alliance disintegrated, but Muslim community self-consciousness, with or without the *Khilafat* to symbolize it, had become a factor in Indian politics. . . . The alternative structures which developed as the vehicles for Muslim consciousness during the *Khilafat* movement provided the techniques, and much of the personnel, for the development of a specifically Muslim nationalism in the subcontinent later"; see Minault, *The Khilafat Movement: Religious Symbolism and Political Mobilization in India* (New York: Columbia University Press, 1982), 212.

10. B. R. Nanda, *Mahatma Gandhi: A Biography* (New York: Barron's Educational Series, 1965), 238.

11. McDonough, *Gandhi's Responses to Islam*, 83, 86, 94–95. See also Abdul Wahid Khan, *India Wins Freedom: The Other Side* (Karachi: Pakistan Education Publishers, 1961), 253.

12. Mushirul Hasan, *A Nationalist Conscience* (New Delhi: Manohar, 1987), 93.

13. S. Abid Husain, *The Destiny of Indian Muslims* (Bombay: Asia Publishing House, 1965), 118; C. Chaudhury, *Gandhi and His Contemporaries* (New Delhi: Sterling Publishers, 1972), 136. Summarizing the motives of affection, Roland E. Miller writes: "We can suggest that Muslim trust of Gandhi was based on four things: his respect for religion and religious commitment; his regard for Muslims as full members of what he once called India's 'joint family'; his peace-loving nature; and his honest friendship"; see Miller, "Indian Muslim Critiques of Gandhi," in *Indian Critiques of Gandhi*, ed. Harold Coward (Albany: SUNY Press, 2003), 194.

14. Exemplifying Muslim suspicions, Muhammad Ali (his one-time friend) in 1930 charged Gandhi's program with being "not a covenant for complete independence of India but of making seventy million Indian Muslims dependent on the Hindu Mahasabha." On his part, the president of the Hindu Mahasabha, V. D. Savarkar, declared in 1938 that the Gandhi-inspired National Congress "has been, since its inception down to this day, a Hindu body"; see Mushirul Hasan, *A Nationalist Conscience*, 173; Mushir U. Haq, *Muslim Politics in India* (Meerut: Meenakshi Prakashan, 1976), 135.

15. Muhammad Mujeeb, *Dr. Zakir Husain: A Biography* (New Delhi: National Book Trust, 1972), 236; quoted in McDonough, *Gandhi's Responses to Islam*, 69.

16. Gandhi stated at one point: "The Moplahs have sinned against God and have suffered grievously for it. Let the Hindus also remember that they have not allowed the opportunity for revenge to pass by" (*The Collected Works of Mahatma Gandhi*, 23:514). See also Roland E. Miller, *The Mappila Muslims of Kerala*, rev. ed. (Madras: Orient Longman, 1992); and Miller, "Indian Muslim Critiques of Gandhi," in Coward, ed., *Indian Critiques of Gandhi*, 202–5.

17. Quoted in Miller, *The Mappila Muslims of Kerala*, 130.

18. See Judith Brown, *Gandhi's Rise to Power: Indian Politics, 1915–1922* (Cambridge: Cambridge University Press, 1972), 331; M. Zaidi, ed., *Congress Presidential Addresses* (New Delhi: Indian Institute of Applied Political Research, 1989), 4:137. The final qualification can be gathered from his additional comment: "In spite of my utter abhorrence of violence I will say with all deliberation that on the Day of Judgment I would rather stand before God's White Throne guilty of all this violence than to have to answer for the unspeakable sin of so cowardly a surrender" (138).

19. See Bhikhu Parekh, *Gandhi's Political Philosophy: A Critical Examination* (Notre Dame, IN: University of Notre Dame Press, 1989), 140, 147; and Raghavan Iyer, *The Moral and Political Writings of Mahatma Gandhi* (Oxford: Clarendon, 1987), vol. 2, pt. 4.

20. Zaidi, ed., *Congress Presidential Addresses*, 4:136.

21. McDonough writes: "Jinnah was negotiating as a lawyer representing his clients, most of the Muslims, who did not trust the majority community to treat them justly and fairly once the British were gone. . . . Jinnah saw Gandhi as a fellow lawyer who was trying to fog up the issues of drawing up a mutually satisfactory contract. A lawyer trying to draw up a contract is not interested in 'heart-unity' with the lawyer from the other side" (see McDonough, *Gandhi's Responses to Islam*, 88). Compare also Stanley Wolpert, *Jinnah of Pakistan* (New York: Oxford University Press, 1984), esp. 230–36; S. K. Majumdar, *Jinnah and Gandhi: Their Role in India's Quest for Freedom* (Calcutta: Mukhopadhyay, 1966).

22. McDonough oversimplifies matters considerably when she presents Jinnah simply as a liberal modernist: "He was not interested in keeping alive and recreating some model society from the remote past, but of moving into the future to create new forms of life." She even compares Jinnah's vision of Pakistan with the Prophet's exodus (*hijra*) from Mecca to Medina, "from the known into the unknown" (see McDonough, *Gandhi's Responses to Islam*, 91).

23. Parekh, *Gandhi's Political Philosophy*, 173. He adds: "The British brought liberal political culture to India but, thanks to the inherent logic of colonialism, corrupted it by embodying it in non-liberal representative institutions" (173–74).

24. Parekh's account of these developments is instructive: "Jinnah's great contribution lay in defining the Muslims as a nation, articulating Muslim nationalism in easily intelligible idioms and mobilizing the masses behind it. . . . [By 1946, however] he radically changed his tune and began to speak the secular language of the modern state. . . . He evidently used the ideological language of nationalism to legitimize and realize his political objectives. Once they were secured and the arduous task of running the state began, the ideological baggage became a grave liability and had to be abandoned at the first opportunity" (see Parekh, *Gandhi's Political Philosophy*, 175, 182); also see M. A. Karandikar, *Islam: India's Transition to Modernity* (Delhi: Eastern Publishers, 1961), 281–82.

25. Parekh, *Gandhi's Political Philosophy*, 121.

26. B. R. Nanda, *Gandhi and His Critics* (Delhi: Oxford University Press, 1985), 103.

27. Gandhi, foreword to *The Sayings of Muhammad*, ed. Sir Abdullah Suhrawardy (New York: Carol Publishing Group, 1990), 7; quoted in McDonough, *Gandhi's Responses to Islam*, 1.

28. Chatterjee, *Gandhi's Religious Thought*, 154, 181.

29. McDonough, *Gandhi's Responses to Islam*, 27–29, 71, 84.

30. See *The Collected Works of Mahatma Gandhi*, 24:153; Abdul Wahid Khan, *India Wins Freedom*, 269. Quoted in McDonough, *Gandhi's Responses to Islam*, 53, 95–96.

31. Parekh, *Gandhi's Political Philosophy*, 123. In a similar vein, McDonough remarks: "As the government of the new secular India swung into action, he [Gandhi]

would most probably have become both a loyal citizen and a hard-working critic. . . .
He would have been an unceasing voice of protest within the structures of a democratic state" (see McDonough, *Gandhi's Responses to Islam*, 93). Gandhi's views on
this matter were echoed by Michel Foucault: "Nothing is more inconsistent than a
political regime indifferent to truth; but nothing is more dangerous than a political
system that claims to lay down the truth. The function of 'telling the truth' must
not take the form of law"; see Foucault, *Politics, Philosophy, Culture*, ed. L. Kritzman
(New York: Routledge, 1990), 43.

32. Quoted in Parekh, *Gandhi's Political Philosophy*, 146. The notion of "heart-
and-mind" is familiar from the Confucian tradition (*hsiao*); it also resonates distantly with Erasmus's motto of *eruditio et pietas* (learning and piety).

33. See Rajmohan Gandhi, "Understanding Gujarat," *Just Commentary* 2, no. 5
(2002): 8; also Rajmohan Gandhi, *Eight Lives: A Study of the Hindu–Muslim Encounter* (Albany: SUNY Press, 1986), ix. For some empirical evidence that interreligious or intercommunal engagement can curb social violence, compare Ashutosh
Varshney, *Ethnic Conflict and Civic Life: Hindus and Muslims in India* (New York:
Oxford University Press, 2002).

CHAPTER SIX. Five Relations Plus One

1. For an eloquent tribute to this tendency, compare Husserl's statement:
"To bring latent reason to the understanding of its own possibilities and thus to
bring to insight the possibility of metaphysics as a true possibility—this is the only
way to put metaphysics or universal philosophy on the strenuous road to realization.
It is the only way to decide whether the *telos* which was inborn in European humanity at the birth of Greek philosophy . . . whether this *telos* is merely a factual, historical delusion . . . or whether Greek humanity was not rather the first breakthrough to
what is essential to humanity as such, its *entelechy*"; see Edmund Husserl, *The Crisis
of European Sciences and Transcendental Phenomenology: An Introduction to Phenomenological Philosophy*, trans. David Carr (Evanston, IL: Northwestern University
Press, 1970), 15.

2. Aristotle, *Politics* 1252a1, 1253a15-16; quoted from *The Politics of Aristotle*,
ed. and trans. Ernest Barker (Oxford: Clarendon, 1946), 1, 7. As Barker elaborates in
his introduction, if Aristotle "speaks of the growth of the household into the village
and of villages in the state [*polis*], he does not rest his belief in the natural character
of political society on the simple fact of such growth. . . . Indeed, it would seem that
Aristotle, true to the general Greek conception of politics as a sphere of conscious
creation in which legislators had always been active, believed in the conscious construction of the *polis*. . . . There is no contradiction in such a sentence; for there is no
contradiction between the immanent impulses of human nature and the conscious
art which is equally, or even more, a part of the same human nature" (xlix–l).

3. Aristotle, *Politics* 1252a2, 1279a9-11; in Barker, ed. and trans., *The Politics of Aristotle*, 1–2, 112. That even in Aristotle's time, this maxim carried a critical edge is revealed by his comment: "Today the case is different: moved by the profits to be derived from office and the handling of public property, men want to hold office continuously" (112). In our own time, the critical edge emerges even more sharply.

4. Aristotle, *Politics* 1252b6, 1253b1, 1254b6-7, 1255b12, 1259b2-3; in Barker, ed. and trans., *The Politics of Aristotle*, 4, 8, 13, 17, 33.

5. Aristotle, *Politics* 1252b4, 1275a6, 1275b12, 1295b7; see Barker, ed. and trans., *The Politics of Aristotle*, 3, 93, 95, 181. Aristotle adds at another point: "The same line of thought is followed in regard to nobility as well as slavery. Greeks regard themselves as noble not only in their own country, but absolutely and in all places; but they regard barbarians as noble only [or at best] in their own country— thus assessing that there is one sort of nobility and freedom which is absolute or universal, and another which is only relative" (16).

6. For the above account, see Barker, ed. and trans., introduction to *The Politics of Aristotle*, lix–lxi.

7. See Thomas Hobbes, *Leviathan* (New York: Dutton & Co., 1953), introduction and chap. 1; also *De Cive or The Citizen*, ed. Sterling Lamprecht (New York: Appleton-Century-Crofts, 1949), 21–22 (1.2).

8. John Locke, *Two Treatises of Civil Government* (New York: Dutton & Co., 1953), 5 (1.2).

9. Ibid., 159, 164–65, 206 (2.7.87; 8.95–97; 15.173).

10. Hannah Arendt, *The Human Condition: A Study of the Central Dilemmas Facing Modern Man* (Chicago: University of Chicago, 1958), 29–30, 268, 292–97.

11. Hall and Ames observe correctly: "What gives the discussion of Confucius' 'sociopolitical theory' such an unfamiliar ring is the absence in his thinking of certain distinctions that Western social and political thinkers have deemed fundamental. The most important of these distinctions is that of the 'private' and 'public' realms. Allied with this distinction is the equally important division between the 'social' and 'political' modes of organization"; see David L. Hall and Roger T. Ames, *Thinking through Confucius* (Albany: SUNY Press, 1987), 146.

12. Herbert Fingarette, *Confucius: The Secular as Sacred* (New York: Harper Torchbooks, 1972), 37, 41, 45, 75–76 (*Analects* 6.28). For a slightly different rendering of these lines, see *The Analects of Confucius*, trans. Arthur Waley (New York: Vintage Books, 1989), 122.

13. Wing-tsit Chan, "Chinese and Western Interpretations of *Jen* (Humanity)," *Journal of Chinese Philosophy* 2 (1975): 109.

14. Tu Wei-ming, "*Jen* as a Living Metaphor," in *Confucian Thought: Selfhood as Creative Transformation* (Albany: SUNY Press, 1985), 81, 88. As he remarks in another context, *jen* not only transgresses the inner/outer, private/public bifurcation, but also mediates between humanity and nature as well as between humanity

and "Heaven" (or celestial immortals). The person striving for *jen*, he writes, "must also be able to realize the nature of the 'myriad things' and assist Heaven and Earth in their transforming and nourishing functions. . . . Unless one can realize the nature of all things to form a trinity with Heaven and Earth, one's self-realization cannot be complete"; see Tu Wei-ming, *Humanity and Self-Cultivation: Essays in Confucian Thought* (Berkeley, CA: Asian Humanities Press, 1979), 97.

15. Tu Wei-ming, "Neo-Confucian Religiosity and Human-Relatedness," in *Confucian Thought*, 133, 137. The "Western Inscription" reads: "Heaven is my father and Earth is my mother, and even such a small creature as I finds an intimate place in their midst. Therefore that which fills the universe I regard as my body and that which directs the universe I consider as my nature. All people are my brothers and sisters, and all things are my companions" (137).

16. Robert N. Bellah, *Beyond Belief: Essays on Religion in a Post-Traditional World* (New York: Harper & Row, 1976), 94–95.

17. Tu Wei-ming, "Selfhood and Otherness: The Father-Son Relationship in Confucian Thought" and "Neo-Confucian Religiosity and Human Relatedness," in *Confucian Thought*, 121–24, 138.

18. *Analects* 1:1; Waley, trans., *The Analects of Confucius*, 83. See also Tu Wei-ming, *Confucian Thought*, 139.

19. David L. Hall and Roger T. Ames, *The Democracy of the Dead: Dewey, Confucius, and the Hope for Democracy in China* (Chicago: Open Court, 1999), 11, 204. They candidly add: "We do not ignore the serious defects to traditional Confucianism illustrated by the isolation of minorities, gender inequities, and an overall disinterest in the rule of law. In spite of these past failings, we argue that, on balance, there are resources within the Confucian tradition for constructing a coherent model of a viable and humane democracy that remains true to the communitarian sensibilities of traditional China while avoiding many of the defects of rights-based liberalism" (12). Compare also Hall and Ames, *Thinking through Confucius* (Albany: SUNY Press, 1987); Hall and Ames, *Anticipating China: Thinking through the Narratives of Chinese and Western Culture* (Albany: SUNY Press, 1995); Hall and Ames, *Thinking from the Han: Self, Truth, and Transcendence in Chinese and Western Culture* (Albany: SUNY Press, 1998); and for some critical comments, see Fred Dallmayr, "Humanity and Humanization: Comments on Confucianism," in *Alternative Visions: Paths in the Global Village* (Albany: SUNY Press, 1998), 123–44.

20. Tu Wei-ming, *Confucian Thought*, 144–46.

21. Masoa Abe, *Zen and Western Thought*, ed. William R. LaFleur (Honolulu: University of Hawaii Press, 1985), 160, 255.

22. Apart from the writings of Hannah Arendt, the above considerations are indebted to the work of Jürgen Habermas, especially Habermas, *The Structural Transformation of the Public Sphere*, trans. Thomas Burger and Frederick Lawrence (Cambridge, MA: MIT Press, 1989), and Habermas, *The Inclusion of the Other: Studies in Political Theory*, ed. Ciaran Cronin and Pablo De Greiff (Cambridge, MA:

MIT Press, 1998). Compare also Craig Calhoun, ed., *Habermas and the Public Sphere* (Cambridge, MA: MIT Press, 1992). For a discussion of the possible role of the public sphere (*kung*) in Asian societies, see, e.g., Wm. Theodore de Bary, *The Trouble with Confucianism* (Cambridge, MA: Harvard University Press, 1991), 100–101; also William T. Rowe, "The Public Sphere in Modern China," *Modern China* 16 (1990): 303–29, and David Strand, "*Civil Society" and "Public Sphere" in Modern China: A Perspective of Popular Movements in Beijing, 1919–1989* (Durham, NC: Asian-Pacific Studies Institute, Duke University, 1990).

23. John G. A. Pocock, "The Ideal of Citizenship since Classical Times," in *Theorizing Citizenship*, ed. Ronald Beiner (Albany: SUNY Press, 1995), 30–31. Compare also the comment of Gershon Shafir: "Citizenship is the legal foundation and social glue of the new communality [of the *polis*]. It is founded on the definition of the human being as 'a creature formed by nature to live a political life' and, in Pocock's words, this is 'one of the great Western definitions of what it is to be human'"; see Shafir, ed., *The Citizenship Debates* (Minneapolis: University of Minnesota Press, 1998), 3.

24. Norberto Bobbio, "Racism Today," in *In Praise of Meekness: Essays on Ethics and Politics* (Cambridge: Polity Press, 2000), 112.

25. Shafir, "Introduction: The Evolving Tradition of Citizenship," in *The Citizenship Debates*, 23–24. For an argument in favor of differentiated citizenship, see especially Iris Marion Young, "Polity and Group Difference: A Critique of the Ideal of Universal Citizenship," in ibid., 263–90. In Bobbio's view, the solution resides in "the reconciliation of the two opposing trends" (of equality and difference) (see Bobbio, *In Praise of Meekness*, 8).

CHAPTER SEVEN. Self and Other

1. Regarding global ecumenicism, compare, for example, Hans Küng, *Global Responsibility: In Search of a New World Ethic* (New York: Crossroad, 1991); and Paul Tillich, *Christianity and the Encounter of the World Religions* (New York: Columbia University Press, 1963).

2. For a perceptive discussion of Gadamer's early writings on dialogical politics, see Robert R. Sullivan, *Political Hermeneutics: The Early Thinking of Hans-Georg Gadamer* (University Park: Pennsylvania State University Press, 1989).

3. Hans-Georg Gadamer, *Wer bin Ich and wer bist Du? Ein Kommentar zu Paul Celans Gedichtfolge "Atemkristall"* (Frankfurt am Main: Suhrkamp, 1973), 7 (translations into English are my own).

4. Ibid., 9–12. Gadamer diminishes the starkness of the ambiguity somewhat by allowing for an occasional specificity of pronouns. Thus, he speaks of the possible substitution of the "reader-ego" for the "poet's ego" and the resulting "determinacy of the meaning of thou" (ibid., 12).

5. Ibid., 14–18.

6. Ibid., 39.

7. Ibid., 110. These comments do not prevent Gadamer from observing at another point that the multivocity or "polyvalence" of words is pinpointed or "stabilized in the course of discourse" and that hence there is "a univocity which is necessarily endemic to every type of discourse, even that of *poésie pure*" (ibid., 113).

8. Ibid., 112–15. For the notion of "phrase families," compare Jean-Francois Lyotard, *The Differend: Phrases in Dispute*, trans. Georges Van Den Abbeele (Minneapolis: University of Minnesota Press, 1988). Regarding "agonistic (or agonal) dialogue," see Fred Dallmayr, *Margins of Political Discourse* (Albany: SUNY Press, 1989), 16–19, 109; see also William E. Connolly, *Identity/Difference: Democratic Negotiations of Political Paradox* (Ithaca, NY: Cornell University Press, 1991), 33.

9. Gadamer, *Wer bin Ich*, 118–21.

10. Ibid., 129–31. Gadamer adds, "There cannot be a 'final' interpretation. Every interpretation only aims at approximation; and its own concrete possibility would be vitiated if interpretation did not assume its historical place and did not insert itself into the 'historical effectiveness' [*Wirkungsgeschehen*] of the text" (ibid., 133–34).

11. See Hans-Georg Gadamer, "Letter to Dallmayr," in *Dialogue and Deconstruction: The Gadamer–Derrida Encounter*, ed. Diane P. Michelfelder and Richard E. Palmer (Albany: SUNY Press, 1989), 96–97. The letter was a response to an essay in which I had tried to compare and counterbalance Gadamer and Derrida; see Fred Dallmayr, "Hermeneutics and Deconstruction:Gadamer and Derrida in Dialogue," also in ibid., 76–92.

12. Hans-Georg Gadamer, "Hermeneutics and Logocentrism," in Michelfelder and Palmer, eds., *Dialogue and Deconstruction*, 118 (in the above citations I have slightly altered the translations for purposes of clarity). Compare also Gadamer, "Destruktion and Deconstruction," in ibid., 102–13.

13. Gadamer, "Hermeneutics and Logocentrism," 123, 125.

14. Hans-Georg Gadamer, "Die Vielfalt Europas: Erbe und Zukunft," in *Das Erbe Europas: Beitraege* [The Legacy of Europe: Contributions] (Frankfurt am Main: Suhrkamp, 1989), 7, 10-11. (Translations from English are my own.)

15. Ibid., 13–14. Regarding Husserl, compare especially his "Vienna Lecture" of 1935, in Edmund Husserl, *The Crisis of European Sciences and Transcendental Phenomenology*, trans. David Carr (Evanston, Ill.: Northwestern University Press, 1970), 269–99. Also compare Martin Heidegger, *Beitraege zur Philosophie: Vom Ereignis*, vol. 65 of *Gesamtausgabe*, ed. Friedrich-Wilhelm von Hermann (Frankfurt am Main: Klostermann, 1989).

16. Gadamer, *Das Erbe Europas*, 15–17, 20–24. Regarding Edmund Husserl's notion of the life-world, see Husserl, *The Crisis of European Sciences*. For a discussion of successive transformations of "world" and "life-world" from Husserl and Heidegger to Derrida, see Fred Dallmayr, "Life-World: Variations on a Theme," in

Life-World and Politics: Between Modernity and Postmodernity: Essays in Honor of Fred Dallmayr, ed. Stephen K. White (Notre Dame, IN: University of Notre Dame Press, 1080), 25–65.

17. Gadamer, *Das Erbe Europas*, 28–30.

18. Ibid., 30–31.

19. Ibid., 32–34.

20. Hans-Georg Gadamer, "Die Zukunft der europaeischen Geisteswissenschaften," in *Das Erbe Europas*, 37–39, 42–45.

21. Ibid., 35, 46–48.

22. Ibid., 45–46.

23. Ibid, 49, 52, 57–58. Regarding Herder, compare R. T Clark, *Herder: His Life and Thought* (Berkeley: University of California Press, 1955), and Isaiah Berlin, *Vico and Herder: Two Studies in the History of Ideas* (New York: Viking Press, 1976).

24. Gadamer, *Das Erbe Europas*, 58–62. Regarding tolerance, see also Robert Paul Wolff, Barrington Moore, Jr., and Herbert Marcuse, *A Critique of Pure Tolerance* (Boston: Beacon Press, 1965).

25. Connolly, *Identity/Difference*. Compare also Anne Norton, *Reflections on Political Identity* (Baltimore: Johns Hopkins University Press, 1988); and Michael Brint, *Tragedy and Denial: The Politics of Difference in Western Political Thought* (Boulder, CO: Westview, 1991). Regarding "lateral" and "interactive" universalism, see Maurice Merleau-Ponty, *Signs*, trans. Richard C, McCleary (Evanston, Ill; Northwestern University Press, 1964), 119–20; and Seyla Benhabib, *Situating the Self* (Cambridge: Polity Press, 1992), 3–6.

26. Cornel West, "The New Cultural Politics of Difference," in *Out There: Marginalization and Contemporary Culture*, ed. Russell Ferguson et al. (Cambridge, MA: MIT Press, 1990), 20–21.

27. Samir Amin, *Eurocentrism*, trans. Russell Moore (New York: Monthly Review Press, 1989), 71–73. Also compare Francis Barker et al., eds., *Europe and Its Others*, 2 vols. (Colchester: University of Essex Press, 1985); Stephen Slemon and Helen Tiffin, eds., *After Europe* (Sydney: Dangaroo, 1989).

28. Stuart Hall, "The Emergence of Cultural Studies and the Crisis of the Humanities," *October* 53 (Summer 1990): 22–23; Paul A. Bové, "Power and Freedom: Opposition and the Humanities," *October* 53 (Summer 1990): 79.

29. Connolly, *Identity/Difference*, 33; Iris Marion Young, *Justice and the Politics of Difference* (Princeton, NJ: Princeton University Press, 1990), 169–71. The path beyond the "logic of complete identity" and that of "pure difference" is also charted in exemplary fashion in Ernesto Laclau and Chantal Mouffe, *Hegemony and Socialist Strategy: Towards a Radical Democratic Politics*, trans, Winston Moore and Paul Cammack (London: Verso, 1985), 105–11, 122–29.

30. Nirmal Verma, "India and Europe: Some Reflections on Self and Other," *Kavita Asia* (Bhopal, 1990), 121, 127.

31. Ibid., 132, 137, 144.

CHAPTER EIGHT. Border Crossings

1. Bernhard Waldenfels, *Deutsch–Französische Gedankengänge* (Frankfurt am Main: Suhrkamp, 1995), hereafter cited as *DFG*; see also Waldenfels, *Phänomenologie in Frankreich* (Frankfurt am Main: Suhrkamp 1983). Among his other publications, compare Waldenfels, *Der Spielraum des Verhaltens* (Frankfurt am Main: Suhrkamp, 1980), Waldenfels, *In den Netzen der Lebenswelt* (Frankfurt am Main: Suhrkamp, 1985), Waldenfels, *Ordnung im Zwielicht* (Frankfurt am Main: Suhrkamp, 1987), Waldenfels, *Der Stachel des Fremden* (Frankfurt am Main: Suhrkamp, 1990), and Waldenfels, *Antwortregister* (Frankfurt am Main: Suhrkamp, 1994). *Ordnung im Zwielicht* has recently been translated: Waldenfels, *Order in the Twilight*, trans. David J. Parent (Athens: Ohio University Press, 1996). For an English-language introduction to this thought, see Fred Dallmayr, "On Bernhard Waldenfels," *Social Research* 56 (1989): 681–712, and also Dallmayr, foreword to *Order in the Twilight*, xi–xv. For a list of English-language essays by Waldenfels, see *Order in the Twilight*, 167–68.

2. Waldenfels, *DFG*, 45, 48–49.

3. Ibid., 50. He adds that the aim is not to produce a "German-French or French-German" mélange, but rather to articulate one idiom in the other and to think it together with the other (11).

4. Ibid., 7, 9–10.

5. Ibid., 7, 27, 31. See also Maurice Merleau-Ponty, "From Mauss to Claude Lévi-Strauss," in *Signs*, trans. Richard C. McCleary (Evanston, Il: Northwestern University Press, 1964), 114–25.

6. *DFG*, 18–20, 29, 39.

7. Ibid, 38.

8. Ibid., 20–21, 40, 42.

9. Ibid., 24–25, 48–49. Compare in this context Paul Ricoeur, *La mémoire, l'histoire, l'oubli* (Paris: Seuil, 2000).

10. *DFG*, 51, 79–80.

11. *DFG*, 84, 91. Compare also Jacques Derrida, *Speech and Phenomena, and Other Essays on Husserl's Theory of Signs*, trans. David B. Allison (Evanston, IL: Northwestern University Press, 1973), in his reading of which Waldenfels comes close to the interpretation of Rudolphe Gasché, *The Tain and the Mirror: Derrida and the Philosophy of Reflection* (Cambridge, MA: Harvard University Press, 1986). Waldenfels, however, also raises some critical reservations regarding Derrida's text, by calling into question an exclusively "phonocentric" construal of Husserl's argument and by insisting on a closer interpretation of time (speech) and space (writing) and of self-other relations in speaking and hearing.

12. *DFG*, 190, 193–94, 261–63, 293, 296, 300.

13. Ibid., 211, 240, 274–76. In the case of Lyotard, Waldenfels refers chiefly to Jean-François Lyotard, *The Differend: Phrases in Dispute*, trans. Georges Van Den

Abbeele (Minneapolis: University of Minnesota Press, 1988). See also Michel Foucault, *The Archaeology of Knowledge*, trans. A. M. Sheridan Smith (New York: Pan-
theon, 1972). Regarding Foucault, it is important to note that Waldenfels's comments do not at all coincide with Habermas's critique, which opposed to Foucault's
"dispersal of reason" a universal metadiscourse animated by universal validity
claims. Waldenfels writes that we have no reason "to fetishize the name of Foucault.
But what cannot at all be avoided is the question how we can and shall philosophically proceed if it is true that the anthropological centering of reason is no longer de-
fensible and if the centrality of 'man' was not so much thought but invented" (*DFG*,
216). Compare also Jürgen Habermas, *The Philosophical Discourse of Modernity:
Twelve Lectures*, trans. Frederick Lawrence (Cambridge, MA: MIT Press, 1987).

14. One may note that the chapter on Levinas in *Phänomenologie in Frankreich* was not written by Waldenfels himself but by S. Strasser (218–65).

15. A similar kind of *Auseinandersetzung*, involving Merleau-Ponty and Derrida, has recently been initiated in the United States. See in this context M. C. Dil-
lon, ed., *Écart and Différance: Merleau-Ponty and Derrida on Seeing and Writing*
(Atlantic Highlands, NJ: Humanities Press, 1997).

16. Waldenfels, *DFG*, 109–11, 119–20, 131–34, 148, 151, 168–69.

17. Ibid., 309–10, 314, 316, 326, 328–30, 334–35.

18. Ibid., 346, 349–50, 352, 354–57.

19. Ibid., 353–54, 357, 362–65, 370–71, 375, 380–81.

20. Ibid., 426–33. For Waldenfels, the main innovation of Habermas's pragmatics is the replacement of the Kantian monologue of reason or conscience by an
intersubjective "communication" in which every participant functions as judge.
The main flaws of this approach are found in the infinite regress of rules (for rule-
governance) and in the deficit of moral motivation (433). Despite his generally critical comments, Waldenfels concedes the limitations of his portrayal and the possibility of retrieving something like an "other Plato" and an "other Kant" (429, 434).

21. Ibid., 434–37.

22. Ibid., 168, 244. However, Waldenfels repeatedly departs from "pure" responsiveness. Thus, we read at various points about the appropriateness and co-
gency (*Triftigkeit*) of a response and also about a "responsive rationality" that seeks
to "meet" a question, thereby avoiding empty chatter (134, 139). One also needs to
recognize that Waldenfels has developed a very complex panorama of possible responses in *Antwortregister*.

23. Ibid., 274–75.

24. Ibid., 118, 282. In my view, terminological aporias also beset the notion of
"otherwise than Being" or "beyond Being," a notion that quickly tends to land one
in the dilemmas of "being and nothingness" (familiar from Sartre). In my view, it is
preferable to follow Heidegger by using being "under erasure."

25. Ibid., 120, 138, 342, 381. On the political level, the Levinasian accent on
separateness seems uncomfortably close to the dominant climate (in the West) of

antisocialism and of a certain libertarianism that condemns any human together-ness as "totalitarian" aberration. A combination of Levinasian disjunction with Carl Schmitt's "friend−enemy" formula has led some political thinkers to an en-dorsement of willful decisionism (harking back to Hobbes). Compare, e.g., Ernesto Laclau, "Deconstruction, Pragmatism, Hegemony," in *Deconstruction and Pragma-tism*, ed. Chantal Mouffe (London: Routledge, 1996), 47−67.

    26. *DFG*, 330, 364−65.

CHAPTER NINE. Hermeneutics and Intercultural Dialogue

    1. Hans-Georg Gadamer, *Truth and Method*, 2nd rev. ed., trans. Joel Wein-sheimer and Donald G. Marshall (New York: Crossroad, 1989), 198−99 (transla-tion slightly altered).

    2. Ibid., 241.

    3. Ibid., 254, 257, 259−60.

    4. Ibid., 267−69.

    5. Ibid., 367−70.

    6. Ibid., 306.

    7. Ibid., 295. This midpoint is well captured by Nikolas Kompridis when he stresses the importance of resisting "two extremes: thinking of ourselves either as standing completely outside our traditions, in no way affected by or indebted to them, or as identical with our traditions, fatefully bound to or enclosed within them"; see Kompridis, *Critique and Disclosure: Critical Theory between Past and Future* (Cambridge, MA: MIT Press, 2006), 7. Compare on this issue also Fred Dallmayr, "Hermeneutics and Deconstruction: Gadamer and Derrida in Dialogues," in *Critical Encounters: Between Philosophy and Politics* (Notre Dame, IN: University of Notre Dame Press, 1987), 130−58; and Dallmayr, "Self and Other: Gadamer and the Her-meneutics of Difference," *Yale Journal of Law and the Humanities* 5 (1993): 101−24.

    8. Gadamer, *Truth and Method*, 293. Continuing this line of thought, Gada-mer perceives in hermeneutical understanding an anticipation or "fore-conception of completeness" (*Vorgriff der Vollkommenheit*) aiming at the disclosure of "truth" (and hence bypassing any kind of relativism) (293−94).

    9. Ibid., 307−9.

    10. Ibid., 309, 324.

    11. Ibid., 329.

    12. Hans-Georg Gadamer, "Hermeneutics as Practical Philosophy" (1972), in *Reason in the Age of Science*, trans. Frederick G. Lawrence (Cambridge, MA: MIT Press, 1981), 93, 101−2.

    13. Ibid., 90−92. The same volume also contains Gadamer's important essay "What Is Practice [*Praxis*]? The Conditions of Social Reason" (1974), 69−87. Al-though he perhaps unduly sidelines Heidegger's influence, Richard Bernstein is

surely correct in saying that Gadamer's hermeneutics stands firmly in "the tradition of practical philosophy that has its sources in Aristotle's *Nicomachean Ethics* and *Politics*" where understanding takes the "form of *phronesis*"; see Bernstein, *Beyond Objectivism and Relativism: Science, Hermeneutics, and Praxis* (Philadelphia: University of Pennsylvania Press, 1983), xiv–xv.

14. Hans-Georg Gadamer, *Das Erbe Europas: Beiträge* (Frankfurt: Suhrkamp, 1989), 28–31. He adds: "And here it may be one of the special advantages of Europe that—more than elsewhere—her inhabitants have been able or were compelled to learn how to live with others, even if the others are very different" (31).

15. Ibid., 31–34.

16. Ibid., 35, 46–48.

17. Thomas Pantham, "Some Dimensions of the Universality of Philosophical Hermeneutics: A Conversation with Hans-Georg Gadamer," *Journal of Indian Council of Philosophical Research* 9 (1992): 132.

18. See, e.g., Charles Taylor, "Gadamer on the Human Sciences," in *The Cambridge Companion to Gadamer*, ed. Robert J. Dostal (Cambridge: Cambridge University Press, 2002), 126–42; and Taylor, "Interpretation and the Sciences of Man," in *Philosophy and the Human Sciences: Philosophical Papers 2* (Cambridge: Cambridge University Press, 1985), 15–57.

19. Charles Taylor, "Conditions of an Unforced Consensus on Human Rights," in *The East Asian Challenge for Human Rights*, ed. Joanne R. Bauer and Daniel A. Bell (Cambridge: Cambridge University Press, 1999), 124–44.

20. Charles Taylor, "The Politics of Recognition," in *Multiculturalism and "The Politics of Recognition,"* ed. Amy Gutmann (Princeton, NJ: Princeton University Press, 1992), 66–68, 72–73. Compare also Paul Ricoeur, "Hermeneutics and the Critique of Ideology," in *Hermeneutics and the Human Sciences*, ed. and trans. John B. Thompson (Cambridge: Cambridge University Press, 1981), 63–100.

21. See, in this respect, especially John Dewey, "Search for the Great Community," in *The Public and Its Problems* (1927), in *John Dewey: The Later Works, 1925–1953*, ed. Jo Ann Boydston (Carbondale: Southern Illinois University Press, 1988), 2:325–27. Compare also David Foot, *John Dewey: America's Philosopher of Democracy* (Lanham, MD: Rowman & Littlefield, 1998).

22. John Dewey, "Nationalizing Education" (1916), in *John Dewey: The Middle Works, 1899–1924*, ed. Jo Ann Boydston (Carbondale: Southern Illinois University Press, 1975), 10:202–4.

23. Maurice Merleau-Ponty, "Dialogue and the Perception of the Other," in *The Prose of the World*, ed. Claude Lefort, trans. John O'Neill (Evanston, IL: Northwestern University Press, 1973), 133.

24. Ibid., 133–34.

25. Ibid., 134–35. On the issue of identity and noncoincidence, compare the exemplary study by Bhikhu Parekh, *A New Politics of Identity: Political Principles for an Interdependent World* (New York: Palgrave Macmillan, 2008).

CHAPTER TEN. Justice, Power, and Dialogue

1. Reference should also be made in this context to such unifying efforts as the Holy Alliance, the Concert of Europe, and balance of power. In the background of national rivalries, there was also something called *ius publicum Europaeum* (European public law), which limited the excesses of nationalist ambitions. On the latter, compare especially Carl Schmitt, *The Nomos of the Earth in the International Law of the Jus Publicum Europaeum*, trans. G. L. Ulmen (New York: Telos Press, 2003).

2. Compare in this context, e.g., Ludwig Wittgenstein, *Philosophical Investigations*, trans. G. E. M. Anscombe (Oxford: Blackwell, 1968); Martin Buber, *I and Thou*, trans. Ronald G. Smith (New York: Scribner, 1986); Gabriel Marcel, *Homo Viator: Introduction to a Metaphysics of Hope*, trans. Emma Craufurd (New York: Harper & Row, 1962); Martin Heidegger, *Being and Time*, trans. John Macquarrie and Edward Robinson (New York: Harper & Row, 1962), and Heidegger, *The Way to Language*, trans. Peter D. Hertz (San Francisco: Harper & Row, 1971); Hans-Georg Gadamer, *Truth and Method*, 2nd rev. ed., trans. Joel Weinsheimer and Donald G. Marshall (New York: Crossroad, 1989); Jürgen Habermas, *Communication and the Evolution of Society*, trans. Thomas McCarthy (Boston: Beacon Press, 1979); David Howarth et al., eds., *Discourse Theory and Political Analysis* (Manchester: Manchester University Press, 2000).

3. See Jürgen Habermas, "On the Pragmatic, the Ethical, and the Moral Employments of Practical Reason," in *Justification and Application: Remarks on Discourse Ethics*, trans. Ciaran Cronin (Cambridge, MA: MIT Press, 1994), 1–17.

4. Compare in this respect Fred Dallmayr, "The Law of Peoples: Civilizing Humanity," in *Peace Talks—Who Will Listen?* (Notre Dame, IN: University of Notre Dame Press, 2004), 42–43.

5. See Hannah Arendt, "On Violence," in *Crises of the Republic* (New York: Harcourt Brace Jovanovich, 1972), 177.

6. Bishop Desmond Tutu (with Douglas Adams), *God Has a Dream: A Vision of Hope for Our Time* (New York: Doubleday, 2004), 58.

7. For this argument, see Moses Mendelssohn, *Jerusalem, oder über religiöse Macht und Judentum* (Berlin: Maurer, 1783), para. 2, 44–47. The argument of Mendelssohn was directed chiefly against Gotthold Ephraim Lessing (1729–81), who had defended a theory of human moral advancement in Lessing, *Die Erziehung des Menschengeschlechts* (Berlin: Voss & Sohn, 1780).

8. Immanuel Kant, "On the Common Saying: 'This May be True in Theory, but it Does not Apply in Practice," in *Kant's Political Writings*, ed. Hans Reiss, trans. H. B. Nisbet (Cambridge: Cambridge University Press, 1970), 88–89.

9. Ibid., 90–92.

10. Kant, *Perpetual Peace: A Philosophical Sketch*, in *Kant's Political Writings*, 107–8, 114. Kant adds in an appendix : "There can be no conflict between politics,

as an applied [practical] branch of right, and morality, as a theoretical branch of right (i.e., between theory and practice)" (116). In recent times, some political "realists" have cast doubt on the emergence of a global civil society and its ethical role in tempering warfare between states. For a critique of this kind of realism, see Fred Dallmayr, "Global Civil Society Debunked? A Response to David Chandler," *Globalizations* 4 (2007): 301–3.

11. Kant, *The Metaphysics of Morals*, in *Kant's Political Writings*, 174.

CHAPTER ELEVEN.   Befriending the Stranger

1. See Bernhard Waldenfels, *Order in the Twilight*, trans. David J. Parent (Athens: Ohio University Press, 1996); and Waldenfels, *In den Netzen der Lebenswelt* (Frankfurt am Main: Suhrkamp, 1985); Waldenfels, *Der Stachel des Fremden* (Frankfurt am Main: Suhrkamp, 1990). Compare also Fred Dallmayr, "Border Crossings: Bernhard Waldenfels on Dialogue," in *Achieving Our World: Toward a Global and Plural Democracy* (Lanham, MD: Rowman & Littlefield, 2001), 129–46.

2. See Thomas Hobbes, *Leviathan*, intro. A. D. Lindsay (London: Dent & Sons, 1953), chaps. 13, 17–18, 21, 26; and *De Cive or The Citizen*, ed. Sterling Lamprecht (New York: Appleton-Century-Crofts, 1949), chaps. 1, 5–6, 13.

3. See Carl Schmitt, *The Concept of the Political*, trans. George Schwab (Chicago: University of Chicago Press, 2007), 25–26; Schmitt, *Political Theology: Four Chapters on the Concept of Sovereignty*, trans. George Schwab (Cambridge, MA: MIT Press, 1985), 5. Compare also Gabriella Slomp, *Carl Schmitt and the Politics of Hostility, Violence and Terror* (New York: Palgrave Macmillan, 2009), and Fred Dallmayr, "The Concept of the Political: Politics between War and Peace" and "The Secular and the Sacred: Whither Political Theology?" in *Integral Pluralism: Beyond Culture Wars* (Lexington: University Press of Kentucky, 2010), 23–44, 45–66.

4. Joseph Lieberman, "Democrats and America's Enemies," *Wall Street Journal*, May 22, 2008, 17. Compare in this context Tom Engelhardt, *The United States of Fear* (Chicago: Haymarket Books, 2011); also Engelhardt, *The American Way of War: How Bush's War Became Obama's* (Chicago: Haymarket Books, 2010).

5. Albena Azmanova, "Against the Politics of Fear: On Deliberation, Inclusion, and the Political Economy of Trust," *Philosophy and Social Criticism* 37 (2011): 401–12. Compare also Azmanova, "Capitalism Reorganized: Social Justice after Neo-Liberalism," *Constellations* 17 (May 2010): 309–406; and Azmanova, *The Scandal of Reason: A Critical Theory of Political Judgment* (New York: Columbia University Press, 2012).

6. See Fred Dallmayr, *Peace Talks—Who Will Listen?* (Notre Dame, IN: University of Notre Dame Press, 2004), esp. chaps. 1 and 2.

7. See Bryan S. Turner, "National Identities and Cosmopolitan Virtues: Citizenship in a Global Age," in *Beyond Nationalism? Sovereignty and Citizenship*, ed. Fred Dallmayr and José M. Rosales (Lanham, MD: Lexington Books, 2001), 202–3.

8. Richard Falk, *The Great Terror War* (New York: Olive Branch Press, 2003), 6–8. He adds: "Megaterrorism is a unique challenge, differing from earlier expressions of global terrorism, by magnitude, scope and ideology, representing a serious effort to transform world order as a whole, and not merely change the power structure of one or more sovereign states" (39).

9. Ibid., 9–10, 29.

10. Ibid., 31, 179.

11. Richard Falk, *The Declining World Order: America's Imperial Geopolitics* (New York: Routledge, 2004), 221.

12. See Joseph S. Nye, *The Paradox of American Power* (New York: Oxford University Press, 2003), and Nye, *Soft Power: The Means to Success in World Politics* (New York: Public Affairs, 2004); Andrew Linklater, *Boundaries in Question: New Directions in International Relations* (New York: St. Martin's Press, 1995). Compare also Paul Gilbert, *New Terror, New Wars* (Washington, DC: Georgetown University Press, 2003); Anthony F. Lang Jr. and Amanda R. Beattie, eds., *War, Terror and Terrorism* (New York: Routledge, 2008); Andrew Schopp and Matthew B. Hill, eds., *The War on Terror and American Popular Culture: September 11 and Beyond* (Madison, NJ: Fairleigh Dickinson University Press, 2009); James F. Hodge and Gideon Rose, eds., *Understanding the War on Terror* (New York: Council on Foreign Relations, 2005); Allen Douglas, ed., *Comparative Philosophy and Religion in Times of Terror* (Lanham, MD: Lexington Books, 2006); and James A. Piazza and James I. Walsh, eds., "Symposium: Torture and the War on Terror," *PS: Political Science and Politics* 43 (July 2010): 407–50.

13. Chandra Muzaffar, *Global Ethic or Global Hegemony?* (London: Asean Academic Press, 2005), 15–16, 165–66. Among other things, Muzaffar is well known as president of the international NGO Just World Trust.

14. See Chandra Muzaffar, *Rights, Religion, and Reform: Enhancing Human Dignity through Spiritual and Moral Transformation* (London: Routledge Curzon, 2002), 105; also Falk, *The Great Terror War*, 180.

15. Schmitt, *The Concept of the Political*, 28–29. The precepts of Abrahamic religions can readily be extended to the Hindu-Jain opposition to violence (*ahimsa*) and the Buddhist stress on compassion (*karuna*).

16. Compare, e.g., Dalai Lama and Fabien Ouaki, *Imagine All the People* (Boston: Wisdom Publications, 1999); Dalai Lama, "The Nobel Peace Prize Lecture," in *The Dalai Lama: A Policy of Kindness*, ed. Sidney Piburn (Ithaca, NY: Snow Lion, 1990); Daisaku Ikeda, *New Horizons of a Global Civilization* (Tokyo: Soka Gakkai, 1997); Bishop Desmond Tutu, *God Has a Dream: A Vision of Hope for Our Time* (New York: Doubleday, 2004).

17. Stanley Hauerwas, "Christian Nonviolence," in *Strike Terror No Move: Theology, Ethics, and the New War*, ed. Jon L. Berquist (St. Louis: Chalice Press, 2002), 246–47.

18. See John B. Cobb, Jr., "A War Against Terrorism," in Berquist, ed., *Strike Terror No More*, 7–9; Walter Wink, "We Must Find a Better Way," in ibid., 335.

19. See John Milbank, "Sovereignty, Empire, Capital, and Terror," in Berquist, ed., *Strike Terror No More*, 75; Max L. Stackhouse, "Theologies of War: Comparative Perspectives," in ibid., 209–10.

20. See *The Spirit of Laws of Montesquieu*, ed. with an introduction by David W. Carrithers (Berkeley: University of California Press, 1977), 107, 117–24, 132–33.

21. John Dewey, "The Ethics of Democracy," in *John Dewey: The Early Works, 1882–1898*, ed. George F. Axtelle et al. (Carbondale: Southern Illinois University, 1969), 1:240. Compare also Fred Dallmayr, "Democratic Action and Experience: Dewey's 'Holistic' Pragmatism," in *The Promise of Democracy: Political Agency and Transformation* (Albany: SUNY Press, 2010), 43–65.

22. John Dewey, "Creative Democracy—The Task before Us" (1939), in *John Dewey: The Later Works, 1925–1953*, ed. Jo Ann Boydston (Carbondale: Southern Illinois University, 1988), 14:228.

CHAPTER TWELVE. Dialogue among Faiths

1. See Gilles Kepel, *The Revenge of God: The Resurgence of Islam, Christianity and Judaism in the Modern World* (University Park: Pennsylvania State University Press, 1994).

2. Leo Strauss, "Reason and Revelation" (1948); cited in Heinrich Meier, *Leo Strauss and the Theologico-Political Problem*, trans. Marcus Brainard (Cambridge: Cambridge University Press, 2006), 6.

3. See Martin Buber, *I and Thou* (Edinburgh: R. Clark, 1937); Buber, *Between Man and Man*, trans. Ronald G. Smith (Boston: Beacon Press, 1955).

4. See Abdulkarim Soroush, *The Expansion of Prophetic Experience: Essay on Historicity, Contingency, and Plurality in Religion*, trans. Nilou Mobasser (Leiden: Brill, 2009); also Nasr Hamid Abu Zaid, *Reformation of Islamic Thought: A Critical Historical Analysis* (Amsterdam: Amsterdam University Press, 2006); Mobasser, *Voice of an Exile: Reflections on Islam* (Westport, CT: Praeger, 2004).

5. The gist of the suspicion is phrased by Martin E. Marty in these terms: "Tolerance has lost its vigorous connotations and now is seen by many as weak and wishy-washy. It is the faith of those who believe little and lightly, and ask you to do the same, so you can meet with each other at low risk, say the critics"; see Marty, *When Faiths Collide* (Oxford: Blackwell, 2005), 65.

6. See Jürgen Moltmann, *God for a Secular Society: The Public Relevance of Theology* (Minneapolis, MN: Fortress Press, 1999), 227–28, 233.

7. Ibid., 234–35.

8. Ibid., 242–43.

9. See John B. Cobb, Jr., "The Meaning of Pluralism for Christian Self-Understanding," in *Religious Pluralism*, ed. Leroy S. Rouner (Notre Dame, IN: University of Notre Dame Press, 1984), 165, 176. For the references to Rahner and Küng, see Marty, *When Faiths Collide*, 158.

10. Compare in this context Richard Madsen and Tracy B. Strong, eds., *The Many and the One: Religious and Secular Perspectives on Ethical Pluralism in the Modern World* (Princeton, NJ: Princeton University Press, 2003); Martin E. Marty, *The One and the Many: America's Struggle for the Common Good* (Cambridge, MA: Harvard University Press, 1997); and Fred Dallmayr, "Conversation across Boundaries: E Pluribus Unum?," in *Dialogue among Civilizations: Some Exemplary Voices* (New York: Palgrave Macmillan, 2002), 31–47.

11. See William E. Connolly, *Pluralism* (Durham, NC: Duke University Press, 2005), 48, 59, 64.

12. Ibid., 48.

13. Jonathan Sacks, *The Dignity of Difference: How to Avoid the Clash of Civilizations* (London: Continuum, 2002), viii.

14. See Fred Dallmayr, "Post-Secular Faith: Toward a Religion of Service," in *Integral Pluralism: Beyond Culture Wars* (Lexington: University of Kentucky Press, 2010), 67–83.

15. Sacks, *The Dignity of Difference*, viii, 19, 22.

INDEX

absolutism, 199
agon. See dialogue
agonistic democracy, 121
ahimsa. See nonviolence, in India
Alexander the Great, 85
al-Qaeda, 186
Amin, Samir, 122–23
Analects (Confucius), 90–92, 93
analytical philosophy, 28, 101, 127
Anselm, 48
anthropocentrism, 16, 132; in
    Maritain, 34–35
apophaticism, 46, 49–50; as
    unknowability, 51
Aquinas, Thomas, 29, 85
Archibugi, Daniele, 25
Arendt, Hannah, 87–88, 172–73
Aristotle, 45, 199, 204; and Aquinas,
    85; and being, 29; criticism of
    Plato's polis, 17–18; ethics, 153;
    as founder of Western political
    philosophy, 82–85; fusion with
    medieval Christianity, 85–86;
    practical philosophy, 155
Asian culture: and interrelationships,
    81, 88; democratic tendencies, 94;
    women in, 94–95
Autobiography (Gandhi), 64
autonomy vs. global oversight, 168

Babel, 15–16
Barth, Karl, 30

Benhabib, Seyla, 121
Bergson, Henri, 29
Bhagavad Gita, 63
Bonaventure, 29
border zones: erasure of
    civilian/combatant border,
    186, 187–88; fences, 183; in
    gender relations ("between-
    world"), 139; as linkages among
    others, 129–30; as zone of
    diversity, 130
Buber, Martin, 167, 196
Buddhism, 95–96

capitalism, as essence of European
    culture, 123
Castoriadis, Cornelius, 135, 139, 142
Catholicism, 27
Celan, Paul, 102, 103–12
Centre for Dialogue, La Trobe
    University, 163–78
Christianity, 189–91, 198–99;
    Yannaras, 45–60
*Church in Post-Communist Europe,
    The* (Yannaras), 58
citizenship: based on public law,
    24; global, 23; "multiple"
    citizenship, 24
Cobb, John, Jr., 191, 198–99
Confucianism, 80–98; five
    relationships of, 88–93;
    modern changes in, 96–97

FRED DALLMAYR

is Packey J. Dee Professor Emeritus in philosophy

and political science at the University of Notre Dame.

He is the author and editor of over fifty books,

including *Spiritual Guides: Pathfinders in the Desert*

(University of Notre Dame Press, 2017).

CPSIA information can be obtained
at www.ICGtesting.com
Printed in the USA
LVHW080006241020
669663LV00013B/241